Welcoming but Not Affirming

Other books by Stanley J. Grenz
published by Westminster John Knox Press

Sexual Ethics:
An Evangelical Perspective

What Christians Really Believe—and Why

Welcoming but Not Affirming

An Evangelical Response to Homosexuality

Stanley J. Grenz

Westminster John Knox Press
Louisville, Kentucky

Scripture quotations, unless otherwise noted, are from
the New Revised Standard Version of the Bible,
copyright © 1989 by the Division of Christian Education
of the National Council of the Churches of Christ
in the U.S.A., and are used by permission.
Scripture quotations marked NIV are from
The Holy Bible, New International Version.
Copyright © 1973, 1978, 1984 International Bible Society.
Used by permission of Zondervan Publishers.

Book design by Sharon Adams
Cover design by Kevin Darst

First Edition
Published by Westminster John Knox Press
Louisville, Kentucky

This book is printed on acid-free paper that meets the American National
Standards Institute Z39.48 standard. ♾

PRINTED IN THE UNITED STATES OF AMERICA
99 00 01 02 03 04 05 06 07 — 10 9 8 7 6 5 4 3 2

Library of Congress Cataloging-in-Publication Data

Grenz, Stanley, 1950–
    Welcoming but not affirming : an evangelical response to homosexuality /
Stanley J. Grenz. — 1st ed.
        p.   cm.
    Includes bibliographical references and index.
    ISBN 0-664-25776-3 (alk. paper)
    1. Homosexuality—Religious aspects—Christianity.
    2. Homosexuality—Moral and ethical aspects.   3. Evangelicalism.
    I. Title.
    BR115.H6G74   1998
    261.8′ 35766—dc21   98-19220

To Paul Couillard,
a dear brother in Christ
who has lived out in
his own personal journey
what I can ony present as theory

CONTENTS

PREFACE

In October 1996, Christian leaders from across Canada gathered in Toronto for the gala "World Shapers '96" conference sponsored by the Evangelical Fellowship of Canada (an umbrella organization for the various evangelical church bodies in that nation). While the thousand conferees were putting the final touches on the opening-night festivities—singing heartily "Bind Us Together"— members of the Word of Life church in nearby St. Catherines broke the unanimity of the event by scattering pamphlets critical of the EFC. The organization's flagship journal, *Faith Today,* had just published an essay on human sexuality that the church's pastor, Peter Youngren, claimed denied the power of the gospel to deliver homosexuals from their sinful, God-dishonoring condition.

Barely a year later, a group of concerned citizens (that included several conservative Christians) sought to hold an open-air public informational forum in downtown Vancouver, focusing on the inappropriateness of using certain literature on homosexuality in the public schools. The meeting, however, never got off the ground. A cadre of shouting gay and lesbian activists took control of the microphones and intimidated would-be attendees, while the law enforcement officers present stood idly by.

These two events—instigated by persons whom we might dismiss as occupying opposite fringes of the political spectrum— stand as reminders of just how emotionally charged and potentially divisive the issue of homosexuality has become, not only in North American society but within the church as well. Such a charged atmosphere seems an inhospitable context to attempt the daunting task of producing an irenic, reasoned treatment of the topic. Indeed, I would not have personally volunteered for the job!

The genesis of this book lies in what I took to be a passing remark during a conversation with Stephanie Egnotovich, executive
editor of Westminster John Knox Press, at the meeting of the
American Academy of Religion in November 1996. But she followed up the remark early in 1997 with the suggestion that I consider responding to what she perceived as the need for a book
presenting the traditional viewpoint in a scholarly and irenic manner. After several weeks of agonizing over the proposal and
against both my initial inclination and the advice of several
friends, I sensed that the overture from the Press, and by extension
from the church, was simply too strong to refuse. As a result, I set
out—not without some trepidation—to carry out the mandate en-
trusted to me to write what to this point has been the most difficult
volume I have produced.

The task of writing this book did not occasion my first serious
thinking about homosexuality as an ethical question. On the contrary, my book *Sexual Ethics,* which initially appeared in 1990,
contained a chapter devoted to the topic. That earlier work, now in
a revised edition, remains foundational for the treatment found in
these pages. Nevertheless, accepting this assignment demanded
that I revisit the question and rethink my position. Although I come
out at the same basic place, this volume reflects some important
development in my thought over the past eight years. The most significant change is that I now see more clearly the significance of
the social constructivist view of homosexuality than I did in 1990.
Ironically, one impetus for this shift was an exchange of letters
with Peter Youngren following his criticism of the *Faith Today* essay in which I was prominently featured. More significant as an
academic source, however, was the careful reading I gave to David
Greenberg's monumental work, *The Construction of Homosexuality* (1988), which I had perused but not fully digested prior to the
publication of *Sexual Ethics.* Social constructivists point out that
we construct who we are—including our sexual identity—in large
part through interaction with others. This parallels the epistemo-
logical idea of the social construction of reality, which speaks

about the power of language to create the world we inhabit. The constructivist insight cautions us against adopting too quickly the language of "sexual orientation," understood as a fixed, lifelong, unchanging given of a person's life.

In many respects, *Welcoming but Not Affirming* is a case study in theological ethics. Although the discussion focuses on one specific ethical question, the current debate about homosexuality raises central methodological issues pertaining to Christian ethics in general. These include such crucial but hotly contested matters as the nature of biblical authority in the church, the role of tradition in contemporary moral understanding, and the importance of current theories in the human sciences for Christian ethical reflection. In a sense, then, what emerges in this volume is an application of the foundational methodological proposal I set forth in *The Moral Quest: Foundations of Christian Ethics* (Downers Grove, Ill.: InterVarsity, 1997).

The completion of this project serves as a reminder of the collaborative nature of all writing. Hence, I gladly acknowledge my indebtedness to several people who have assisted me in so many ways in my work. For his willingness to take charge of the painstaking work of confirming endnote references and preparing the indexes, I thank Paul Chapman, who served as my very capable teaching assistant for the past two academic years, but has now gone on to bigger and better things at Microsoft in Seattle. The board of administration and Principal Brian Stelck, of Carey Theological College, together with the College support staff—Beverley Norgren and Felicity Fok—provide a context conducive to scholarly pursuits. The staff at the Regent College Library, under the direction of Ivan Gaetz, are always willing to lend a helping hand. I benefit from interaction with faculty members and students at Carey/Regent College in Vancouver, who form my primary academic context, as well as my colleagues at Northern Seminary in Lombard, Illinois, who graciously allow me to appear on the campus intermittently over the academic year.

Several persons read the initial draft of the book and offered both strong encouragement and helpful comments. Among them was Dr. Bruce Milne, Senior Pastor at First Baptist Church in Vancouver and hence my pastor, who encouraged me to accept the challenge when I thought I might not. I am also deeply grateful to Professor William Placher of Wabash College for his positive endorsement of a manuscript that takes a position with which he disagrees. Above all, I thank Stephanie Egnotovich, together with the staff at Westminster John Knox Press. Without Stephanie's unrelenting conviction that I was the one to undertake this project the book never would have gotten off the ground.

Paul Couillard, writer, activist, and architect, also provided unswerving encouragement to me in this project. In fact, his affirmation of the final product as a fair and much needed statement is in a certain sense the endorsement I cherish the most. For Paul would readily admit that as a Christian who is gay he knows firsthand what it means to experience the grace of God, divine grace that is received in the context of a welcoming—but not automatically affirming—church. By relying on this divine grace, Paul has sought to embrace true biblical chastity and sexual integrity. For this reason, it is my privilege to dedicate this volume to him.

Introduction

Homosexuality and Christian Sexual Ethics

On January 13, 1996, after a heated debate, representatives from the congregations of the American Baptist Churches of the West voted to disfellowship four member churches. The infraction that led to their ouster was quite simple. These congregations were self-styled "welcoming and affirming churches"—they had become convinced that the Christian mandate involved not only ministering to homosexual persons but also sanctioning same-sex relationships.

The Northern California decision marked yet another incident in the decades-long controversy over homosexuality within many North American church bodies, a controversy that shows no sign of subsiding. The debate has become so sharp in recent years that several mainline denominations have teetered on the brink of division over the proper Christian response to homosexuality and homosexual persons.[1] Although not faced with the prospect of outright schism, even many evangelical groups are finding the issue divisive.

In this book I speak in this context of disagreement within the church. Although homosexuality is a broad issue today, having found its way into North American society as well as into the North American church, my focus will be on its specifically ecclesiastical dimension. At the heart of the current controversy is a basically ethical question: Should the church continue to condemn homosexual behavior, or has the time come for it to affirm gays and lesbians in its midst? My goal is to indicate that the mandate we have received from our Lord calls the church to welcome homosexual persons on the same basis that all persons are to be welcomed. But this same mandate prohibits the church from condoning same-sex sexual behavior as well as same-sex sexual unions.

Homosexuality as a Contemporary Issue

Once a taboo topic, homosexuality is now among the most widely discussed and emotion-laden issues in North American society. From the halls of state and federal legislatures to school board meetings and curriculum design committees, the debate over public policy issues relating to homosexual persons continues to simmer. And the media—from television and films to newspapers and tabloids—keep the debate before the public eye.

Why is this issue so prominent? Why is homosexuality debated so widely—and hotly—today? The single most significant incident that gays and lesbians themselves look to as marking the beginning of the gay rights movement occurred in New York City on June 28, 1969. On that day, police raided the Stonewall Inn, a bar frequented largely by homosexual persons. Unlike previous raids, on this occasion the customers retaliated. So vehement was the response that the police found it necessary to barricade themselves inside the bar for protection from the angry mob forming outside.

As crucial as Stonewall was to the emerging gay and lesbian psyche, it was not what catapulted the issue into the public eye. What actually did so was the Anita Bryant crusade that began in Dade County, Florida, in 1977. This campaign served both to galvanize the gay rights movement and marshal forces within the churches. And the attention the press devoted to the Bryant crusade brought an awareness of the hotly contested issue into the American heartland.

Taken together, these two events marked a turning point in the relationship of homosexual persons to the wider society. They served to heighten public awareness of the presence of gay and lesbian persons in society, of course. But, more important, they inaugurated an era of new boldness among homosexual persons themselves.[2] Since the Stonewall raid and the Bryant crusade, an increasing number of gays and lesbians have "come out of the closet" (publicly affirming their own sexual orientation). And in the wake of these incidents, homosexual activists have relentlessly campaigned for change in societal attitudes toward homosexuality.

The goal of many contemporary gay activists is more than mere tolerance of homosexuality. They demand that society view homosexuality as a sexual preference on equal footing with heterosexuality. In the words of one spokesperson,

> We want the elimination of homophobia. We are seeking equality. Equality that is more than tolerance, compassion, understanding, acceptance, benevolence, for these still come from a place of implied superiority: favors granted to those less fortunate. . . . The elimination of homophobia requires that homosexual identity be viewed as viable and legitimate and as normal as heterosexual identity. It does not require tolerance; it requires equal footing.[3]

Such demands would at one time have been dismissed as the ranting of radicals on the fringes of society. Now, however, voices calling for change include respected Christian theologians and ethicists representing a broad range of ecclesiastical traditions.[4] Whether in the wider society or within the church, we find ourselves living in the era of "gay rights."

What We Are Talking About

The word "homosexual" is not difficult to define.[5] Basically, as an adjective, it means "of one sex" (or "of one gender"). As a noun, it means "a homosexual person, especially a male." Yet what exactly are we talking about when we use this designation?

According to the *Encyclopedia of Bioethics,* a homosexual person is one who sustains "a predominant, persistent, and exclusive psychosexual attraction toward members of the same sex. . . . feels sexual desire for and a sexual responsiveness to persons of the same sex and who seeks or would like to seek actual sexual fulfillment of this desire by sexual acts with a person of the same sex."[6]

This definition is noteworthy because it assumes a widely held contemporary understanding of human sexuality. Many sexologists today differentiate among several aspects of a person's sexual makeup. Our "biologic sex" consists of those basic physical characteristics that mark us as either male or female. Our "gender identity" is the personal sense of being a man or a woman that emerges from cultural understandings of masculinity and femininity, and generally arises early in life.[7] Our "sexual orientation," in turn, involves our actual erotic feelings or the source of the sexual attractions we feel—specifically, whether we find ourselves erotically attracted to persons of the same sex, of the other sex, or perhaps of both sexes. Viewed from this perspective, homosexuality may be defined simply as the state of being erotically aroused by persons of the same sex. A homosexual person is someone who is "homoerotic."

How widespread is homosexuality, understood in this manner? In 1948, sex researcher Alfred Kinsey published the conclusions he drew from studying the sexual histories of fifty-three hundred American men. He reported that 37 percent admitted at least one homosexual experience since the beginning of adolescence,[8] while 10 percent claimed to have been homosexual for at least three years.[9] The shocking news was out: One in ten males in America was homosexual!

The 10 percent figure became lodged in the public awareness, even though Kinsey's data was later discredited.[10] A 1972 survey revealed that one-fourth to one-third of adult males had some overt homosexual feelings or experience, generally between the onset of puberty and age sixteen.[11] Yet in a 1993 poll of 3,321 American men, only about 2 percent indicated that they had engaged in homosexual behavior within the previous ten years and a mere 1 percent reported being exclusively homosexual.[12] Psychologist

Joseph Nicolosi cites the 1989 and 1992 findings of the National Opinion Research Center in Chicago, which reported a 2.8 percent incidence; this in turn mirrors a Danish study in 1989 that reported a 3 percent rate of homosexuality among males.[13] Today, researchers place the instance of exclusive homosexuality somewhere between 1 percent and 4 percent of males, half that figure among females.[14]

The *Encyclopedia of Bioethics* definition is likewise interesting because it reflects the contemporary distinction between sexual "orientation" and actual behavior. It suggests that homosexuality has to do primarily with feelings and only secondarily with behavior, with the result that a person can be homosexual without having acted upon his or her homoerotic attractions.[15] This distinction is widely held today among practitioners, whether secular or Christian.

For example, evangelical scholars Stanton Jones and Don Workman of Wheaton College define "homosexual behavior" as "acts between two persons of the same sex that engender sexual arousal (usually to the point of orgasm)," whereas they use "homosexual orientation" or "homosexuality" to refer to "a stable erotic and/or affectional preference for persons of the same sex." The authors then add, "Persons can engage in homosexual behavior without being homosexual; others can have a homosexual orientation without ever engaging in overt homosexual behavior."[16]

Further, the definition focuses exclusively on the erotic aspect of our existence as sexual beings. Hence, it suggests that homosexuality is primarily a matter of being sexually attracted to persons of the same sex.

While this is the most common understanding, some theorists today reject it as too narrow. For example, a gay Roman Catholic priest offered this comment:

> The genital aspect of sexuality (genitality) is a part of a much broader phenomenon: Whom do we love and how? How do we bond with one another? How is a person's affective life organized,

centered, focused? Being gay touches the very core of our being. It delineates and illuminates our characteristic way of coming to know ourselves and entering into relationships with others, our way of freeing up our energies so that they may produce life as they allow us to share love.[17]

Similarly, for some women, calling themselves "lesbian" is not so much a declaration of their sexual preference as a political statement. Specifically, it is a poignant way of asserting their radical rejection of patriarchy. This is reflected in an illuminating declaration from Roman Catholic activist Mary Hunt:

> A lesbian is not defined by her sexual partner any more than she is defined by those with whom she does not sleep. This is to fall into the patriarchal trap of defining women according to sexuality, which only serves to divide us. What we need is to be united in order that our strength will free all of us. A lesbian is an outlaw in patriarchy. But she is the herald of the good news that patriarchy is in its decline. A lesbian is a woman who in the face of heterosexist patriarchal messages not to love women—the others, the outsiders, the despised—indeed not to love herself as woman, in fact does both. . . . To be a lesbian is to take relationships with women radically seriously, opening oneself to befriend and be befriended, so that by loving, something new may be born. When all women are free to have this experience, then, and only then, can we say that any women are free.[18]

The use of "gay" and "lesbian" in these contexts indicates how fluid language can become!

Homosexuality as an Ethical Question

While not intending to minimize the possible broader aspects of homosexuality, in the discussion that follows I will restrict my focus to the explicitly sexual dimension of the question. I will look at homosexuality as a question for Christian theological ethics. My central concern is with the ethical aspects of the phenomenon of homosexuality understood in the sense of persons being homoerotic and then acting out these impulses. Specifically, I will focus on two questions, which I take to be central to the contemporary debate.

First, I am interested in the ethical stance of the homosexual preference. Should we view heterosexuality as the "normal" pattern or condition for all humans? That is, should biologic sex and gender identity lead a person to become solely heteroerotic? Second, I am concerned with the ethical question of behavior—how persons respond to their erotic feelings: Is it ethically proper for a person to act on homoerotic desires?

Homosexuality as an Issue in the Church

In recent years, the "gay movement" has become increasingly visible within the church. Homosexual Christians have joined their counterparts outside the church in "coming out of the closet." Rejecting the traditional negative appraisal of homosexuality as inherently evil, some gay Christians (Christians who affirm their homosexuality) have even affirmed that homosexuality is—to cite award-winning Roman Catholic writer Jerry Bartram—"a sacred gift from God." Bartram goes so far as to assert, "It is simply a fact . . . that homosexuality and the love of God go together."[19]

In this claim, gay Christians have been joined by others within the church. For example, in April 1995 a group of twelve United Church of Christ members, including ethicist James B. Nelson, drafted what they called the "Silver Lake Challenge." This document declared,

> We believe that there are many ways rather than just one to live as men. . . . We claim the goodness of our bodies, seek ways of wholeness, and celebrate healthy male energy. We reclaim the inseparability of sexuality and spirituality, and seek the healing of this split in men's lives. Men of all different sexual orientations can gather together in a place of respect, honor, and mutual empowerment.[20]

Voices such as these within the church have demanded that homosexuality be acknowledged as a gift from God and, as a consequence, that homosexual persons be placed on equal footing with heterosexual believers in all aspects of church life. In practical terms, this entails a call for the church to bless same-sex unions and to ordain practicing homosexual persons to the ministry on the same basis as heterosexual candidates.

In keeping with this goal, at the 1994 Episcopal convention more than fifty bishops signed what they called "A Statement of Koinonia (Collegiality)," which asserted that "both homosexuality and heterosexuality are morally neutral, that both can be lived out with beauty, honor, holiness and integrity." On this basis, the statement affirmed that homosexual persons should not be excluded from ordination. Instead, "those who know themselves to be gay or lesbian persons . . . [and who] forge relationships with partners of their choice that are faithful, monogamous, committed, life-giving and holy, are to be honored."[21]

At the same time, the push toward the recognition of homosexuality and heterosexuality as two equally valid sexual preferences has met with stiff opposition from others within the church. In fact, Christians today appear to be divided into two increasingly well-defined and seemingly mutually exclusive hostile camps. The one seeks to maintain the traditional Christian teaching on the topic, whereas the other is attempting to foster more open attitudes toward homosexuality within the church.

Both groups are convinced that the gospel is at stake in the controversy. Those who uphold the traditional teaching express concern for homosexual people who they believe are in a sinful situation but who can experience healing and transformation (whether or not they become heterosexual). Proponents of the traditional view believe that the historic strictures against homosexual activity are not arbitrary but are in fact for the benefit of homosexual persons themselves. Jerry Kirk, a pastor in the Presbyterian Church (U.S.A.), spoke for many when he asked rhetorically, "When God says such acts are sinful in His sight and contrary to His intention, is it loving for us to tell such persons that their active sexual conduct is not sinful? Should we tell them that it is really okay, and even good?"[22]

Conservatives such as Kirk see themselves as fighting for the future of the family, society, and even humankind. Fuller Seminary professor Don Williams offered this telling appraisal:

> For the church at this point to surrender to gay advocacy and gay theology and thus to give up her Biblical faith would bring not only disaster upon herself, it would bring more havoc to the world as well. If the church simply blesses homosexuality, the hope for change in Christ will be destroyed. Millions of potential converts will have the only lasting hope for wholeness cut off from them. Untold numbers of children and adolescents who are struggling with their sexual identity will conclude that 'gay is good,' deny their heterosexual potential and God's heterosexual purpose for them, and slip into the brokenness of the gay world. Untold numbers of adults will follow suit.[23]

Unsurprisingly, those who advocate a more open stance toward homosexual activity are equally convinced that the integrity of the gospel is bound up with their cause. They believe that faith in Christ demands that they take up the cause of homosexual people who have been hurt by moral and ecclesiastical strictures against homosexual practices. As Choon Leong-Seow, professor of Old Testament at Princeton Theological Seminary, noted, some Christians are "convinced that the authenticity of the church is in question if it is unchanging and exclusivistic." For them, "nothing less than the survival of the faith is at stake," for "the church is unfaithful if it turns its back on those who are marginalized in various ways by society or if the church itself excludes people on the basis of their race, gender, or sexual orientation from full participation in its life and leadership."[24]

The Anglican bishop Peter Coleman summed up the concern of both sides in this poignant manner:

The moral dilemma about homosexuality presents itself to some Christians in the form: How dare I feel sympathy for gay people and their sexual behaviour if my basic commitment is to Christ, and to the truth of God's will as revealed in the teaching of scripture and the tradition of the church throughout the ages? In hard cases, loyalty to Christ has to override human sympathy. Other Christians can and do sense the dilemma in a directly opposite way. Since loyalty to Christ and scripture requires the acceptance of all people in love not judgment and that has to include not only inadequate, unfortunate and handicapped people but also those who are simply different, therefore I must accept homosexuals and allow them to express their sexuality in the only ways open to them. I cannot order them to be celibate because that is a vocation, not a rule, even if traditional Christianity tried to make it one.[25]

Unfortunately, this shared concern for the gospel and the authenticity of the church's witness is often clouded by the strong rhetoric many protagonists use to defend their viewpoint. Despite the decades-long discussion, a climate of suspicion reigns on both sides of the divide. Such suspicion fosters a polarizing "us-them" attitude. In this emotionally charged climate, attempts to engage in meaningful dialogue are often hijacked by combatants who resort to ad hominem arguments.

Proponents of change often dismiss their opponents as intolerant bigots. To this end, they invoke the contemporary code word "homophobia." Strictly speaking the word refers to an irrational "fear or hatred of homosexuals and homosexuality."[26] But since the early 1970s, it has taken on a more sinister meaning, being seen as referring to an irrational social prejudice.[27] More often than not "homophobia" now refers to any belief that values heterosexuality above homosexuality or claims that heterosexuality is more natural to our human makeup.[28] Hence, gay activists and their sympathizers repeatedly protest loudly against the twin evils of "heterosexism" and "homophobia."

For their part, certain upholders of the traditional view propagate elaborate conspiracy theories replete with descriptions of the doomsday scenarios that will inevitably follow if this battle is lost.

Such apocalyptic approaches to the issue tend to view anyone who is at all sympathetic to the situation of homosexual persons in church and society as either a duped participant or a willing collaborator in a grand plot to undermine sexual morality in general and thereby to destroy the family, the nation, and even the Christian church.

Homosexuality as an Issue for Christian Theological Ethics

In this book, I hope to cut through the rhetoric on both sides and focus on what I see as the central ethical question: Are same-sex relationships a viable, God-given way of giving expression to our sexuality? Or are such relationships contrary to God's intention for human life and conduct?

But exactly how should we proceed? Lying behind the current debate over homosexuality is another issue, that of the way in which the church ought to reach conclusions on matters touching the life of the believing community. More specifically, the debate over homosexuality raises the question as to the proper method of theological and ethical reflection.

I believe that as Christians we ought to seek answers to questions of faith and practice by means of a conversation involving three "voices." A proper Christian theological method involves a trialogue consisting of the interplay among the biblical message, the heritage of reflection found within the historical life of the church, and the contemporary culture in which God has called us to live and minister.

Viewed from this perspective, the fundamental question now being debated is whether or not contemporary understandings of homosexuality demand that the church revise its long-standing declaration that homosexual behavior is sinful. More specifically, has our contemporary cultural situation given us such important new insight into the reality of homosexuality that our traditional reading of scripture is woefully inadequate and therefore in dire need of revision? The central task of this volume is to attempt to answer this question.

The book begins with the contemporary pole of this trialogue. In chapter 1, I explore current thinking about homosexuality. Here I seek to pinpoint what the human sciences are saying about the nature of this sexual preference as well as about the causes of homosexuality.

Chapter 2 moves from contemporary psychology and biology to the biblical texts. I look at the specific verses in the Bible that opponents of homosexual activity claim speak to the issue. My chief aim is to determine whether or not—or in what sense—the biblical writers declare homosexuality to be sinful.

This leads to chapter 3, which focuses on church tradition. My goal here is to document the trajectory of Christian teaching on homosexuality in an attempt to determine the extent to which the church has consistently rejected homosexuality as sinful and to discover exactly what the church has consistently condemned.

In chapter 4, I raise the question of the place of the Bible in the life of the church today. The purpose of this discussion is to seek clarity as to the manner in which the biblical teaching ought to serve as our authority in determining the ethical stance of the church toward homosexuality.

In the light of these conclusions, my discussion in the crucial fifth chapter focuses specifically on the Christian ethical response to the issue. This, in turn, forms the foundation for chapter 6, in which I apply this understanding of the Christian sex ethic to the practical issues the church now faces, such as the blessing of same-sex unions, the ordination of practicing homosexual persons, and the church's public stance on issues surrounding gay rights.

In the epilogue, I then draw the discussion to a close by inquiring as to how it is possible for Christian communities to welcome homosexual persons while not affirming homosexual conduct— that is, how the church can seek to minister to gays and lesbians while claiming that their sexual conduct runs counter to God's desires for humans.

Homosexuality in Contemporary Perspective

Homosexuality is no new phenomenon. On the contrary, sexual practices involving persons of the same sex have been present among a wide range of human societies.[1] For example, the Old Testament writers warned Israel against participating in homosexual behavior practiced by Israel's neighbors. So widespread were certain practices in the Roman Empire that they found their way into Paul's list of the sins of the pagans. And even the Christianization of the Western world did not lead to the eradication of homosexual activity. Instead, Christian leaders grappled with the presence of homosexual behavior throughout church history.

Despite the apparent presence of homosexuality in various forms since ancient times, the contemporary discussion is in several respects unlike that of previous epochs. Prior to the modern era homosexuality was understood almost exclusively in connection with certain specific activities. The contemporary outlook, in contrast, looks at homosexuality primarily as a sexual orientation—as a fixed, lifelong pattern—and only secondarily as actual behavior.

What marked this shift in understanding? And when did the change occur? Many scholars look to the rise of modern medical science, beginning in the nineteenth century, for the answer. Although the idea of homosexuality as a relatively stable trait is perhaps as old as the Renaissance, the first use of the term "homosexual" to refer to an underlying, ineradicable trait is routinely attributed to Karl Maria Kertbeny (née Benkert), a Vienna-born writer, who published a pamphlet on the topic in Leipzig, Germany, in 1869.[2]

Despite its relatively short pedigree, since the mid–twentieth century the belief that homosexuality is a sexual orientation and that it may be the normal condition for some people has gained wide acceptance in professional and academic circles. The relatively quick and seemingly thorough acceptance of this theory has led the postfeminist writer Maggie Gallagher to observe in a somewhat hyperbolic manner,

> Two hundred years ago . . . homosexuality did not exist. There was sodomy, of course, and buggery, and fornication and adultery and other sexual sins, but none of these forbidden acts fundamentally altered the sexual landscape. A man who committed sodomy may have lost his soul but he did not lose his gender. He did not become a homosexual, a third sex. That was the invention of the 19th century imagination.[3]

In this chapter, I offer a survey of contemporary opinion as to the nature and causes of homosexuality. I embark on this task conscious, however, that a number of writers look askance at research into the "causes" of homosexuality. They worry that these endeavors are intrinsically hostile to homosexual persons, because they believe such research is motivated by the premise that homosexuality is a deviation from the heterosexual norm.[4]

Although opinions vary greatly, scientific attempts at understanding homosexuality have followed two basic approaches, generally paralleling the long-standing question as to whether humans are the product of "nature" or "nurture." Modern psychologists have tended to look for a connection between homosexuality and upbringing ("nurture"), whereas other medical researchers have generally sought a basis for the phenomenon in a person's biological inheritance ("nature").

Homosexuality and Psychology:
The Disease Model

It is not surprising that from the beginning the fledgling field of psychology would concern itself with the question of the cause of homosexuality. More than any other figure, the "father of modern psychology," Sigmund Freud, set the basic categories for the psychological probing into the phenomenon.

Freud suggested that a newborn infant is ambisexual, deriving pleasure from a variety of bodily sensations. As the child matures, he or she moves through a series of stages, each of which involves a new object of love: first the self, then the mother and the father, and finally, normally someone of the other sex. Freud theorized further that a person can become fixated at, or later regress to, one of the intermediate states, which accounts in part for homosexual tendencies in some persons.[5]

In this manner, Freud removed sex from the realm of morality and placed it squarely in the domain of scientific reflection. Invoking the language of sickness and cure rather than sin and redemption when speaking of "aberrant" sexual behavior, Freud replaced the traditional focus on standards of morality with a therapeutic system designed to help people adjust to their own characteristic perversions.[6] Hence, he maintained that one could live happily and productively with one's homosexuality.[7]

Freud himself denied that homosexuality is a sickness.[8] Yet by moving the discussion into the realm of psychology, he in effect opened the door for others to construct an understanding of the phenomenon that viewed homosexuality as a disease.

Homosexuality, Parenting, and Arrested Development

In the wake of Freud's pioneering work, many psychologists appealed to a disease model to explore the nature and causes of homosexuality. Even the decision of the American Psychiatric

Association to remove homosexuality from its list of psychopathological disorders in 1973 did not immediately spell the demise of this approach. In fact, a survey four years later (1977) found that 69 percent of the psychiatrists polled held that homosexuality usually represents a pathological adaptation in human development.[9]

Psychological theories about homosexuality often elevate heterosexuality as the goal of personal development and consequently treat homosexuality as an unhealthy condition resulting from a disruption in the normal developmental process. Psychologist Elizabeth Moberly, for example, asserts that persons are not born either homosexual or heterosexual, but grow to become heterosexual persons. Consequently, she concludes the homosexual situation is due to arrested development:

> God did not create homosexuals *as* homosexuals, but as men and women who are intended to attain psychological maturity in their gender identity. . . . The mistake of some homosexuals is to assume that the goal has already been reached, when in fact development has been checked and still requires completion.[10]

If homosexuality is the condition of arrested growth, the role of the therapist becomes that of assisting the homosexual person in making a transition from homosexuality to heterosexuality. Such a transition, of course, requires an awareness of the cause of the developmental disruption, which in turn demands that psychologists determine the roots of homosexuality.

Building from Freud, the classic psychoanalytic theory of causation looks to a person's family of origin. Foundational for this view was the work of Irving Bieber, who asserted that serious disturbances during child development, especially in the area of parent-child relationships, are responsible for homosexuality.[11] Such disturbances, he argued, result in confusion in the child's sexual identity.

In keeping with this basic theory, Moberly stated categorically, "a homosexual orientation does not depend on a genetic predisposition, hormonal imbalance, or abnormal learning processes, but on difficulties in the parent-child relationship, especially in the earlier years of life." On the basis of her work with homosexual persons she concluded, "one constant underlying principle suggests itself: that the homosexual—whether man or woman—has suffered from some deficit in the relationship with the parent *of the same sex;* and that there is a corresponding drive to make good this deficit—through the medium of same-sex, or 'homosexual,' relationships."[12] Homosexual longings, therefore, are an attempt to make up for arrested growth in relationship with the same sex.[13] The homosexual person seeks to compensate for this deficit through a same-sex relationship with another, which in the process becomes eroticized.

Following the same line of reasoning, Michael Saia explained how this confusion works:

> Most homosexually oriented men do not enter into relationships with other men just to have sex. Rather, they are trying to fulfill their needs for unconditional love and a sense of identity. But sex often plays a part in these relationships, and after a while confusion may occur. The man may begin to think sex will meet his basic needs, so he attempts to satisfy his needs in that way. Since sex is such a powerful, pleasurable experience, it can quickly reinforce any behavior associated with it. This is how the patterns of thinking (sexualization) and behavior (promiscuity) can so quickly become entrenched in the homosexual's life.[14]

In Moberly's estimation, this realization of the cause of homosexuality places the question of homosexual behavior outside the realm of ethics and into the concern of the therapist. Such acts are prohibited, she asserts, simply because "sexual expression is not appropriate to pre-adult relationships."[15]

Psychologists holding to the dysfunctional parent-child model have attempted to devise a profile of the family situation most likely to produce a male homosexual child. Lawrence J. Hatterer sketched the classic description: "a dominant, aggressive, hostile,

binding, but hypercritical mother . . . combined with a passive, in-
effectual, rejecting, indifferent father."[16] Such a situation can frus-
trate the developing boy's desire to identify with his father, and as
a result he does not fully internalize a male gender-identity.

Joseph Nicolosi articulated a widely held explanation as to why
this occurs. For nearly all infants, the first source of nurture and
care is the mother, who therefore becomes the parent with whom
they first identify. Whereas girls maintain their primary identification with the mother, boys later face the additional developmental
task of shifting their primary identification to the father. Through
his relationship with the father a boy gains the masculine identification necessary for the development of a normal male sense of
personal identity. Through his example, the father models for his
son that it is possible to maintain a relationship with the mother
that is intimate while autonomous. Here problems can easily arise.
Nicolosi claims that a homosexual man's family background typically gives evidence to an overly close relationship to his mother
and a father who is distant from both of them.[17]

Not surprisingly, the dysfunctional-parent theory lies at the
foundation of a range of proposals, whether ascribed to by secular
psychologists or Christian counselors,[18] that promise help for the
homosexual person.

Homosexuality as a Learned Behavior

Although it continues to enjoy wide acceptance, the view that
the cause of homosexuality lies in arrested development due to
dysfunctional child-parent relationships is not the only prominent
psychological theory. In keeping with the findings of Masters and
Johnson,[19] some psychologists believe that homosexuality is a
learned behavior or a learned preference. Hence, they prefer what
is often called "learning theory" to explain the genesis of homosexuality. These theorists build from the idea that pleasure posi-
tively reinforces behavior by encouraging its repetition, whereas
pain discourages repeating the behavior.

Learning theory suggests that childhood or adolescent experiences, especially sexual experience, shape erotic orientation. Such experiences color a child's self-perception, sexual fantasies, and subsequent choices. For example, a boy who tends to engage in actions generally perceived as "sissy"[20] or who struggles with troubled family relationships and a tendency toward effeminate behavior may interpret his early erotic experiences in a homosexual manner and pursue subsequent experiences on this basis. When these early experiences lead to difficulties in establishing, or an inability to establish, successful heterosexual relationships in adolescence, the result may be the development of a homosexual condition. Homosexuality offers a way of freeing the person from what he or she perceives to be the awesome responsibilities of heterosexuality.[21]

An important variation on this theme came from the work of C. A. Tripp. According to Tripp, the focus of a person's sexual response is the result of a process that begins in childhood. Tripp noted that young children "show an utterly polymorphous sexuality." (Pre-puberty boys, for example, respond with erections to a variety of stimulations.) But beginning in puberty, this diversity of response begins to narrow, leading finally to the narrowing of one's sexual interests "to specific channels of expression. In this process, most people come to a fork in the road and move toward either the homosexual or heterosexual alternative.[22]

What leads a person in one direction or another? Tripp rejected the idea that the origins of homosexuality lie in family structure. Lying behind the choice, according to Tripp, is a person's set of sexual values that eliminate weaker alternatives while guiding him or her toward certain kinds of partners, situations, and acts. And he argued that society itself plays a role in this process. In Tripp's words, "Human sexuality is exceedingly variable, deriving its directionality (especially its final targeting) from what is individually learned and experienced in personal and social settings."[23]

More specifically, Tripp asserted that the way a society views and values maleness is a central factor in the rise of homosexuality. In societies that foster the male ideal as the "winner" or the "hero," Tripp theorized, homosexuality is readily activated.[24] Why? Young boys who already suffer from identity problems or who desire to exceed their present achievements readily discern a sharp contrast between themselves and the culture's male ideal. As a result, they tend to eroticize that ideal and then seek to possess it sexually with the hope of being able thereby to import more masculinity into themselves.[25] Tripp then concluded, "In all their essentials, the sought after rewards of homosexual and heterosexual complementations are identical: the symbolic possession of those attributes of a partner which, when added to one's own, fill out the illusion of completeness."[26]

Although offering differing understandings of the source of homosexuality, adherents of both theories generally agree that homosexuality is a negative situation. Richard Hettlinger drew the two theories together in concluding, "Most authorities attribute the homosexual condition to a combination of psychological and sociological factors which prevent the individual from achieving full and free personal relationships with the other sex."[27] And despite differences about the exact trail that leads to a specific case, followers of both theories tend to agree that homosexuality is the result of "nurture," not "nature." Thus, Lawrence J. Hatterer spoke for many of his colleagues when he declared that homosexuals "are not born but made and that genetic, hereditary, constitutional, glandular, or hormonal factors have no significance in causing homosexuality."[28]

Despite the wide acceptance of the disease model of homosexuality, psychological theories have not won universal acceptance. A study by researchers Alan Bell, Martin Weinberg, and Sue Hammersmith found that family backgrounds had little or no effect on a person's eventual sexual orientation:

> For the benefit of readers who are concerned about what parents may do to influence (or whether they are responsible for) their children's sexual preference, we would restate our findings another way. No particular phenomenon of family life can be singled out,

on the basis of our findings, as especially consequential for either homosexual or heterosexual development. . . . *What we seem to have identified . . . is a pattern of feelings and reactions within the child that cannot be traced back to a single social or sociological root;* indeed, homosexuality may arise from a biological precursor (as do left-handedness and allergies, for example) that parents cannot control.[29]

On the basis of findings such as these, the Roman Catholic scholar Gerald Coleman offered this somewhat neutral conclusion: "It seems that there is not enough evidence to prove the psychoanalytic hypothesis, but there is too much evidence to dismiss it at this time."[30]

Homosexuality and Medicine: Searching for a Biological Cause

Since the early 1950s researchers have moved in a quite different direction—that of "nature" or biological inheritance. Motivated in part by disappointment over the inconclusive results of psychiatric research,[31] biologists have sought to determine whether or not certain biological features might be responsible for the presence of homosexuality in a person. The quest for a biological foundation for homosexuality has looked in three general directions: genetic makeup, prenatal (or postnatal) hormonal levels, and the anatomy of the brain.[32]

By the end of the 1980s the idea that homosexuality has a genetic foundation had fallen on hard times. Since then, however, the hypothesis has enjoyed a revival. In fact, the appeal to genetic makeup, especially when paired with considerations of the role of hormones in brain development and differences in brain structure, has reemerged today as the central theory of the biological origins of homosexuality. Several types of widely touted scientific experiments have led to this renewed interest in a biological foundation for homosexuality.

Researchers have explored the possibility of a genetic basis by focusing on the siblings of homosexual persons in general and twins in particular. Studies conducted by Michael Bailey and Richard Pillard indicated that homosexual persons were two and one-half to five times as likely to have homosexual siblings as heterosexuals were.[33] In a set of related studies in 1991 (males) and 1993 (females), the researchers suggested that the concordance of homosexuality among identical twins was higher than among fraternal twins, nontwin siblings, or adopted siblings,[34] although these findings seem to be at odds with another study conducted in 1992.[35] Then in 1993, a published study seemed to confirm a genetic connection, for it appeared that a team from the National Institute of Health had discovered a small stretch of genetic material on the tip of the long arm of the X chromosome (contributed by the mother) that may be linked to male homosexuality.[36]

A second approach to determining a biological foundation for homosexuality investigates the role of prenatal hormones in influencing the development of both the sex organs as well as the brain. The hypothesis is that male homosexuality is the result of a decreased level of testosterone during a critical period of prenatal development resulting in a "feminization" of the brain. Female homosexuality, in turn, results from an overexposure to testosterone during the same period.

One interesting recent study conducted by neuroscientist Sandra Witelson and psychologist Cheryl M. McCormick sought to confirm this hypothesis by investigating possible differences in innate skills such as visual-spacial ability and verbal fluency, as well as such other characteristics as left-handedness. The researchers noted "a different pattern of cerebral asymmetry between gay and heterosexual individuals . . . compatible with different courses of brain development." These results suggest that "prenatal hormonal factors may be a factor in the origin of sexual orientation."[37] Hence, some scientists theorize that homosexual persons are exposed to atypical levels of prenatal sex hormones producing in turn atypical development of susceptible areas of the brain.

A third related direction of study explores the purported difference between the brain structure of homosexual and heterosexual men.[38] In 1991 biologist Simon LeVay published the findings of research indicating that part of the anterior hypothalamus (a brain region that governs sexual behavior) in homosexual men resembles the anatomical form usually found in women rather than in men.[39] LeVay's findings came on the heels of research in the Netherlands published in 1990 that also discovered a related difference in brain structure.[40]

Despite the repeated use of studies such as these by persons sympathetic to the gay activist movement,[41] no biological factor has emerged as the sole cause in determining sexual preference.[42] Even the scientists who conduct the research are often wary of attempts to draw sweeping conclusions from their work.

One problem is the correlational nature of biological factors. Although scientific experimentation can suggest that certain genetic or physiological factors are associated with homosexuality, such research is hard-pressed to prove the causal direction of the connections. In the words of Joseph Nicolosi, "a biological outcome does not necessarily mean a biological cause."[43]

Hence, we are left wondering whether brain structure or homosexual behavior—to cite one example—comes first. Does brain structure cause homosexuality? Or does homosexual behavior result in changes to brain structure? The possibility that the latter may be the case is suggested by evidence that behavioral therapy can produce changes in brain circuitry. More recently, the work of neuroscientist Marc Breedlove on rats has indicated that sexual behavior itself can alter the nervous system and the brain.[44]

In addition, even if there is a causal connection between biological makeup and sexual orientation, the question remains as to whether this connection is direct or indirect. For example, William Byne and Bruce Parsons of Columbia University propose an "interaction model" of the connection. They suggest that genes and hormones do not themselves determine a person's sexual orientation. Instead, a person's biological makeup results in the development of certain personality traits. The interaction of these traits with the environment is what leads to the development of homosexuality.[45]

Perhaps we are left with the cautious conclusion Byne and Parsons offered at the end of their survey of the contemporary search within "nature" for the foundation of homosexuality:

> There is no evidence at present to substantiate a biologic theory, just as there is no compelling evidence to support any singular psychosocial explanation. While all behavior must have an ultimate biologic substrate . . . critical review shows the evidence favoring a biologic theory to be lacking.[46]

This quotation illustrates a growing consensus within the scientific community that homosexuality is likely the product of both inheritance and environment. Rather than determining sexual orientation, biology provides the predisposition; biological influences increase the probability that under certain environmental circumstances a person will engage in homosexual behavior.[47] As Joseph Nicolosi reported, "we have begun to realize that biology and psychology cannot be so neatly separated but are inseparably linked."[48] In keeping with this outlook, Gerald Coleman, who himself favors a more open stance toward homosexual persons in the church, has offered this appraisal:

> There is a general consensus today that no one theory of homosexuality can explain such a diverse phenomenon. . . . There is no single genetic, hormonal or psychological cause of homosexual orientation. There appears to be a variety of factors which can provide a "push" in the direction of homosexuality for some persons. The complex of factors which result in the orientation toward homosexuality probably differs from person to person. While we do not know what causes the orientation, we undoubtedly know that the forces that go into the creation of a homosexual person are more complex and mysterious than most had earlier appreciated. There is, then, substantial reason to approach the scientific topic of homosexuality with caution, respect and humility, as the overwhelming complexity of the issue merits.[49]

Homosexuality and Change
in Sexual Orientation

The modern discussion about the nature and causes of homosexuality is closely connected to another question, one which for many people carries far-reaching existential ramifications: Can a person undergo a change in sexual orientation? This question has been the topic of heated debate in recent years.

Helping Homosexual Persons Change

In 1962 psychologist Irving Bieber and his colleagues published a set of research findings based on a nine-year study of male homosexual persons, concluding that:

> The therapeutic results of our study provided reason for an optimistic outlook. Many homosexuals became exclusively heterosexual in psychoanalytic treatment. Although this change may be more easily accomplished by some than others, in our judgment, a heterosexual shift is a possibility for all homosexuals who are strongly motivated to change.[50]

Seventeen years later, Bieber offered confirmatory evidence to this earlier conclusion. He reported: "We have followed some patients for as long as ten years who have remained exclusively heterosexual. Reversal estimates now range from 30% to 50%."[51] That same year (1979) Masters and Johnson published a controversial study[52] in which they concluded from their research an overall failure rate for the treatment of male homosexual dissatisfaction of about one-third.[53]

Other studies seem to confirm expectations of long-term significant change in behavior and perhaps even orientation for 30 percent to 50 percent of homosexual persons who undergo therapy.[54] Some reports suggest that the figure may be as high as 65 percent.[55]

Armed with statistics such as these, many counselors attempt to assist homosexual persons to alter their sexual preference. Secular psychotherapist Martin Hoffman, for example, inaugurates the process by seeking to help his clients assess their motivation for change,[56] for motivation is a crucial factor determining the likelihood of successful treatment. His next step is to aid them in accepting themselves as they are, reminding them that acceptance does not preclude change, but may in fact actually enhance change. The ultimate goal of such efforts, he maintains, is to help clients achieve a sense of their own value as persons.

Conservative Christian counselors are often even more confident about the likelihood of genuine change. One therapist offered this optimistic conclusion:

> My experience as a Christian therapist and ministry leader is that I have seen most overcomers experience a great degree of freedom from homosexuality. Over time they report an almost complete absence of homosexual thinking, feeling, and attraction. They are able to go on with their lives as 'normal' in all respects with a very small 'h' remaining. This means that they may still experience some homosexual feelings or interests from time to time; some temptations, but with a minimum of tension, conflict, or difficulty.[57]

In the task of effecting a change in sexual orientation, many evangelical therapists draw from the work of Elizabeth Moberly. Moberly has asserted that in many cases such change can arise as the consequence of meeting the need for parental relationship that originally gave rise to a person's homosexual orientation. And because she is convinced that the homosexual situation arises from a deficit in same-sex, not opposite-sex, parent-child relationships, the key to meeting this need lies in creating loving, nonsexual, same-sex relationships.[58]

Douglas A. Houck of Outpost ministry in St. Paul, Minnesota, has constructed Moberly's theories into a four-stage program. First, the homosexual person responds to God's call to obedience by changing his or her behavior. The second stage focuses on building self-esteem on the basis of God's grace. During the third stage the person seeks to establish healthy same-sex relations that can meet the needs of same-sex love lacking in his or her past. Only then is the person ready for stage four, namely, acceptance of heterosexuality.

Moberly's basic position also echoes in the approach developed by Paul D. Meier, psychiatrist at the Minirth-Meier Clinic, Richardson, Texas. He too focuses on the needs that remained unmet in childhood. In the case of males, he advocates giving primary emphasis to developing friendships with men their own age and older. Such male mentors become same-sex role models with whom the homosexual person can begin to identify. These mentors also provide the emotional and spiritual affection that will help fill the "father vacuum" in the homosexual person's life.[59]

Motivated by the belief that homosexual persons can change, a variety of "help" groups, such as Homosexuals Anonymous and Exodus International (an umbrella organization for about fifty ministries), have sprung up in recent years.[60] Others, however, flatly disagree with that belief. They maintain that a person simply cannot change his or her sexual orientation.[61] Rather than attempting to assist homosexual persons in doing the impossible, some Christians—including conservative organizations such as Evangelicals Concerned—put their energies in promoting monogamous relationships between homosexual persons.

After studying a variety of evangelical groups, *Christianity Today* writer Tim Stafford could offer only "cautious optimism" about the prospects for change in sexual orientation. "The degrees of healing vary," he wrote. "But the possibility of living an adjusted, hopeful, and fruitful life in a sin-distorted world—and the possibility of growing more joyful and consistent in life—remain."[62]

All researchers are in agreement on one point. Whatever change actually occurs comes with great difficulty. According to Jones and Workman,

No study suggests that change comes from willingness to change or some simple set of procedures. There seems to be a consensus of opinion that change is most likely when motivation is strong, when there is a history of successful heterosexual functioning, when gender identity issues are not present, and when involvement in actual homosexual practice has been minimal. Change of homosexual orientation may well be impossible for some by any natural means.[63]

Sexual Orientation: Static or Dynamic?

Can a person's sexual orientation change? Our answer to this question is in part dependent on how we view the durability of sexual orientation. That is, it confronts us with the question, Is homosexuality (and heterosexuality for that matter) static or dynamic?

Many people today assume that a person's sexual orientation is a fixed reality, a given. Consequently, "homosexual"—like "heterosexual"—is primarily something that people are. And they are one or the other even before they engage in certain behaviors. At this point, proponents of this view are careful to differentiate between static homosexual persons and "situational" homosexuals, that is, persons who engage in homosexual acts under extreme circumstances, such as while incarcerated, but otherwise are heterosexual in behavior. It is the former who are characterized by a fixed homosexual orientation.

The static view of sexual orientation carries an important implication. If sexual orientation is fixed, to try to change a static homosexual person is not only futile but actually entails an attack on the sacredness of his or her personhood. And because homosexual persons have no reasonable chance for change, they will probably suffer more, not less, as a result of any treatment geared toward changing their sexual orientation.[64]

The static view of human sexual orientation stands as an important reminder that we never act in a biological and psychological vacuum. Any act occurs in the context of a personal disposition that in a certain sense predates the moment of our acting. This disposition is the product of a variety of dimensions of personal existence, such as personal biological makeup, what we have experienced at the hands of others, and even our own past behaviors.

Despite its popularity, the understanding of homosexuality as a static reality has by no means gained universal acceptance. Opponents argue that human nature is not purely static, but in flux or dynamic. Human nature, they maintain, is malleable, adaptable, and changing. As humans we are constantly learning and relearning. Consequently, a person's sexual orientation may also be in flux. This leads naturally to what we might call a "dynamic" understanding of homosexuality.

Some proponents accept the assertion that human sexuality comprises a continuum between the homosexual and heterosexual poles, with most of us falling somewhere between the two. Further, these theorists suggest that in some sense we all have within us the potential toward both heterosexual and homosexual behavior and that our "place" on this continuum is not necessarily static but subject to fluctuation. Rather than following by necessity a fixed pattern of conduct, therefore, a person might in fact move in and out of homosexual behavior. This means that the label "homosexual" does not designate how a person *must* act but only characterizes what appears to be his or her present conduct.

Dynamic conceptions such as these keep before us the role of personal choice and personal behavior in determining who we are. Yet the debate between disposition and personal choice does not appear to tell the whole story.

The missing dimension seems to be supplied by the "social constructivist" theorists.[65] David Greenberg, for example, sides with the dynamic view in that he rejects the idea that homosexuality is a fixed, pre-social given common to different societies and different periods of time. Against the "static" theorists, he notes that sexual practices and the conceptual categories through which people understand them—including practices involving persons of the same sex—vary greatly from society to society. Hence, the contemporary Western concept of homosexuality as a fixed, biologically based sexual orientation that is "normal" for a select group of people is in fact the product of a constellation of ideas present in our society and not the transcultural reality proponents assume it is.

Like other proponents of the dynamic view, Greenberg argues that homosexual behavior is learned. But he quickly adds that this learning always occurs within a specific social context. In his view, cultural conditioning is able to override whatever seemingly innate factors might otherwise be operative in a person's life. He writes, "Where social definitions of appropriate and inappropriate behavior are clear and consistent, with positive sanctions for conformity and negative ones for nonconformity, virtually everyone will conform irrespective of genetic inheritance and, to a considerable extent, irrespective of personal psychodynamics."[66]

Should Homosexual Persons Change?

At first glance, the social component of homosexuality provides a powerful foundation from which to argue that a person's sexual orientation could potentially change. More specifically, it opens the door to the possibility that homosexuality might be altered through a reinculturalization process. By joining a community characterized both by a fluid understanding of sexual orientation and by strong strictures against homosexual behavior, a homosexual person could conceivably expect to find his or her propensity toward such behavior diminish over time.

Some psychologists conclude, however, that awareness of the social dimension of homosexuality provides the conceptual tools to move in a quite different direction. If sexual orientation is in part a cultural construct, then a crucial social question emerges: Which orientation—if any—ought society to inculcate in its members? Or to reframe the question in our context, On what basis ought Western society to continue to "privilege" heterosexuality?

Already in the 1970s several psychologists took important steps in this direction. George Weinberg rejected the heterosexual ideal propagated by our society. In fact, he saw the widespread acceptance of this ideal as the source of the real problem we face, which in his estimation is not the incidence of homosexuality but the homophobia propagated by our society. He argued that Western society has created homophobia by inculcating in children the mistaken idea that the goal of life is monogamous, heterosexual marriage replete with offspring.[67] Instead of inciting homophobia, Weinberg challenged, our concern ought to be the creation of healthy homosexual persons.

Don Clark took the matter even further. He asserted that homosexuality, not heterosexuality, is the human norm. Clark theorized that we are all born "gay." That is, we have an innate capability of "moving toward pleasant homosexual sensations."[68] Why do most of us not do so? According to Clark, the reason lies with society: Society socializes out our homosexual feelings. Despite the socialization process, however, these feelings remain beneath the surface ready to reemerge. Full self-awareness arises when we recognize that we are "gay"—that is, capable of loving the same sex and able to act on that love.

But why is homosexuality the norm? Clark's answer lies in his rejection of "our society's obsession with seemingly polar opposites and dualities." Persons who are attracted to their sexual opposite, Clark avers, have been socialized to devalue themselves and to launch the "love search" in a quest for "some sort of integration or completion."[69] The homosexual person, in contrast, has rejected the male-female polarity and recovered the "gay" reality given in infancy. As a result, the "gay" person is more whole than the heterosexual. In Clark's words, "While most of the rest of the population struggles with the *half-lives assigned to them* . . . we can be whole as humans."[70]

Proposals such as Weinberg's and Clark's provide the intellectual foundation for a perceived shift in mood both in the American Psychiatric Association and in society in general. Within the realm of therapy we have witnessed a strong movement away from attempts to provide treatment that facilitates a change in behavior if not in orientation itself. This focus is being replaced by "gay affirmative counseling,"[71] which tries to help homosexual persons embrace their own sexuality and cope with their fear of that sexuality,[72] that is, to move beyond their socially induced latent "homophobia." Some activists have even gone so far as to demand an official ban on therapy that encourages homosexual persons to undergo a change in orientation.[73] In the wider society, recent years have brought a marked increase in efforts, whether through educational incentives in the marketplace or school curricular changes, to combat the supposedly twin "evils" of "heterosexism" and "homophobia."

The Bottom Line

Where does the contemporary discussion leave us?

First, we seem no closer to a definitive conclusion as to what homosexuality actually is. Following the *Encyclopedia of Bioethics,* we may continue to define the word as involving "a predominant, persistent and exclusive psychosexual attraction toward members of the same sex." We may continue, albeit with great caution, the contemporary practice of differentiating between homosexuality as a seemingly consistent sexual orientation—that is, as the propensity to be sexually aroused by persons of one's own sex— and overt homosexual acts.

Yet scientific research—whether psychological, biological, or sociological—has not substantiated that this attraction is either innate or an ineradicable trait that for this reason can be said to be normal for some persons. Instead, by "normal" we can only assert that certain persons "sense" that their homosexuality precedes any conscious choice on their part, at least any choice that they can remember making.

This observation becomes important as we turn to the Christian teaching on homosexuality. It provides a crucial contemporary background for an assessment of the significance of the biblical texts and the trajectory of church tradition that ought to inform the Christian community's outlook toward homosexuality.

Before reassessing this teaching, however, I must offer one additional observation. Perhaps the various dimensions of the contemporary discussion stand as a reminder that in the end, the controversy over homosexuality involves our understanding of humanness. While not assuming that everyone would engage in overt sexual behavior, the older consensus nevertheless connected intrinsic humanness with what we today would likely call "heterosexuality." The social mood, however, has begun to change. Increasingly the focus on difference so characteristic of the postmodern ethos has led to the loss (or the welcomed destruction) of the concept of normative humanness. Consequently, we face today the crucial question, Is there a normative humanness or has the idea of "norm" lost its meaning?

In any attempt to answer this question we quickly find ourselves confronted with the quest to determine our human purpose. And this quest leads eventually beyond the pale of science and into the realm of the transcendent vision that informs our understanding of ourselves as persons and as a people.

The Bible and Homosexuality:
The Exegetical Debate

Even though homosexual conduct is not a major theme in the Bible, certain biblical passages do in fact speak of some type(s) of same-sex acts. The central texts are relatively few: the story of Lot and Sodom (Gen. 19:4–11) as informed by other references to the sin of Sodom, together with the incident in Gibeah (Judges 19); the prohibitions found in the Holiness Code (Lev. 18:22 and 20:13); and Paul's inclusion of homosexual practices within his condemnation of Gentile society (Rom. 1:26–27) and in his list of moral infractions (1 Cor. 6:9; 1 Tim. 1:10).

Traditionally, Christian ethicists have found in these texts a clear rejection of all genital homosexual behavior. However, in recent years a growing chorus of exegetes has voiced disagreement with this conclusion, arguing that the church has misread the texts. These scholars argue that the sin of Sodom and Gibeah involved inhospitality, attempted rape, or even the desire to cohabitate with angels;[1] the prohibitions in the Holiness Code refer to idolatrous sexual relations; and the Pauline injunctions speak about practices known in Roman culture, such as pederasty or homosexual prostitution.[2] In none of these texts, proponents of the new exegesis conclude, do we find reference to homosexuality as a natural sexual orientation for some people nor condemnation of its behavioral expression within the context of committed same-sex relationships. In addition, proponents of an affirming stance toward conscientious homosexual persons suggest that certain biblical heroes, such as David and Jonathan, might have been homosexual lovers, and they note the silence of Jesus on this topic.

I now revisit these texts to determine the extent to which the newer suggestions are compelling. My intent is not to offer a complete exegesis of any one text, but to determine whether recent scholarship has provided sufficient new insight into these texts to warrant our rejection of the traditional interpretation.

The Sins of the Cities

The idea of same-sex behavior is first encountered in the Bible in the story of the destruction of Sodom and Gomorrah (Genesis 19). A similar event occurs later, in the narrative of the Levite and his concubine who overnight in Gibeah (Judges 19). According to traditional Christian exegetes, the townspeople in both accounts sought to engage in homosexual acts with the visitors in their midst. In the first narrative, God subsequently destroys the Sodomites because of their grievous sins, which included homosexual behavior.[3]

Important to the traditional interpretation is the meaning of the Hebrew verb *yadha,* found twice in the Sodom story (Gen. 19:5, 8), as well as in the account of the Levite and his concubine (Judg.` 19:22). Generally, *yadha* means "to know" in the sense of "being acquainted with." But on as many as ten occasions in the Old Testament it carries the idea of sexual intercourse. Apart from these two stories, such intercourse is heterosexual and results in the conception of a child. Thus, the desire of the men of the town in each case was "to know" the visitors in the sense of engaging in same-sex intercourse with them.

Throughout church history Christian exegetes generally interpreted these stories as referring to an attempted homosexual assault. The first radical questioning of that interpretation came in 1955 with Derrick Sherwin Bailey's *Homosexuality and the Western Christian Tradition.* In rejecting the traditional view, Bailey argued that the narratives make better sense if we interpret *yadha* according to its more general meaning. In so doing, we discover that in both stories the true intent of the townspeople was to establish the identity of the strangers, not to engage in homosexual intercourse. Bailey explained that by taking the travelers into his house, Lot—himself a resident alien (Hebrew: *ger*) and hence already suspect—had perhaps exceeded his rights as a foreigner. The wickedness of the townspeople was not homosexuality. Instead, they demonstrated their sinfulness in refusing to allow the host to fulfill the obligation of hospitality.[4] Building on Bailey's suggestion, John Boswell went so far as to state categorically, "There is no sexual interest of any sort in the incident."[5]

Bailey's interpretation suffers from one debilitating flaw. According to the Sodom narrative, Lot responds to the demand of the men of the city by offering them his daughters who, he declares, have "never slept with a man." Similarly, after they were given the Levite's concubine, the men of Gibeah "wantonly raped her, and abused her all through the night until the morning" (Judg. 19:25). In each case, the same word, *yadha,* is clearly used to refer to sexual relations. Bailey's conjecture leads inevitably to the highly unlikely assumption that in both stories the narrator has used *yadha* in two very different senses in close proximity to each other.

Perhaps more telling, however, is the actual alternative the host proposes to the unruly crowd at his doorstep. Could either of them possibly think his offer of a woman would placate the townspeople, if their only intent was to "become acquainted with" the strangers?

The best reply Bailey could provide to this quandary was to suggest that the offer was the hosts' ad hoc attempt to get out of a sticky situation. Concerning Lot's bold suggestion, he commented,

> No doubt the surrender of his daughters was simply the most tempting bribe that Lot could offer on the spur of the moment to appease the hostile crowd; and the fact that he could contemplate such a desperate course may well indicate his anxiety at all costs to extricate himself from a situation which he had precipitated . . . by action incompatible with his status in Sodom as a *ger*.[6]

Despite its wide influence, most scholars find Bailey's innovative conjecture unconvincing. Even those who advocate a more open stance toward homosexuality find his exegesis suspect at this point. Biblical scholar Victor Paul Furnish, for example, admits that the townspeople did indeed plan to engage in same-sex rape. However, Furnish then quickly dismisses this intention as "incidental to the main point" of the narrative.[7]

Despite Bailey's ingenious proposal, both narratives seem to indicate quite clearly that the townspeople were intent on engaging in same-sex intercourse with the strangers. But does this mean that homosexuality was the crucial sin that gained the narrator's disapproval? Was the homosexual dimension of the act the townspeople planned what made it so despicable? Perhaps other biblical references to this incident provide a clue.

On several occasions subsequent biblical writers invoke Gibeah (Hos. 9:9; 10:9) or more importantly Sodom as a negative example. Yet as Bailey pointed out, such texts do not focus on homosexual behavior per se. Instead, they paint the wickedness of these cities in broad terms. Sodom was guilty of arrogance, apathy toward the poor, and a haughty attitude, as well as engaging in "abominable things" (Ezek. 16:49–50). The prophets drew a connection between Israel and Sodom, for God's people are also guilty of insincere sacrifice, injustice, and oppression (Isaiah 1), as well as adultery and hypocrisy (Jer. 23:14). In short, Sodom came to be an archetype of ungodliness, unrighteousness, and lawlessness (2 Peter 2:6).

Nor does homosexual behavior itself lie at the heart of either story. Seemingly more central in each is the importance of hospitality. In the narrative of Sodom, this theme emerges in the broader context, as Abraham offers genuine hospitality to the three messengers. And upon their arrival in the city, the angelic messengers seem intent on testing the reputation of its inhabitants for inhospitality by stating that they planned to overnight in the city square.

Without a doubt, the sin of Sodom involved inhospitality. But how does the attempted homosexual gang rape fit into this situation? There is evidence of a practice among certain ancient cultures that sheds light on the connection between inhospitality and the desire of the townspeople to engage in a sexual act. In these cultures, male-to-male anal violation was thought to be the kind of indignity that would add to the humiliation of a defeated enemy, for it would treat the conquered foe as a woman.[8] Hence, the intent of wicked residents of these two cities may not have been to participate in homosexual acts merely for their own sake. Instead, they perhaps planned to use the heinous practice of gang rape to assert their superiority over and declare the subordinate status of the strangers Lot (and the old man in Gibeah) harbored.[9]

In short, showing utter disregard for the social rules of hospitality, they demand that the visitors submit to the most demeaning treatment conceivable. In the eyes of the narrator (and presumably the reader), this confirmed that the citizens "were wicked, great sinners against the LORD" (Gen. 13:13).

But is this the only dimension of the sexual sin of Sodom? We already noted that Ezekiel chastised Sodom for, among other sins, engaging in "abominable things" (Ezek. 16:50). The Hebrew term (*to'ebah*) found here is also used in the Holiness Code to describe homosexual acts (Lev. 18:22). This at least opens the door to suggest that whatever act came to be prohibited under the Levitical injunction characterized the men of Sodom as well.

One additional scriptural text must be mentioned. In a somewhat obscure reference, Jude appeals to the Sodom story as an example of "those who suffer the punishment of eternal fire" (Jude 7, NIV). Here Jude is speaking against godless people who both deny Jesus and turn God's grace into "a license for immorality" (v. 4, NIV). The specific sins Jude mentions in connection with Sodom are fornication and going after "strange flesh" (v. 7, KJV). And Jude links their example to sinful angels (v. 6; see also 2 Peter 2:4), whom God has reserved for punishment.

What can this seemingly strange reference mean? Bailey suggested that Jude is alluding to the ancient story of angels cohabitating with humans (Gen. 6:1–4). On this basis, he concluded that according to Jude God did not punish the Sodomites for homosexual behavior itself, but because they desired to have sexual relations with angelic beings. Hence, the emphasis of the text is upon the sexual incompatibility of the angelic and human orders.[10]

Bailey's interpretation may have some merit. However, he seems to have drawn too much from it. In contrast to Bailey's interpretation, Jude ought to be read as another instance of the type of argument from nature Paul offers in Romans 1. Jude may well be using the angelic cohabitation with humans and the homosexual practices of the Sodomites evidenced in their intended homosexual gang rape as parallel instances of the wickedness of violating the sexual order God has placed in creation. This would suggest that the male-on-male gang rape practiced by the Sodomites (and intended by the Gibeathites) was abhorrent not merely because it violated the norm of hospitality but because it violated that norm in an especially heinous manner. The men of Sodom were guilty of twisting God's good intention for human sexuality into a vehicle for unjust treatment of visitors to their city. In short, such violence involved perverting the sexual function as God had designed it into an act diametrically opposed to God's intent for human sexual expression.

These considerations suggest that Bailey and others have not been able to substantiate the claim that the homosexual dimension of the sin of Sodom was purely incidental. At the same time, we must readily admit that what is depicted and condemned in these texts is violent homosexual rape. As a result, we come away from these texts with a crucial question not satisfactorily answered: What about homosexual relationships between consenting adults?

The Prohibitions in the Holiness Code (Lev. 18:22; 20:13)

Two explicit commands within the Law provide traditionalists with the clear answer to this question of consensual homosexual relationships between adults. The first forthrightly prohibits male-

to-male sexual intercourse (Lev. 18:22). And the second pre-
scribes the death penalty for offenders (Lev. 20:13).

The commands occur within a lengthy section containing injunctions for personal and family conduct within the context of
God's covenant people. This section is called the Holiness Code
because the various precepts flow out of the central command:
"You shall be holy, for I the LORD your God am holy" (Lev. 19:2).
Thus, a holy God desires that the covenant people also be holy.
They must abstain from certain practices that characterize the surrounding nations, as well as the Canaanites who had inhabited the
land (Lev. 18:1–4, 24–28). One crucial dimension of such holiness
is proper sexual conduct (Lev. 18:5–23). And sexual propriety, traditionalists conclude, precludes homosexual behavior.

Today this traditional understanding is under attack. One widely
held alternative asserts that the Leviticus texts do not condemn homosexuality as we know it today. Instead, they warn Israel against
a certain, specific type of activity found in the ancient world,
namely, same-sex acts associated with idolatry.[11]

Proponents of this view point out that male-cult prostitutes were
an important aspect of the fertility rites that occurred as part of certain pagan temple practices. These practices, in turn, formed the
historical context for many of the prohibitions of the Holiness
Code.[12] Because the prohibited homosexual acts had a cultic significance they no longer have today, advocates of this theory add,
to cite these injunctions outside the context of idolatry and thereby
offer a biblical foundation for a blanket condemnation of homosexuality is misleading.[13]

The seemingly intrusive prohibition of sacrificing children to
idols (Lev. 18:21; 20:2–5) may offer some warrant for the suggestion that the primary interest of this section of the Holiness
Code is the prohibition of practices connected to idolatry. Some
proponents would add that the injunction against bestiality is
also connected to a cultic ritual involving intercourse between humans and sacred animals at Canaanite shrines.[14] And even the distinction between clean and unclean animals (Lev. 20:25), they

surmise, may have arisen from the realization that the unclean animals were used in pagan religious rites.[15]

This theory is dependent, of course, on the assumption that sexual acts with shrine prostitutes were actually a part of the religious practices in the ancient Near East. There is some evidence to suggest that Canaanite fertility rites did involve not only female but also male prostitutes (e.g., Deut. 23:17–18) and that such practices may have been propagated even within Israel (1 Kings 15:12; 22:46; 2 Kings 23:7). But the exact role of male cult prostitutes is an open question: Did they function solely with women who might have participated in a fertility rite in the hope of curing barrenness? Or were they available for male-to-male sexual acts?[16] To date, no compelling theory has emerged as to how male homosexual intercourse might have functioned within the context of a fertility rite,[17] especially given the widespread ancient understanding of the sex act that viewed taking the role of the female as shameful for an adult male.[18]

Another alternative to the traditional interpretation looks to ancient concerns for ritual cleanness as the key to understanding the prohibitions in the text. In this view, the Holiness Code contains precepts that define the life of a "clean" Israelite, that is, the one who is fit to worship God as a member of the covenant community. Simply stated, a true worshiper maintains ritual cleanness by avoiding whatever defiles.

This understanding leads some exegetes to conclude that the injunction against homosexual acts is not an ethical but rather a ceremonial prohibition. John Boswell, for example, declared that the Levitical texts speak about "ritually unclean" acts, rather than offenses that are "intrinsically evil, like rape or theft."[19] Similarly Furnish asserted that rather than being among the moral laws found in the Holiness Code, the prohibition of same-sex intercourse is concerned with ritual purity. It speaks about what is objectively (rather than morally) clean and unclean.

And what makes a homosexual act unclean? Furnish explains that ritual cleanness was in part connected to the concern to keep like things together and unlike things separate. Hence, whenever two things belonging to different categories become mixed together—such as planting different kinds of seeds in a field, wearing different kinds of fiber at once, or crossbreeding (Lev. 19:19)—they are both polluted. In a similar manner, same-sex intercourse is a "mixing" of two things that belong to different categories, for it involves a male taking the role of a female. In this manner, the act becomes perverted and both participants are polluted.[20]

This theory is a helpful reminder that the Holiness Code arose partly out of a concern for ritual purity. However, it is not completely clear that the injunctions against sex acts such as bestiality and same-sex intercourse fall in this category. As William Morrow notes, the Holiness Code generally views impurity as a condition that is involuntarily contracted, whereas it presents these forbidden sexual practices as willful.[21]

Further, proponents overstate the matter when they introduce a disjunction between cleanness and morality, and conclude from this disjunction that ritual purity is the sole concern—to the exclusion of morality—motivating the Levitical laws. The Holiness Code does acknowledge that certain forms of ritual uncleanness are not intrinsically immoral. Examples include childbirth (12:2–5), emission of semen (15:16–18), and menstruation (15:19–30). However, unlike homosexual acts, such things are not designated by the word to'ebah, which is more likely to be applied to actions that are contrary to "a being's true identity" than actions that result in ritual uncleanness.[22] And rather than resulting in punishment or even the death penalty (20:13), through bathing and sacrifice a person can be purified from such pollutions (e.g., 15:17–18, 29–30).[23]

Further, by claiming that the Holiness Code prohibition of homosexual acts arises merely out of concern for ceremonial purity and not for morality, the argument assumes a disjunction between ethics and ritual cleanness that is foreign to Leviticus. The Holiness Code presents everything Yahweh prohibits as a matter requiring due seriousness. In opposition to those who would dismiss the injunction against homosexual acts because it is merely a stipulation for Old Testament ritual cleanness, sociologist David Greenberg noted, "That intercourse with a menstruating woman is also classified as an abomination along with homosexuality is an indication not . . . that the latter offense was considered trivial, but rather that the former was considered extremely grave."[24]

Considerations such as these make it difficult to get around the conclusion that the Holiness Code prohibits homosexual acts in general and that it did so on the basis of concerns that were at least in part moral. But why did the Hebrews view such behavior as abhorrent?

One possibility emerges from a consideration of how male-to-male intercourse would have been interpreted in the Old Testament era. As we have noted already, in ancient patriarchal societies to be the recipient of anal penetration constituted a grave affront to masculine dignity. Consequently, to force another man to such an act entailed a violation and degrading of his male glory. Perhaps this concern motivated the prohibitions in the Holiness Code.

Unfortunately this interpretation fails, for it cannot explain why the second text stipulates the punishment of death for both participants. We would expect that only the perpetrator of the affront to the dignity of the other should bear the punishment of the act, as appears to be the case in strictures found among other ancient cultures.[25] Of course we might argue that the penalty simply forms a strong deterrent to anyone who might voluntarily submit to such degradation. But given the assumed cultural understanding of being penetrated, it seems highly unlikely that such a forceful warning would be needed. We are left searching for a deeper motivation at work in this law, which in the punishment it demands is unique among ancient cultures.

A second suggestion builds from the assumption that the chief concern of this entire section of the Holiness Code is the misuse of semen.[26] Homosexual activity is an abomination because it does not produce offspring, a grave concern in an agrarian society such as Israel.

As plausible as this theory may sound, it is difficult to substantiate. Nowhere does the Bible explicitly put forth this type of argument in speaking against any sexual behavior, let alone male homosexual acts.[27] Hence, the concern of the ancient writers was likely not limited to semen and its role in reproduction per se.

A more promising possibility looks to the created order as the foundation for the injunctions. The sexual strictures were intended to prohibit certain acts which because they were contrary to the fixed order of creation crossed the boundary between natural and unnatural behavior.[28]

Drawing from the biblical designation of such acts as an "abomination," Bailey found a point of connection between this dimension and the context of the threat of idolatry in which the Holiness Code was written. The term "abomination," he noted,

> is closely associated with idolatry, and designates not only false gods but also the worship and conduct of those who serve them. By a natural extension of meaning, however, it can also denote whatever reverses the proper order of things, and this seems to be the connotation of *to'ebhah* as applied to homosexual acts in Leviticus. Such acts are regarded as 'abomination' not . . . because they were practised by Egyptian or Canaanite idolaters (for of this there is no proof), but because, as a reversal of what is sexually natural, they exemplify the spirit of idolatry which is itself the fundamental subversion of true order.[29]

H. Darrell Lance, who himself favors an openness to homosexuality, arrived at a similar conclusion. "Both Leviticus 18:22 and 20:13 are unambiguous in their practical effect: homosexual relations between Israelite men are forbidden and are punishable by death." This prohibition, he added, is grounded not only in the connection to idolatry, but also creation. "Such acts violated the created order of male and female and are *to'ebah:* they are an idolatrous affront to the integrity of the deity."[30]

This suggestion pinpoints a crucial factor in the biblical rejection of homosexual acts. Yet it does not account for the prohibitions that place limitations on sexual activity that surround the injunction against homosexual acts found in both texts within the Holiness Code. Taken together, these commands suggest that an even more central, albeit related, theme is at work here. The injunctions of the Holiness Code regulating sexual behavior appear to have as their intention the safeguarding and preservation of the marital context in which sexual acts are to occur. Hence, Peter Coleman is on the right track in declaring, "Old Testament morality concerning sexual relationships is in basic principle committed to the defence of family and married life, and everything outside it is seen as a threat and an outrage, an abomination not to be permitted in Israel."[31]

One additional question remains, however. To what extent does the prohibition of homosexual behavior continue to have binding authority into the present? Many people today argue that consistency demands that we reject whatever injunctions against homosexual acts we find in the law as no longer valid. To this end, they remind us that we exempt ourselves from many of the commands in the Holiness Code, such as the ban on intercourse during a woman's menstrual period and the injunction against wearing clothes made from different types of cloth.[32] And they rightly point out that most people would no longer demand the death penalty for homosexual activity.

To reject the moral teaching of the text on this basis, however, fails to understand why the Holiness Code stipulated the death penalty for certain acts and why that stipulation is no longer in force. At the heart of these chapters of Leviticus is the warning that Israel's disobedience will defile the land, and as a consequence the land will "vomit" them out, as it did the former inhabitants (Lev. 18:24–30). With a view toward this dire threat, the Holiness Code provides a way for the people as a whole to separate themselves from those who transgress the laws. Thereby they are able to purge themselves of corporate responsibility for the offenses of the few and avoid the awful fate that disobedience would otherwise bring upon them.[33]

Further, under the Old Covenant the severity of the penalty was an indication of the importance of the precept. Certain acts resulted in an Israelite becoming ritually unclean for a set period of time, after which he or she might again join the worshiping community. Other offenses, however, were so heinous that the holiness of the community could only be preserved though the expulsion of the transgressor from their midst. The death penalty marked the complete eradication of such offenders from Israel not only for the sake of the purity of the community but also to ensure Israel's ongoing presence in the land.

In contrast to ancient Israel, the New Testament community is not localized within a particular physical land given them through divine promise. Consequently, according to the New Testament writers eradication of those who commit abhorrent offenses occurs through excommunication (which is connected with spiritual death) rather than through the death penalty itself. For this reason, Christians may continue to cite the ethical normativity of the stricture of the Holiness Code against homosexual behavior, while not advocating that the physical penalty it stipulated remains in force.

The argument from consistency suffers from an additional weakness as well. Taken to the limit, the logic of the argument could in effect negate every attempt to find moral guidance in the Old Testament law. Hence, the same argument could lead us to dismiss the strictures against such practices as incest (Lev. 18:9), slander (Lev. 19:16), or even cruelty to the physically challenged (Lev. 19:14).

What prevents us from doing so? One crucial factor is our discovery that the New Testament writers reiterate certain Old Testament prohibitions while ignoring others.[34] This, of course, leads us to consider the texts in the Pauline writings that seem to reaffirm the strictures of the Holiness Code.

Paul's Critique of
Pagan Society (Rom. 1:26–27)

Without a doubt, the central biblical text around which the contemporary debate over homosexuality revolves is Paul's condemnation of same-sex relations found within the context of his critique of the pagan society of his day. Traditionalists see in these verses a clear New Testament confirmation and expansion to females of the prohibition of male-to-male intercourse articulated in the Holiness Code. Here, they contend, the apostle forthrightly declares that all forms of same-sex genital behavior are immoral. This interpretation of Paul's words is hotly contested today.

Some contemporary exegetes simply downplay the importance of the reference to homosexual behavior in this text. For example, Furnish asserted, "Paul's remark about same-sex intercourse is incidental to his main point in Romans 1:18–3:20 and to his exposition of God's grace in the following chapters."[35]

It is certainly correct that the apostle devotes little space to such acts—two verses in a lengthy letter. Yet his statement is hardly "incidental." Margaret Davies, who herself considers Paul's view on this topic "an anomalous emotional blindspot in an otherwise radical transformation of tradition," nevertheless advised, "We should notice that Romans 1 includes a much longer list of vices which intimate the general corruption in vv. 29–31, but it is still true that homosexual practice is particularly highlighted."[36]

A more common approach is to claim that Paul was not voicing a blanket rejection of all homosexual acts, but that his intention lay elsewhere. Where? One proposal claims that the apostle's remarks were aimed at some specific practice widespread in the Roman Empire of his day, such as temple prostitution or, more likely, pederasty (i.e., homosexual relations between an adult and a youth).[37]

While it is likely that Paul meant to include pederasty, narrowing the focus to this form of behavior alone seems to go against the whole tenor of his indictment. The apostle speaks of the behavior he has in mind in general terms. It involves "males with males"

(v. 27), not "men with boys," as would be the case if pederasty alone were in view and as Plato had said in his critique of this practice.[38]

That Paul is not concerned merely with pederasty is evident as well in his inclusion of a reference to "females" who "exchanged natural relations for unnatural ones" (v. 26). Of course, it is possible that the apostle means certain heterosexual practices he—like others of his day—supposedly considered "unnatural" (perhaps anal intercourse or women adopting the "superior" position in intercourse).[39] This is how certain early Christian exegetes understood the text. Yet the conclusion of most interpreters today is that the apostle's words do in fact refer to lesbian behavior.[40]

A second alternative to the traditional view claims that Paul was condemning "perverts" rather than "inverts." The objects of the apostle's indictment were heterosexual persons who by engaging in homosexual behavior were acting against their own nature.[41] Thus, he was not thinking about persons who find in themselves a "natural" homosexual preference (inversion) and who as a result enter into loving, stable homosexual relationships, a situation about which the apostle supposedly knew nothing. In fact, proponents add, for a person who is naturally homosexual to engage in a heterosexual act would be to violate the spirit of the text.

While packing a fair amount of appeal, upon closer inspection this interpretation collapses.[42] The apostle did not have in mind the personal life histories of some specifiable group of his contemporaries. One clue that this is the case lies in the wording Paul uses. He does not state these people changed *their* natural, but *the* natural sexual functioning (although we might not want to push this literal reading of the Greek construction too far). This also indicates that in Paul's mind there is a natural way as well as an unnatural way to have sexual relations and that the standard is not merely the preferences of the individual himself or herself.[43]

Further, the verse does not speak of natural and unnatural *feelings,* but natural and unnatural *function.*[44] Hence, Paul does not suggest that the morality of sexual acts is to be judged on the basis of the inner disposition of the actor but in accordance with what the apostle considered to be our "natural" functioning as humans. As Peter Coleman concluded about the pervert-but-not-invert theory, "it is probably unrealistic to suppose that Paul himself could have thought in this way. . . . this is really an attempt to read the old texts with modern presuppositions."[45]

But the most telling clue lies in the context in which Paul couches his critique. Although there are ample examples in the Western interpretive tradition of commentators who have seen an individual focus in this text, many contemporary exegetes aver that rather than referring to any specific collection of individuals, Paul is offering a corporate indictment of pagan society.[46] To cite L. William Countryman's words, "Paul did not, of course, mean that every Gentile . . . began to experience homosexual desire as a direct result of individual sin. He was thinking in terms of Gentile culture as a whole, not of individuals."[47] Hence, the text is best understood as Paul's description of a digression that he believed to have taken place as a consequence of idolatry. The apostle is assuming that heterosexual expression had once been the universal human practice, but somewhere along the line homosexual acts had become prevalent.

Perhaps the most challenging alternative to the traditional view claims that the text does not articulate Paul's own moral conclusions but summarizes the typical Hellenistic Jewish picture of Gentile society and in so doing lays the foundation for Paul's subsequent attack on Jewish hypocrisy (Romans 2).[48] To this end, the apostle avoids describing homosexual acts as sinful. Instead, thinking in terms of Jewish understandings of ritual cleanness, he speaks of such behavior as "unclean."[49]

Although this theory has been cogently articulated, it has not gained a strong following.[50] In contrast to those who interpret Paul as saying that homosexual acts merely lead to Jewish ritual uncleanness or invoke social disapproval, Greenberg offered this summary appraisal:

> That Paul did not regard deviations from what is natural as *invariably* bad is shown by his use of the term elsewhere. . . . Neverthe-

less, it is clear that he did view *this* deviation negatively. He is describing a people who, in ignorance of God, plunged into many forms of vice and wickedness, homosexuality among them. The enormity of their crimes was so great that they deserved to die.[51]

As Greenberg's statement suggests, it appears that Paul did consider the same-sex genital behavior prevalent in his day, whether between males or females, to be morally condemnable because such acts were "unnatural." But this raises the crucial question, On what basis did the apostle come to this conclusion? What does Paul mean by "nature"? What leads Paul to assert that heterosexual intercourse is "natural" whereas homosexual behavior is "unnatural"?[52]

Some interpreters argue that for Paul "nature" simply means convention. As in 1 Corinthians 11:14, the term refers to the generally accepted practice in a particular time and place.[53] Yet Paul knew full well that in the Gentile culture of his day homosexual acts were not "against convention." On the contrary, there was a powerful group within the Roman Empire that either favored or practiced various same-sex behaviors.

A more promising approach looks to the various ancient sources Paul had at his disposal for the source of his view of "nature." This approach then seeks to understand the apostle's condemnation of homosexual acts in the context of these sources.

From his reading of the literature, Furnish claimed to have found two main concerns that motivated such opposition among ancient authors. First, same-sex intercourse is unnatural because it necessarily transgresses the widely accepted "patriarchal" understanding of sex roles. Male-to-male intercourse demeans the partner who takes the woman's inferior, passive role, whereas lesbian acts require that one or both usurp the man's superior, aggressive role. Second, the ancients believed that same-sex intercourse is unnatural because humankind would be doomed to extinction were everyone to opt for it.[54]

It is, however, not obvious that either of these two concerns actually motivated Paul. Rather than being slavishly tied to the hierarchical sex roles of his day, the apostle was quite able to display a countercultural egalitarian attitude toward sexual relations within marriage (1 Cor. 7:3–5).[55] Nor did he ever indicate that he was overly concerned about the demise of the human species. In fact, he was imbued with an apocalyptic eschatology that anticipated the immanent consummation of human history. And in view of the distressing times in which he thought he was living, Paul actually counseled people to forgo marriage and hence having children (1 Cor. 7:26).

Although the specific concerns Furnish cited may not provide the key to understanding what motivated Paul, the apostle no doubt was borrowing language and imagery from other ancient writings. But which ones?

Some exegetes look to Greek sources, especially the Stoic writers, for the background to Paul's understanding of "nature." While this literature is a likely candidate, for the Stoic moralists regularly differentiated between natural and unnatural acts,[56] it is unlikely that the apostle appropriated Stoic ideas unmodified. Paul had at his fingertips a Hellenistic Jewish tradition that wedded Greek philosophical ideas to the Old Testament heritage. This tradition, exemplified by such intertestamental writings as the Wisdom of Solomon,[57] offered an elaborate account of the rise of idolatry with the attendant plunge of Gentile culture into degradation.

Because the concept of "nature" crossed the boundary between Jewish and Greek thought, Paul's choice of this term was ingenious. His entire readership—both Jew and Gentile—could identify with the word. As Peter Coleman helpfully observed:

> Among the Christians in Rome, therefore, those converted from Judaism would find little new or strange in Paul's argument at this stage of the Epistle. Gentile converts would probably have heard such condemnation from Stoic sources, and perhaps be aware that Roman law officially disapproved of homosexual behaviour, irrespective of rumours about disgraceful goings-on in the dissolute imperial court.[58]

Although Stoic ideas were no doubt present, it is likely that Paul was more consciously drawing from Hellenist Jewish sources. From the assumption that Paul was following this literature, Dale Martin has constructed what he takes to be the narrative lying behind the apostle's diatribe:

> Once upon a time, even after the sin of Adam, all humanity was safely and securely monotheistic. At some point in ancient history most of humanity rebelled against God, rejected the knowledge of the true God, made idols for themselves, and proceeded to worship those things that by nature are not gods. As punishment for their invention of idolatry and polytheism, God "handed them over" to depravity, allowing them to follow their "passions," which led them into sexual immorality, particularly same-sex coupling. Homosexual activity was the punishment meted out by God for the sin of idolatry and paganism.[59]

This reconstruction of the Hellenistic Jewish myth of the origins of idolatry led Martin to conclude that Paul does not appeal to the narrative of creation and fall to establish the sinfulness of same-sex behavior. Hence, the apostle is not presenting an indictment of a universal human condition but of Gentile culture. Martin then questions the apostle's entire characterization, noting that the ancient myth Paul borrows is simply out of keeping with modern ideas: Most people do not believe that all humankind was once monotheistic nor that homosexuality is the consequence of polytheism.[60]

Martin's suggestion raises a crucial question. He leads us to ask, What narrative would the Jewish contingent in Paul's audience "hear" when they read his indictment of Gentile society? They might recall the myth of the rise of idolatry developed during the intertestamental period, as Martin asserts. But is this the only or even the most likely possibility?

Paul's readers would undoubtedly also hear overtones to another, related narrative—that of the creation account in the opening chapters of Genesis. The apostle's lament that the Gentiles "exchanged the glory of the immortal God for images made to look like mortal human beings and birds and animals and reptiles" (Rom. 1:23, NIV) would readily take the reader back to the primordial divine intention to make human beings "in our image" and to give humans dominion over "the fish of the sea and the birds of the air, over the livestock . . . and over all the creatures that move along the ground" (Gen. 1:26, NIV).

Further, in referring to humankind as male and female, Paul uses the more general Greek words *arsen* and *thelus,* rather than *gune* and *aner,* which more readily denote the marital relationship of husband and wife. In so doing, the apostle follows the Septuagint rendering of the narrative of the creation of humankind as male and female (Gen. 1:27).[61]

Paul may have had the Jewish myth of the rise of idolatry in view. But standing behind that myth is a wider story—a story of which this myth is but one more installment—that of God's intention for humankind as delineated in the Genesis creation narrative and our human failure to live according to the Creator's good purposes.

This observation is in keeping with the Hellenistic Jewish tradition from which Paul was borrowing. These religionists characteristically filtered Stoic ideas through Jewish monotheism, so that "nature" became identified with God's creative intention.[62] And as Paul's writings repeatedly indicate, his foundational standard for human conduct lay in God's ultimate purpose for humankind, a *telos* announced in the Genesis creation narrative but more fully disclosed in God's saving act in Jesus, which, in the words of Wolfgang Schrage, "reveals the world once more as God's creation."[63] Hence, we ought to view Paul's concept of "nature" as a broad idea that refers to the world and human life as intended by God, so that conversely everything that runs contrary to God's intention is "unnatural."

But what about Martin's claim that unlike Paul, we do not take the Jewish idolatry myth as historically factual? Even if the myth is not actual history, it does not for that reason necessarily lose its appeal. Paul is offering a theological, rather than a modern, historical narrative. He is recounting the story of human sin and divine grace. In this story, Gentile society constituted the continuation of the trajectory of human sin that began in our common primordial past, whereas Israel and, more recently, the church are signs of God's salvific intervention into human history. In keeping with this theological narrative, Paul places idolatry and its consequences (including homosexual behavior) in conjunction with Gentile culture and not in his subsequent indictment of the Jews, who for all their shortcomings have been the bearers of the tradition of the knowledge and worship of the true God (e.g., Rom. 3:1–2).

Paul's critique of homosexual behavior as an expression of idolatry does not rise and fall with the historical validity of the Jewish myth that may lie behind the text for another reason as well. Paul may be saying little more than that cultic idolatry and homosexual activity as phenomena within human society have their genesis in a common source. This source is the primordial sin of "idolatry" understood as the rejection of the truth of God together with willful departure from the design of the Creator.

At the same time, it seems that Martin may have overstated the point. Some biologists today believe that humankind has a single origin. If so, it is at least as conceivable that the first humans were characterized by a common primordial religious ethos from which subsequent generations fell away as it is that our primeval religious ethos was polymorphous.

In addition, the recent sociological studies of David Greenberg offer an interesting, indirect confirmation of Paul's point. There may in fact be a parallel between the rise of polytheism and the advent of homosexual activities within ancient human culture. Greenberg concluded that ancient societies did not generally repress male homosexuality when practiced within certain limits. On the contrary, in many agricultural societies, "male homosexual relations were invested with sacramental significance." Greenberg found two major exceptions, however: "when a nomadic people that lacked institutionalized cult homosexuality conquered another that had it," and, more importantly for our purposes, "when religion shifted from the veneration of deities who are immanent in the world, to the worship of transcendent gods."

Greenberg explained this latter connection: "Immanent deities, imagined on human or animal models, are gendered and can be sexual; the latter are more abstract, and cannot express themselves sexually."[64] Given this sociological connection, it is not surprising that Paul would include homosexual behavior in his critique of the idolatrous Gentile world that had refused to honor the only true God, the God of Israel.

To summarize: In his critique of homosexual acts as practiced in Gentile society, Paul is upholding as his standard God's intention for woman and man. In keeping with the injunctions of the Holiness Code, the apostle declared that this model is natural, for it alone fits with the Creator's design for sexual activity. Homosexual relations, whether between men or women, are "against nature," because they are contrary to this divine intent. And for Paul it comes as no surprise that in an idolatrous culture, which sacrifices the truth of God, homosexual acts would emerge.

The Pauline Rejection of Same-Sex Acts (1 Cor. 6:9; 1 Tim. 1:10)

In Romans 1, Paul spoke of homosexual behavior in the context of a forceful critique of Gentile society. In two other texts the apostle singles out certain specific acts. Both references occur in the context of short lists of sins. In composing such lists, Paul was following a typical practice among both pagan and Jewish moralists.[65]

The contemporary exegetical debate focuses on the exact meaning of the Greek words *malakos* and *arsenokoites* in 1 Corinthians 6:9. In 1 Timothy 1:10, the latter term occurs again, lodged between two possibly related terms, *pornos* and *andrapodistas*.

Some exegetes have concluded that these texts are in fact irrelevant to the discussion. Boswell, for example, is convinced that neither of the terms used in 1 Corinthians 6:9 "connoted homosexual-ity in the time of Paul or for centuries thereafter."[66] If any sexual behavior was in view, it was simply masturbation and perhaps male cult prostitution.[67] While some exegetes see in the text evidence that Paul linked the homosexual acts he condemned with idolatry,[68] Boswell's thesis has failed to win widespread agreement.[69]

Certain other interpreters agree that the two terms do refer to sexual misbehavior. But they come away with the sense that we have insufficient information to offer any definitive pronounce-ments as to the exact meaning of the terms. Hence, as Furnish de-clared, "neither of these lists nor their respective contexts actually discuss same-sex practices, so it is impossible to know exactly what is in mind."[70]

Most exegetes, however, agree that Paul did have some type of same-sex behavior in view. But they are divided as to exactly what he was condemning.

With the notable exception of Boswell and Countryman,[71] nearly all interpreters begin by observing that the two terms in 1 Corinthians are closely related. More specifically, these words— to cite Bailey's succinct statement—"denote respectively those males who engage passively or actively in homosexual acts."[72]

The first of the pair, *malakos,* is actually an adjective meaning "soft" or "weak." In the ancient world, the word was often used negatively to denote men who others considered to be "effemi-nate." It was only a short step to the sexual use of *malakos* as re-ferring to the more passive male in a same-sex relationship and adolescent boys who sold themselves for sex with older men.[73] Hence, the Bauer Greek-English lexicon offers the more general meaning: "men and boys who allow themselves to be misused ho-mosexually."[74]

The second word, *arsenokoites,* is related to the noun *koite,* the usual euphemism in the Septuagint for the emission of semen and hence a Greek term for "seminal emission."[75] Thus, *arsenokoites* designates the one who takes the active genital role in male-to-male intercourse.[76] This observation together with the connection to *malakos* suggests that *arsenokoites* refers to the one who assumes the more active role in such intercourse. With this in view, Furnish renders 1 Corinthians 6:9–10: "Don't deceive yourselves: Neither the sexually immoral, nor idolaters, nor adulterers, nor effeminate males, nor men who have sex with them . . . will get into God's kingdom."[77]

Because the word is unique to these two texts in the New Testament, scholars have sought to determine its origin. Scroggs theorized that *arsenokoites* is simply a literal rendering in Greek of the Hebrew phrase *mishkav zakur,* "lying with a male," the usual way of referring to male homosexual intercourse in early rabbinic literature.[78] David Wright demonstrated that the Greek term in all likelihood arose from the Septuagint rendering of the two injunctions against homosexual behavior in the Holiness Code, especially Leviticus 20:13, which reads, *hos an koimethe meta arsenos koiten gynaikos.*[79] Wright's work provides an important link between Paul's injunctions and the prohibitions in Leviticus.

Despite this exegetical spadework, there is a lack of consensus as to whether the references are to specific acts or are more general in scope. Many exegetes gravitate to the possibility that Paul was only speaking against "youthful callboys and their customers."[80] For example, Robin Scroggs asserted that in 1 Timothy 1:10 *pornos* is juxtaposed to *arsenokoites* in a manner similar to *malakos* in 1 Corinthians. Drawing from what he saw as the normal Greek use of *pornos* as "prostitute"—whether one who sells himself or who is a slave in the brothel house—and linking all three terms together, he offered the translation: "male prostitutes, males who lie [with them] and slave dealers [who procure them]."[81]

Others, however, are convinced that Paul is speaking against any type of male-to-male intercourse. From his survey of the pertinent literature, David Wright concluded, "It is difficult to believe that *arsenokoitai* was intended to indict only the commonest Greek relationship involving an adult and a teenager." Rather, Paul meant it to be a more generic term for male activity with males.[82]

Finally, we must remind ourselves that Paul's list in the Corinthian epistle occurs in the wider context of matters related to proper sexual conduct and the believing community (1 Cor. 5— 8). As his subsequent discussion indicates, Paul was convinced that the only proper context for sexual intercourse was heterosexual marriage. The apostle apparently did not see any reason to elaborate further why homosexual behavior violated this basic view.[83]

The Silent Texts

The contemporary exegetical debate has rightly focused on the biblical texts that apparently speak against certain same-sex acts. Yet it has not been limited to the passages we have discussed so far. Some scholars suggest that a few seemingly silent texts in fact speak volumes to this issue.

The Story of David and Jonathan

One important attempt to let the silent texts speak involves the search for the presence of homosexual relationships within the narrative of ancient Israel. Although a few scholars suggest that the bond between Ruth and Naomi may have been that of a lesbian couple,[84] by far the stronger candidate is the close bond between David and Jonathan.[85]

Drawing from possible parallels to the Babylonian *Epic of Gilgamesh,* Greenberg, for example, finds homosexual overtones in the story of Jonathan and David.[86] According to Greenberg's reading of the story, the context for the drama was set when David, whom Saul loved, entered the king's service as his armor-bearer (1 Sam. 16:21). After David killed Goliath, however, a potential rivalry emerged: "Jonathan became one in spirit with David, and he loved him as himself. . . . And Jonathan made a covenant with David because he loved him as himself" (1 Sam. 18:1, 3). Soon Saul turned on David to the point of attempting to kill him. And when Jonathan sided with David, the king flew into a rage, even cursing his own son (1 Sam. 20:30). While acknowledging that

Saul feared David's growing popularity, as the text itself indicates, Greenberg nevertheless concluded, "sexual jealousy runs through the narration like a red thread."[87]

Whereas Greenberg finds innuendos of a homosexual love triangle, others focus on the relationship between David and Jonathan. The central clue that leads to speculation that theirs is a story of homosexual love comes in David's lament after the death of his friend: "your love to me was wonderful, passing the love of women" (2 Sam. 1:26).[88]

Critics are quick to point out that there is no explicit mention of a sexual relationship in the biblical texts. In response, Greenberg appeals to the possibility that subsequent redactors altered the original narrative: "The Hebrew Bible underwent extensive editing before being put into final form, and an explicit homosexual relationship between David and Jonathan could easily have been deleted by priestly editors."[89]

Despite various attempts to uncover a deeper-lying story of homosexual love, most scholars remain unconvinced. Whatever feelings David and Jonathan had for each other, both were definitely heterosexual in behavior, for both were married and fathered children.[90] And rather than looking for a tone that fits with modern homosexuality, several exegetes suggest that we are closer to the story if we view the language it uses to describe their relationship as typical of the treaty terminology of the day.[91]

Jesus' Silence and Its Significance

Perhaps more significant to the discussion is what from one perspective appears to be the enigmatic silence of Jesus on this matter. Proponents of an affirming stance toward homosexual love today suggest that this silence indicates that our Lord did not find this issue at all important.[92] Further, they point out that on the occasions when Jesus could have legislated against homosexual conduct, namely, when he mentioned Sodom, he chose to speak instead of inhospitality (Matt. 10:12–15; Luke 10:10–12) and unbelief (Matt. 11:23–24).[93] Finally, some even see hints in the story of the healing of the centurian's servant (Matt. 8:5–13; Luke 7:1–10) and in Jesus' statement about eunuchs (Matt. 19:10–12) that our Lord was not at all hostile to persons who had had homosexual relationships.[94]

While these observations ought not to be dismissed too quickly, arguments from silence are notoriously difficult to substantiate. We might just as easily conclude that other acts about which Jesus was silent were equally unimportant to the Master. For example, does his silence about incest mean that we are no longer bound to the Old Testament prohibitions in this area? It would seem that the same logic might demand that we affirm loving, committed relationships between a brother and a sister.

But why Jesus' silence? One possibility is that homosexual behavior was simply not a major problem in first-century Palestine. Bailey indicates that the mainstream of rabbinical literature did not tend to speak of the sin of Sodom as homosexual acts, in contrast to the writings of those Jews who faced the potential inroads of Greek practices.[95] Jesus appears to stand more in this dominant Jewish tradition. Perhaps this was to a great degree because the conflicts out of which much of his teaching arose, especially as it pertained to his attempt to interpret the Hebrew scriptures correctly, were almost exclusively with the Pharisees and Sadducees in the Jewish enclave of Palestine.

Jesus did indeed speak about the proper expression of human sexuality, however. He condemned sexual immorality, which he differentiated from adultery (Mark 7:21). What Jesus meant by immorality we can only conjecture. But nowhere did he condone genital sexual activity outside the context of a lifelong heterosexual commitment. In fact, the only option he mentioned other than marriage was celibacy (Matt. 19:11–12). Moreover, whenever Jesus engaged with questions involving human sexual conduct, he appealed to God's intention in creation (e.g., Mark 10:11–12; Matt. 19:4–9).

Conclusion

Recent exegetical discussions of biblical literature have deepened our understanding of the ancient world and have given us deeper insight into the texts that mention homosexual acts. Nevertheless, scholars who propose that the church accept committed same-sex relationships have yet to produce a sufficient basis for revising the traditional belief that the biblical writers condemned homosexual conduct, at least as they had come to know it.

Robin Lane Fox, who favors a more open stance, offered this conclusion:

> As for homosexuality, Paul and the early epistles agreed with the accepted Jewish view that it was a deadly sin which provoked God's wrath. It led to earthquakes and natural disasters, which were evident in the fate of Sodom. The absence of Gospel teaching on the topic did not amount to tacit approval. All orthodox Christians knew that homosexuals went to hell, until a modern minority tried to make them forget it.[96]

Of course, there remains the possibility that the ancient texts have become passe. Perhaps what the biblical writers were referring to in their contexts was so totally different from the modern phenomenon that we simply cannot transfer their condemnatory response to the ancient phenomena to the present situation. I will look more closely at this possibility in chapter 4. But before tackling it, I must survey the historical teaching of the church about same-sex behavior.

Homosexuality
and Church Teaching

Until recently, most Christians assumed that the church had spoken with nearly total consistency on homosexuality. Church teaching on this topic, they believed, formed an unbroken line from the biblical documents to the present. The church had condemned homoerotic behavior as sinful, as a violation of God's intention for human sexuality.

In the last half of the twentieth century this understanding of Christian history came under fire, as voices both inside and outside the church called for a more nuanced reading of the tradition. The publication in 1955 of *Homosexuality and the Western Christian Tradition,* by Derrick Sherwin Bailey, marked an important turning point in the reappraisal of the historical trajectory. Even more challenging to the assumed understanding, however, was the appearance twenty-five years later of John Boswell's *Christianity, Social Tolerance, and Homosexuality* (1980). A third volume, *The Construction of Homosexuality* (1988), by David F. Greenberg, offered a social constructionist view not only of Christian teaching but of the concept of homosexuality in other cultures as well.

Boswell argued that apart from isolated exceptions, homosexual people in Christian society were not significantly censured during the first millennium of church history. Beginning in the 1200s, however, they—together with other minorities such as the Jews—became the victims of rising intolerance. According to Boswell, this change was precipitated in part by a general movement toward uniformity in society and by an acute fear of heretics and non-Christians that came in the wake of the crusades.

In this chapter I revisit the trajectory of church history in order to provide an overview of ecclesiastical teaching on homosexuality. My goals are to determine the extent to which the church has consistently rejected homosexual behavior as sinful, as well as to consider the significance of that rejection.

Censuring Behavior:
Church Teaching on Homosexuality

From the early centuries (commonly known as "the patristic era") to the twentieth century, Christian moralists have censured homosexual behavior. But what activities have drawn ecclesiastical condemnation? And in what contexts have Christian moralists warned the faithful against involvement in such acts?

The Patristic Era:
Standing Apart from Corruption

The early church leaders, like the biblical writers, were not preoccupied with the issue of homosexuality. Nevertheless, Christian moralists deemed certain same-sex behaviors significant enough to warrant their attention. The response of these leaders was an unambiguous rejection of such activities.[1] Bailey offered this appraisal: "Although the matter is never discussed extensively, nor in general otherwise than incidentally, there can be no doubt that the early Church regarded homosexual practices with unqualified disapproval, particularly when committed by men with boys, or with one another."[2] The teachings of the moralists in the patristic era set the foundational position of the church, a position that remained largely intact until the twentieth century.

The initial target of the church's censure was pederasty. Ecclesiastical response to this widespread practice in Roman society came as early as the *Epistle of Barnabas* (written sometime between 70 and 135 C.E.): "Do not fornicate; do not commit adultery; do not practice pederasty; do not let the Word of God escape your lips in the presence of any that are impure."[3] A warning against pederasty likewise found its way into the "household code" of the *Didache,* written in the late first century C.E. The second chapter includes this injunction: "Do not murder; do not commit adultery; do not corrupt boys; do not fornicate; do not steal; do not practice magic."[4] The *Apostolic Constitutions,* a late–fourth-century Syrian writing, offered a somewhat lengthier admonition concerning this practice. After speaking out against adultery, this document declares, "Thou shalt not corrupt boys; for this wickedness is contrary to nature, and arose from Sodom, which was therefore entirely consumed with fire sent from God."[5]

Church synods also spoke against homosexual practices. For example, the church leaders gathered at the Council of Elvira in Spain (305–306 C.E.) voiced an official condemnation of pederasty by denying communion even at the hour of death to men who "defiled" boys.[6] In addition, such documents as the Irish Penitentials — a somewhat ad hoc group of writings that offered guidance for confessors in the administration of private penance by assigning an appropriate penance for each sin based on the perceived gravity of the act[7] — established penances for persons who sinned in this manner.[8]

Although many of these early statements specifically condemned sexual relations with "boys," Boswell and others caution against interpreting the term too narrowly. Rather than being limited to a youth, a "boy" could mean a homosexual partner of any age. Thus, references to "pederasty" frequently had no relation to the age of the objects of desire.[9] Instead, as Bailey observed about the Council of Elvira, "subsequent legislation and Church opinion suggests that at this time no distinction was made between different kinds of homosexual offenders."[10]

The statements cited thus far also suggest that male homosexual acts were the special target of censure in the patristic era. While this is no doubt true, church leaders also went on record opposing sexual relations between women, partly under the assumption that on the basis of Romans 1:26–27, sexual relations between women, as well as between men, violated nature.[11]

In response to what they saw as the immorality of Roman society, Christian moralists took seriously the New Testament call to chaste living with its focus on marriage as the only context for genital sexual expression and its elevation of celibacy as an alternative vocation for believers. To this end, these teachers admonished their flock to avoid a host of sexual temptations, including fornication, adultery, and sex with prostitutes. Whether these activities were heterosexual or homosexual was beside the point. They viewed all such conduct as sinful.

In keeping with this appraisal, the admonitions of the patristic era placed homosexual sins on the same level as other sexual transgressions.[12] Even as late as the close of the fourth century, in their disciplinary regulations for homosexual behavior, Basil[13] and Gregory of Nyssa[14] assessed the gravity of this offense as similar to adultery, greater than fornication, but less than murder or apostasy. In addition, church leaders admonished the celibate among the clergy and the monastic orders to refrain from homosexual relations. In such exhortations they not only singled out males[15] but spoke to nuns as well.[16]

In their condemnation of homosexual practices, church leaders appealed to several authoritative sources. Of course, the biblical texts were high on their list. As the citation from the *Apostolic Constitutions* I noted earlier indicates, the Sodom story was one such authoritative biblical text. Paul's mention of homosexual behavior in his diatribe against pagan society loomed significant as well.[17] But several of the early moralists, including Tertullian,[18] Origen,[19] Clement of Alexandria,[20] and Eusebius of Caesarea,[21] also appealed to the prohibitions in the Leviticus Holiness Code, which they considered binding on Christians.[22]

Following Paul, many church fathers condemned homosexual acts as being "contrary to nature."[23] Yet it is not always obvious what they meant by this phrase.[24] Augustine, for example, declared that such practices violate one's relationship with God.[25] Like many others, Clement of Alexandria argued that homosexual behavior is unnatural because it is intrinsically nonprocreative.[26]

In condemning homosexual acts, the early church leaders also appealed to Greek sources. Yet their appropriation of the Greeks was selective and never uncritical. John Chrysostom, to cite one example, denounced Plato for the great philosopher's support of pederasty.[27]

The moral stance of the Christian leaders eventually influenced governmental policy of the Christianized empire.[28] Whereas the pagan emperors had tolerated homosexual prostitution, even using it as a source of revenue for the state, by about 250 C.E. this practice was the target of official suppression.[29] In 390, the emperors Valentinian and Theodosius increased the penalty for homosexual offenses: "All persons who have the shameful custom of condemning a man's body, acting the part of a woman's, to the sufferance of an alien sex (for they appear not to be different from women), shall expiate a crime of this kind in avenging flames in the sight of the people."[30]

In the sixth century, the emperor Justinian provided an interesting augmentation to the civil legislation. To the legal condemnation of homosexual practices, he added exhortations to those guilty of such offenses, calling on offenders to repent and seek forgiveness. Justinian voiced a concern that the divine vengeance visited on Sodom would likewise destroy the empire, if this vice continued.[31]

After surveying the two-hundred-year development of "sodomy" laws, Bailey offered this striking conclusion:

> the picture, conjured up by certain writers, of panic-stricken imperial religious fanatics obsessed with fear of the consequences of sodomy and committed by their Faith to an implacable persecution of the 'love' which the Greeks had esteemed, is a mischievous travesty of the facts. On the contrary, the edicts of the emperors . . . were the acts of responsible legislators and . . . were directed against abuses which are incontestably injurious to the well-being of society.[32]

Speaking of Justinian in particular, Bailey then added,

> Justinian, who is often castigated as the chief and most fanatical of the Christian emperors who penalized homosexual practices, is in

fact notable as the only one who showed himself concerned as much for the repentance and reformation of offenders as for their punishment.[33]

The Middle Ages:
Official Church Condemnation

In the Middle Ages the various teachings about homosexual behavior that had been set forth in the patristic era solidified into an official ecclesiastical stance against such activities. This posture came to expression in several ways.

One means of official expression was to offer forgiveness to penitent offenders. This attempt is evident in the Penitentials. The Penitentials listed homosexual activity among various sexual sins, which included less consequential infractions such as masturbation and engaging in intercourse in the wrong posture, as well as grave vices like fornication and adultery. Within this context, the Penitentials also distinguished among a variety of homosexual behaviors, ranging from mere same-sex kissing to the use of an artificial phallus in lesbian relationships and male-to-male intercourse. The manner in which the Penitentials treated such acts suggests that medieval spiritual leaders did not consider homosexual practices as categorically different in gravity from heterosexual misconduct.[34]

By the advent of the Middle Ages, same-sex sexual behavior had become especially problematic among the clergy and in the monasteries. Hence, when Charlemagne became emperor in the eighth century, he attempted to reform the monastic orders, for he believed that they had grown lax toward homosexual sin.[35]

Charlemagne's attempts indicate the continuing role the civil sphere undertook in seeking to suppress same-sex practices. Boswell claims that such civil sanctions occurred without ecclesiastical advice or support, and that they may have even been partly directed against church leadership.[36] While this conjecture is perhaps correct, there is little evidence that the church hierarchy disagreed with the underlying principle, namely, that homosexual conduct was morally repugnant.

Bailey offered what appears to be a fair assessment of ecclesiastical legislation from the second through the twelfth centuries. His comment reveals the growing connection between the church and civil strictures that emerged in the Middle Ages. The person who engages in homosexual activity, Bailey wrote, "is certainly denounced as one guilty of very grave sin, but he is not singled out for any sadistic persecution; he is offered reconciliation with God and man through the Church's penitential discipline, but if he refuses the means of grace, he has to take the eternal consequences of his sin and the temporary consequences of his crime."[37]

In addition to providing forgiveness through penance and influencing—even if indirectly—the attitude of civil rulers, the church sought to deal with homosexual behavior through official pronouncements. Edicts in Gothic Spain (650) and Jerusalem (1120) condemned both active and passive participation in homosexual acts. But the first general church ruling on homosexual behavior came at the Third Lateran Council (1179). According to the council directive:

> Let all who are found guilty of that unnatural vice for which the wrath of God came down upon the sons of disobedience and destroyed the five cities with fire, if they are clerics be expelled from the clergy or confined in monasteries to do penance; if they are laymen they are to incur excommunication and be completely separated from the society of the faithful.[38]

Subsequent councils at Paris (1212) and Rouen (1214) added an interesting additional prohibition: nuns were not to sleep together.[39] Penance and the threat of excommunication became two powerful weapons the church could wield among a people concerned with their prospects of gaining access to heaven.

As the Middle Ages unfolded, church leaders became increasingly concerned about matters of morality. Homosexual activity among the clergy, who were now to be strictly celibate, was a special cause for concern.[40] Moralists also worried about a connection they perceived between theological heresy and moral laxity—including homosexual practice—among certain religious groups that stood outside the mainstream of ecclesiastical and civil life. During this time, public attitudes toward homosexual activity hardened as well.[41]

In the wake of this growing concern, church leaders increased the penance required for sexual sins, including homosexual behavior. This ecclesiastical response found its parallel in the civil realm in the form of laws mandating strict punishments for "sodomy"[42] (which, however, was not consistently defined solely as homosexual activity[43]).

Despite the stiffening stance, the church of the high Middle Ages had not declared "open season" on homosexual offenders. Bailey concluded,

> there is no proof that large numbers of persons were put to death simply and solely because they had committed some homosexual offence. Indeed, it is doubtful whether such delinquents were ever handed over by the Church to the civil power after conviction in the ecclesiastical courts—and it is to be noted that the various canons against sodomists go no further than the imposition of an appropriate penance. Generally, it seems that in practice homosexual offenders only became liable to the severity of the law if their behaviour was attributable to heretical ideas, or if immorality in conduct was accompanied by grave error in belief.[44]

In addition, official strictures retained their focus on behavior. As Greenberg observed, "Someone who wanted to engage in sodomy but did not do so was no sodomite, and someone who had done so but had stopped was one no longer. The category was defined by the act, not the person."[45]

In the writings of Thomas Aquinas, the Middle Ages produced perhaps the most carefully reasoned moral argument against homosexual behavior constructed prior to the modern era. Aquinas placed homosexual practices among the six species of lust (the other five being fornication, adultery, incest, seduction, and rape), which are contrary to the proper end of the sex act. Of the six, homosexual acts, whether among males or females, are the most grievous because they—together with masturbation, bestiality, and unnatural heterosexual sex—are also "contrary to the natural order of the venereal act as becoming to the human race." That is, these practices are devoid of the potential for procreation.[46] In this manner, Aquinas paved the way for the subsequent elevation of homosexual behavior as an especially grievous sin.

The Post-Reformation Climate: Rejection and Reconsideration

The Protestant Reformation saw no marked change in church teaching on homosexuality. Initially, the crucial issue of sexual ethics was not whether homosexual behavior was sinful, but whether those who as monks and nuns had vowed celibacy were now free to marry.[47] Nevertheless, the Reformers' commitment to follow the biblical texts as they understood them led these church leaders to condemn homosexual behavior, whenever they took a stand on the issue.[48] Almost without exception the denominations that emerged out of the Reformation viewed homosexual acts as sinful, some even refusing practicing homosexual persons entrance into the church.

Meanwhile, the Roman Catholic Church of the Counter-Reformation strengthened its stance against homosexual behavior. Ignatius of Loyola, for example, supported the censuring of priests and monks involved in homosexual acts. Habitual offenders—whether lay or cleric—were to be excommunicated.

In the wake of the Reformation, many Western nations enacted legislation banning homosexual behavior. Such activity was illegal in Calvin's Geneva and Puritan New England.[49] In England under Henry VIII (1533), homosexual intercourse became a felony, sodomy cases were transferred from ecclesiastical to civil courts, and the death penalty for offenders was imposed. Similar legislation was reenacted under Elizabeth I (1563).[50]

As late as 1750, two homosexual offenders were publicly executed in Paris.[51] Although the death penalty was removed from English law in 1861, the statute against homosexual intercourse remained in effect until 1967.[52] Greenberg offers this summary of the legal situation in the post-Reformation era: "The conjuncture of extremely harsh legislation justified primarily on religious grounds, erratic enforcement, and popular indifference, punctuated by infrequent episodes of repression, remained characteristic of social responses to homosexuality from the Renaissance through the eighteenth century."[53]

Signs of change, however, eventually began to appear. A limited degree of social and civil toleration emerged in such places as France during the Enlightenment and Russia under Peter and Catherine.[54] More significantly, the eighteenth century became a period of "cognitive transition," to cite Greenberg's helpful characterization:

> Some continued to view homosexuality as a vice anyone might find attractive. Those who thought that found homosexuality especially frightening, because they believed it had the potential for spreading and reaching epidemiclike proportions. Others began to see effeminacy and homosexuality as defining a distinct type of person whose sexual orientation was fairly stable, and whose distinguishing essence was determined in some way by factors outside his own control.[55]

The stage had been set for a rethinking of homosexuality in general and same-sex conduct in particular.

The Implications of the Tradition

There is little debate today about the main features of the historical trajectory as outlined above. More controversial, however, is its significance. For this reason, I must offer a preliminary statement as to what conclusions can be drawn from the tradition.

The Focus on Male Homosexuality

Contemporary discussions about the implications of the Christian tradition repeatedly ask why Christian moralists devoted so much attention specifically to male same-sex activity. Why do we find in church history repeated strictures against male-to-male intercourse (i.e., "sodomy"), whereas so little is said about lesbian practices?

Historians generally respond by suggesting that from ancient times to the present people have tended to view male-to-male intercourse as especially degrading or disgusting. But why? Bailey voiced the typical explanation:

> There has been a marked tendency to regard sodomy in particular as though it were, so to speak, 'playing the woman' to another man, or using another man 'like a woman.' . . . In other words, this act has been looked upon as one which involves the degradation, not so much of human nature itself as of the male, since in it he simulates or encourages or compels another to simulate the coital function of the female—a 'perversion' intolerable in its implications to any society organized in accordance with the theory that woman is essentially subordinate to man.[56]

In short, the "standard" theory looks to the patriarchal nature of Western culture for the answer. In the eyes of the patriarchalist, homosexual acts are disgusting chiefly, if not solely, because they transform a male into a lowly female.

At first glance, this theory appears to have merit. Certain circles in our society today promote a "macho" image of what it means to be male and react with revulsion toward any male who fails to fit that image. This macho mystique explains, at least in part, the widely held belief that the male homosexual is an especially despicable "pervert." If the present is a trustworthy indicator of the past, we can well imagine that similar ideas were widespread in previous centuries as well.

Despite its appeal, as an explanation of what provided the foundation for the consistent rejection of homosexual behavior in the

Christian tradition, the theory is inadequate. Even if patriarchal macho images of maleness were prevalent in previous eras, this ethos would not necessarily have led to an elevation of male same-sex relations as more grievous than female practices. Patriarchal ideals might just as easily have produced concern about lesbian activities. Although female homosexual acts tend to be less structured and readily allow for a blurring of roles, persons influenced by patriarchal understandings generally assume that in every lesbian liaison, one partner must play the male role. What could be more unthinkable from a patriarchalist perspective than for a lowly woman to usurp the position of a man?

The theory falls short in another, more important way as well. If such acts are morally reprehensible merely because they efface a preconceived male ideal, as this explanation assumes, only the one who actually plays the "female part" ought to be seen as culpable, for only this person is truly guilty of degrading or bringing shame upon "maleness." We see overtones of this mindset in the Sodom story. And it is clearly evident in situations today, such as prisons and gangs, where males use roles in homosexual acts as a way of asserting personal supremacy and of degrading rivals. In such contexts, social "rules" generally attribute no guilt to the "male" partner in an act by which another is degraded or degrades himself.

The suggestion that animosity toward homosexual acts arose out of concern to preserve the male ideal fails to account for the evenhanded manner in which the traditional injunctions treat the parties involved in male-to-male intercourse. Like the biblical writers before them, Christian moralists did not limit their admonitions to those who willingly play the "female" role (and hence efface their maleness). Instead, they also spoke out against the perpetrators of homosexual acts—in fact, against anyone who plays the "male" role—and hence are not themselves guilty of degrading their own maleness. This suggests that the moralists' concern moved beyond merely trying to propagate a patriarchal image of maleness.

The theory is suspect as well because it reads too much into the language of "playing the woman's part" found in ancient writings. Rather than providing the rationale for the condemnation of homosexual acts, such language may have been merely descriptive. In using this image, the moralist offered a vivid, readily understood picture of the behavior being condemned.

It is, however, instructive to note why such language (e.g., "You shall not lie with a male as with a woman"—Lev. 18:22) would carry such descriptive force, for this may in fact indicate the actual reason why homosexual acts were deemed loathsome. In using the image of "playing the woman's part," moralists drew from the widely held biblical assumption that sexual intercourse by its very nature involves a male and a female partner.

Another reason often proposed as to why male homosexual acts became the special target of censure appeals to ancient misunderstandings of how conception occurs. At one time, people believed that the male plants human "seed" in the female much like a farmer sows seed in a field. According to this model the male is directly responsible for conception, whereas the female provides the context in which the offspring develops prior to birth. This ancient understanding led to what Bailey called "a superstitious reverence for semen,"[57] which he in turn cites to explain why ancient moralists considered male same-sex intercourse reprehensible: Unlike female homosexual behavior, such acts involve the emission of semen.

At first glance this theory also seems plausible. But it too is flawed. Essentially it draws from an unsubstantiated conjecture.[58] Nowhere in the writings of the Christian moralists do we find an argument against homosexual behavior based on an appeal specifically to the loss of life-carrying semen. Further, if concern for the loss of semen did provide the foundation for the rejection of homosexual practice, we would anticipate that the introduction of a more adequate understanding of conception would evoke a sustained call to revise the strictures against male-to-male intercourse. Yet this did not occur.

Concern for the loss of semen itself was likely not of central interest to the Christian moralists. Yet in certain early moral codes the
juxtaposing of strictures against homosexual behavior and such
heterosexual practices as intercourse in the "wrong" position point
to a possible deeper concern. The Christian teachers seemed to have
desired to preserve a higher good, namely, reverence for the joining together of male and female in the great wonder of procreation.

If neither of these theories provides the complete picture, what is
the answer? Why did Christian moralists devote so much more attention to male homosexual acts than to offenses involving females?

Before venturing an answer, a cautionary word is in order. We
ought to avoid overstating the disparity. Without a doubt the ma-
jority of statements in the tradition speak about male homosexual
acts. Nevertheless, we also find strictures against female same-sex
behavior in every major epoch of church history. Christian moralists—whose ranks include Tertullian, Augustine, and the leaders at
the Council of Rouen—were not indifferent to this phenomenon.

At the same time, I readily admit that Christian teachers did
speak less often about female same-sex behavior. Why? Perhaps
the most obvious reason is also the most illuminating: It simply
was not as pressing a problem.

Like the epistles in the New Testament, most of the writings
produced during the early years of church history were occasional
pieces, composed for the purpose of dealing with problems that
had arisen in the church. Lesbian behavior was not one of them.
Hence, Greenberg came close to the truth when he noted matter-
of-factly, "sexual relations between women received so little discussion in secular and religious sources that they could not have
been common or publicly visible."[59]

Again we are pressed to ascertain why this was so. Here we do
well to invoke Bailey's first suggestion cited earlier. The answer
may lie with patriarchal social structures that dominated ancient
and medieval culture. The world into which the gospel first
came—whether Jewish Palestine or the ancient Roman Empire—
was deeply patriarchal, as was the Christianized empire that even-

tually emerged from that world. These social structures were far more conducive to male than to female homosexual relationships.

However, there developed relatively early in church history the one place within the broader patriarchal context where lesbian relationships might readily emerge, namely, among nuns in the cloistered context of the convent. Therefore, it comes as no surprise that female same-sex behavior did in fact emerge in the convent. So pressing was this problem that it attracted the attention of church leaders.

The Motivation for Church Strictures

In the quest to determine the implications of the Christian tradition I must raise another, more crucial question as well: What motivated the condemnation of same-sex behavior we find in that tradition? More specifically, what lay at the foundation of the censuring of such acts in the patristic era?

Some scholars suggest that the initial rejection of same-sex relations arose as an outworking of the general ascetic antipathy to sex that quickly came to characterize the patristic church.[60] The early church was "antisex," this argument charges; consequently, church moralists opposed homosexual sex not because it was categorically different from heterosexual sex, but merely because it was one variety of sexual expression, which was itself an evil.

The ascetic impulse was doubtless one important factor, and a bias against sexual activity of any type was certainly a strong motivation for some Christian moralists. Yet the theory is wide of the mark. It assumes a greater antipathy to sexual expression than was in fact the case in the patristic era. While gnostic influences that deprecated the physical dimension of human existence remained a struggle in the early church for several centuries, the orthodox teachers never elevated celibacy as the norm for all believers. Instead, they followed the main trajectory of biblical teaching (which included Paul) in acknowledging marriage as a viable option, albeit one which also required a type of chastity in the form of sexual fidelity.

Rather than being one particular case reflecting an opposition to sexual expression in general, the condemnation of homosexual activities was embedded in a much larger ethical stance Christian moralists enjoined on the Christian community. Although Roman laws prohibiting certain forms of homosexual conduct likely predated Jesus' birth, the ancient Roman Empire tolerated some same-sex practices, especially involvement of male citizens with slaves or foreigners. In addition, homosexual behavior among adult males as well as pederasty were routinely practiced, at least among the upper classes.[61]

Patristic moralists were concerned that the Christian community be holy and that believers in Jesus stand apart from the moral corruption and sexual vice widespread in the surrounding pagan society. The homosexual practices of the Romans were but one of many expressions of the general moral debauchery Christian leaders saw around them. These acts stood on the same level as a host of sins—of other transgressions of God's holiness. Some of these were sexual. But many were not; they involved other dimensions of human life.

The increased prominence of the church in the empire did not lessen the danger that sexual vice posed to the community. But it did alter the focus of concern. The great influx of people from pagan backgrounds brought immoral practices into the very heart of the church. Even clergy were guilty of immorality, including homosexual behavior. Chrysostom offered this sobering appraisal of the church in fourth-century Antioch:

> But these persons who are, so to speak "rational," who have had the benefit of divine instruction, who say to others what should be done and what should not be done, and who have heard the scriptures which have come down from heaven—these men have intercourse more fearlessly with young boys than with prostitutes![62]

Faced with this crisis situation, Christian moralists shifted their attention to the clergy. They became concerned for purity among church leaders. Sexual purity was especially crucial, as celibacy became first the more desirable option for clergy, then the norm, and finally a requirement.

Although the shift in focus precipitated the unfortunate perception that the clergy were called to a higher standard of morality than the laity, the concern for purity among church leaders was well placed. In the Middle Ages, people looked to priests, monks, and nuns to give shape to societal attitudes and values. Christian moralists were wisely attentive to the ethical example such persons offered to the populace. In a sense, the very survival of Western society was at stake.

Celibate shepherds of Christ's church, however, faced a grave difficulty, namely, how to handle the erotic impulse. This impulse did not disappear at the moment of ordination to the priesthood; it could not be parked at the doorway to the monastic order. Nor did the spiritual focus that pervaded life in the Middle Ages banish eroticism from the Christianized society that typified the era. Instead, the erotic and the spiritual often coalesced.

For persons called to the celibate life this coalescence ideally ought to have come to expression in devotion to Jesus (which was a far easier pathway for nuns to tread than for monks and priests). But rather than being limited to this divine-human relationship, the spiritualized eroticism of the age regularly found an outlet in friendships among colleagues. Such relationships sometimes expressed themselves in heterosexual physical acts. But given the close contact available in monasteries and convents, they could more easily result in homosexual expressions of various types.

Boswell, who celebrates the erotic friendships within the ranks of the medieval clergy, warned against confusing this eroticization of same-sex friendship with contemporary homosexual bonding.[63] He is surely correct in this. Such caution prevents us from finding in church strictures intended largely to suppress homosexual behavior among a celibate clergy a sure-fire precedence for a rejection of same-sex coupling today. But Boswell's caution cuts both ways. It also ought to alert us to the impossibility of finding in erotic same-sex friendships among celibate medieval clergy the foundation for the homosexual partnerships often operative today. Where does this leave us? This much I would conclude from the tradition: Whenever the church was confronted with sexual practices involving persons of the same sex, Christian teachers spoke out against such behaviors. Despite differences among them, the ecclesiastical sources Boswell and others cite never expressed moral approval of, or even indifference to, same-sex activity. On the contrary, explicit moral references to such behavior in the Christian tradition were consistently negative.[64]

This suggests that Christian ethicists from the second century to the twentieth forge an unbroken chain. Their teaching, which condemned a variety of behaviors, occurring as they did in differing social contexts, nevertheless connects all such actions together. The Christian trajectory draws together the varieties of pederasty prevalent in pagan Roman society; the conduct of medieval clergy, monks, and nuns, who expressed their deep affection through sexual acts; certain acts of sexual licentiousness prevalent among heterodox groups in the Middle Ages; and the homoerotic activities present in post-Reformation Western society. In each era, Christian moralists rejected the same-sex practices of their day. And they consistently found the basis for such condemnation in the several scriptural texts in which the biblical authors appear to pronounce divine judgment on the homosexual behavior with which they were confronted.

That all such practices were lumped together under the misleading name "sodomy" is unfortunate. Yet this error in judgment does not negate the insight shared throughout the tradition, namely, that the call to godly holiness entails vigilance on many fronts, including the sexual. When taken seriously, such vigilance demands that believers avoid illicit sexual practices, among which are fornication, adultery, and—the tradition would add—same-sex behavior.

Homosexuality and Biblical Authority

What does the Bible teach about homosexuality? In chapter 2, I engaged this question in a preliminary manner by looking at the major texts that purportedly condemn same-sex intercourse. The goal of my earlier deliberations was to determine the extent to which recent exegetical findings provide a sufficient foundation for revising the traditional understanding of these central texts.

My conclusion was quite modest: Contemporary explorations do shed light on several of the passages. Nevertheless, recent findings do not provide sufficient warrant to reject completely the traditional exegesis, which, as I outlined in chapter 3, has formed the biblical foundation for the church's nearly consistent condemnation of same-sex intercourse.

Although crucial, this conclusion does not bring the interaction with the Bible to a close, for it does not yet provide a satisfactory answer to the question, What does Scripture teach *us* about homosexuality? For this reason we must take another look at the biblical material. Now, however, we step back from the individual texts themselves and consider a crucial topic that the contemporary debate has placed on center stage, namely, biblical authority.

My purpose in this chapter is to come to a more explicit conclusion about the manner in which biblical texts ought to function in the construction of a contemporary Christian outlook toward homosexuality. Thus, I now raise the controversial matter of the authority of the Bible in Christian sexual ethics.

How Does the Bible Speak to Homosexuality Today?

En route to understanding the role of scripture in shaping the church's outlook toward homosexuality today, I must attempt to determine more explicitly whether, in what sense, and to what extent the Bible speaks to the contemporary question. Here four basic options present themselves.

Total Biblical Silence

We might answer these questions by simply concluding that the Bible is silent on the issue. That is, exegetical deliberations could lead us to surmise that scripture nowhere speaks about homosexual behavior of any type; Christians who find precepts in scripture condemning same-sex intercourse are simply misreading the texts. Certain abusive homosexual practices may be unethical, but one ought not attempt to build a case against homosexuality in general by appeal to specific biblical passages that purportedly speak directly to the issue.

As I indicated in chapter 2, Derrick Sherwin Bailey and others have claimed as much in their consideration of the story of Sodom (Genesis 19) and the narrative of the Levite and his concubine (Judges 19). The focus of these texts, they argue, is not homosexual acts at all. Instead, these narratives address what in ancient society was an inexcusable sin—inhospitality.

This position requires only a brief response. Recent exegesis has effectively shown that there are markedly fewer biblical texts that refer directly to same-sex intercourse than Christian ethicists once thought. Yet, as the discussions in chapter 2 suggest, almost no contemporary biblical scholar would go so far as to assert that *none* of the texts considered earlier touches on homosexual practices of any type. Consequently, we may quickly dismiss this first proposal.

Partial Biblical Silence

More widely held, and thus far more important, is a second suggestion. Many persons who call for a more open stance toward homosexuality readily admit that the Bible condemns certain same-sex practices. But they add that the target of such injunctions is a set of specific abuses found in biblical times. John McNeill represents this view well. Drawing from the work of the Dutch scholar Herman van de Spijker, he acknowledges that "wherever the Bible clearly seems to refer to homosexual activity, we must recognize a judgment of condemnation." But McNeill immediately adds,

> Every text dealing with homosexual activity also refers to aggravating circumstances such as idolatry, sacred prostitution, promiscuity, violent rape, seduction of children, and violation of guests' rights. As a result one can never be sure to what extent the condemnation was of homosexual activities as such or only of homosexual activities under these circumstances.[1]

Proponents then take an additional step. The biblical texts, they aver, are not relevant to the issue standing at the heart of the contemporary debate.[2] These passages cannot be invoked against the loving, committed, stable homosexual relationships that today's gays and lesbians are interested in maintaining.[3]

Why not? The standard answer[4] is simple: Such relationships are expressions of a reality about which the biblical writers knew nothing, namely, homosexuality as a fixed "sexual orientation," a sexual "inversion," or a lifelong pattern of sexual preference. Marilyn Bennett Alexander and James Preston speak for many in declaring, "The original biblical languages of Hebrew and Greek have no word for homosexuality, let alone specific vocabulary to connote any particular understanding of sexuality, gender identity, or sexual orientation."[5]

The implication of this assumption is far-reaching: If the biblical writers knew nothing of homosexuality as a constitutional or congenital reality, we are wrong in reading the biblical texts discussed in chapter 2 as condemning the loving expression exhibited between two persons whose sexual preference is toward persons of the same sex. In fact, for the invert—for the one for whom homosexuality is a natural condition—to engage in homosexual acts is morally and ethically right, so long as such acts occur within a loving and responsible relationship.[6]

Ethicist James Nelson capsuled this conclusion:

> The specific New Testament judgments against homosexual practice simply are not relevant to today's debate about the validity of caring, mutual relationships between consenting adults. Nor does the Bible directly address today's question about the appropriateness of homosexuality as a psychosexual orientation.[7]

This position, however, builds from certain assumptions that require further scrutiny. For example, proponents presuppose that the same-sex character of the acts condemned in Scripture is incidental to that condemnation. Hence, they argue, the Levitical Holiness Code found involvement in male cult prostitution problematic only because of its connection to idolatry and not because it involves homosexual intercourse.

Yet such an assumption is difficult to maintain. The Old Testament writers do not generally condemn religious rituals solely because such practices were associated with the worship of pagan gods. On the contrary, certain of the sacrifices the Israelites offered closely resembled those of their neighbors.[8] And rather than banning the sacrifice of bulls because this animal was the symbol of Baal, the Torah actually prescribed its use in certain sacrifices.

The argument is predicated on another presupposition as well. Its proponents assume that the biblical writers were ignorant of homosexuality as a stable sexual preference. However, this assumption is not as self-evident as some would have us believe. Certain thinkers in the Greco-Roman world were aware of a type of constitutional homosexuality, even though they did not understand it in the psychosexual categories in vogue today.

Ptolemy, for example, spoke about certain "diseases of the soul" which he believed were the product of astrological influences. Among these, he included homosexual predilections. Although admitting that this condition was not the result of a deliberate choice rooted in sexual appetite, he nevertheless viewed homosexual affection as "contrary to nature."[9] For Ptolemy, the "natural" served as an objective standard by which conduct could be measured, regardless of what inclinations the persons involved might sense as "normal" for them.

Other philosophers appealed to Greek or Roman mythology to explain homosexual attraction. In the first century, Phaedrus suggested that the phenomenon occurred because Prometheus, after a drinking party with Bacchus, mistakenly affixed male sexual parts to some women and female parts to some men.[10]

In a somewhat similar manner, in Plato's *Symposium,* Aristophanes appeals to a Greek creation myth in which humans originally had four arms, four legs, and two faces. Some of these primordial creatures were androgynous, while others were double males or double females. To preclude a potential revolt, Zeus sliced each of them in half. This led to the emergence of love, understood as the innate desire to be restored to wholeness by fusing with another person of the "missing" sex. Those persons who were originally double females "are inclined . . . to women," whereas a formerly double male is "born to be a lover of boys or the willing mate of a man."[11] So well known was this myth that several Hellenistic Jews of Paul's day appealed to one aspect of it, the idea that the original human was androgynous, to resolve what they saw as an apparent contradiction in the Genesis creation narratives.[12]

In his monumental study, John Boswell acknowledged that "the idea that homosexuality represented a congenital physical characteristic was widespread in the Hellenistic world." Yet he quickly added, "it is not clear that Paul distinguished in his thoughts between gay persons (in the sense of permanent sexual preference) and heterosexuals who simply engaged in periodic homosexual behavior. It is in fact unlikely that many Jews of his day recognized such a distinction."[13]

In the end, Boswell's cautious stance is a conjecture, an argument from silence. It is just as likely that Paul was aware of the prevalent ideas about constitutional homosexuality. But like other thinkers of his day, he believed that acts springing from a person's inner constitution need not necessarily be deemed "natural." Indeed, this conjecture looms even more probable in the light of Paul's hypothesis that the human heart is "darkened" (Rom. 1:21).

Proponents of this second approach to the texts are correct in reminding us that we ought not simply equate the same-sex behavior that drew Paul's fire with the type of homosexuality being socially constructed in our day. Nevertheless, unless our vision is clouded by a cultural hubris, we surely ought to find some significance in the attempts of several of the apostle's contemporaries — as premodern as these attempts unavoidably were — to make sense out of the kind of congenital or constitutional condition they saw as expressing itself in pederasty and other objectionable behaviors.

Biblical Incorrectness

More radical than, yet often closely connected to, the second proposal is a third option. Many gay/lesbian activists readily acknowledge that the biblical writers condemn homosexuality. But, they quickly add, no one need take seriously their injunctions.

Why not? Some proponents appeal to the paltry nature of the biblical witness. Because homosexuality was of such minimal concern to the biblical writers, they argue, the scriptural condemnation of it ought not to occupy us today.

Canadian scholar Christopher Levan represents this position, asserting:

> The Bible cannot act as a solid basis upon which to make ethical judgments about homosexual practice when, on the whole, the biblical record treats same-gender sexual intimacy as a peripheral concern. How can Christian theology declare a law to be significant when the biblical record treats the issue against which the law is written as an inconsequential problem?[14]

Of course this conclusion begs the question as to how much attention the biblical writers must give to any issue before we take it seriously. The documents are equally reserved in speaking against a host of other matters, including such matters as incest and child abuse. Yet this relative silence does not dissuade us from rightly seeing such practices as necessitating our attention.

More significant is the claim that in condemning same-sex intercourse the biblical writers were simply wrong. Writing in *Christian Century,* Walter Wink declared forthrightly, "The Bible clearly considers homosexuality a sin. . . . I freely grant all that. The issue is precisely whether that biblical judgment is correct." Wink's position on this issue is clear, for he then asked rhetorically, "Are we not . . . free to re-evaluate the whole issue in the light of all available data and decide, under God, for ourselves?"[15]

In a similar manner, James Nelson announced that Paul's conclusions on the topic are not necessarily binding on Christians today:

> Perhaps we should just accept him for what he was: a faithful apostle and a profound interpreter of the central message of the gospel, yet one who was also a fallible and historically conditioned human being. . . . If the norm of the new humanity in Jesus Christ together with our best current moral wisdom and empirical knowledge would cause us to question some of Paul's moral convictions about the status of women and about the institution of human slavery, surely his moral judgments about homosexual acts ought not be exempt.[16]

Gay theologian Gary Comstock's comments are even more pointed. Referring to the various texts in the traditionalists' arsenal, he concluded, "Those passages will be brought up and used against us again and again until Christians demand their removal from the biblical canon or, at the very least, formally discredit their authority to prescribe behavior."[17]

On what basis do contemporary thinkers judge these texts so harshly? For many proponents, the Bible—or at least the prohibitions and admonitions of scripture—cannot stand as the foundational source for a Christian sexual ethic.[18] These theorists look to some other norm, seeing it as at least on a par with biblical teaching.

For their overarching authority, gay and lesbian activists typically appeal to personal experience. Foundational to them is the quest for acceptance and a sense of personal well-being as gay or lesbian persons. In the words of John McNeill,

> We lesbian and gay believers have the right and the duty to carefully scrutinize all religious belief systems and distinguish between those belief systems that support our need to achieve healthy self-acceptance and those that are destructive of our psychic health and maturity.[19]

This "given," in turn, sits in judgment over the biblical texts as well as over church teaching. Indeed, with this criterion in place, lesbian and gay critics can pick and choose what in the Christian tradition they find affirming, while rejecting whatever is critical or demands behavioral change. Gay theologians like McNeill are forthright in claiming this prerogative. He asserted, "We must ask ourselves which of the church's values we continue to want, respect, and love; in other words, which values are compatible with who we are and are not destructive of our dignity as persons."[20]

The gay/lesbian criterion leads many activists to place high value on personal autonomy. Comstock, for example, describes salvation as the promotion of autonomy: "Salvation is 'to choose *your* self,' not to 'be afraid of yourself,' to 'live your individuality to the full—but for the good of others.'"[21] This, in turn, allows Comstock to look within himself, and not to the external norms of scripture and tradition, in his quest for acceptance: "I skirt established Christian Scripture and tradition to gain autonomy, to locate myself within my own life, to escape an external authority and find an internal authority, to respond to my own need for the company of others." In Comstock's estimation, so doing does not entail an act of "rebellion," but a bold step of "independence."[22]

Some gay/lesbian readers offer a second basis for rejecting the biblical voice. They critique the texts as being legalistic reflections of ancient cultural prejudices.[23] More specifically, they argue that the injunctions against same-sex intercourse are the product of a deeply ingrained bias toward heterosexual males that arose out of the patriarchal nature of ancient society.[24]

Comstock finds this patriarchal bias reinforced by four themes running throughout the Bible:

> male lineage and genealogy,
> the tragedy of "barren" women and the value of women as childbearers,
> the use of "harlotry" as a metaphor for Israel's corporate sin,
> the wickedness of lesbians and gay men.

This bias, he proposes, accounts for the unfortunate condemnation of homosexual behavior present in scripture. "Within such a patriarchal framework," Comstock cautions his readers, "lesbians and gay men should not be surprised to find passages that malign us."[25]

Obviously, this third approach raises the question, In what sense can the biblical documents be said to be authoritative sources for theology and ethics in any ultimate way?

Biblical Normativity

Posing this question leads to yet a fourth option. Perhaps the Bible does speak to homosexuality as we know it today, and what it says is normative for Christians. Viewed from this perspective, Marion Soards is correct in observing that "the decision one makes about the validity of homosexual behavior for members of the Christian community is effectively a decision about the authority of the Bible in the life of the church."[26]

But exactly how ought the biblical statements to function in a normative manner today? To this central hermeneutical question I now turn.

How Should We Understand the Biblical Statements?

Most participants in the current debate about the proper Christian stance toward same-sex behavior would agree that the Bible ought to function authoritatively in the church. The question that divides the conversation participants is, How? What role should the biblical texts play in the construction of a Christian sex ethic? How can the Bible help us respond constructively to the issue of homosexuality? How should we be reading scripture in the midst of this controversy? In short, what hermeneutical key can bring the Bible into constructive conversation with our contemporary situation?

The Bible versus the Texts

In attempting to develop an ethic that can speak to this situation, proponents of a more inclusive stance toward homosexuality generally appeal to the Bible as a whole over against the texts that purportedly condemn homosexual behavior. By drawing from scripture certain themes they believe capture the heart of the biblical witness, they assert that the gospel itself—when properly understood—demands the affirmation of homosexual persons, despite the presence in the Bible of passages that at first glance appear to censure same-sex relations.

What are these themes? Here opinions vary. James Nelson has offered a constellation of principles he believes form the scriptural foundations for a Christian sex ethic. In Nelson's estimation, sexual acts ought above all to be "shaped by love, justice, equality, fidelity, mutual respect, compassion, and grateful joy."[27] Other scholars offer a more theologically focused foundation.

Covenant

The British ethicist Michael Keeling, for example, suggests that the Christian sex ethic must draw from "the fundamental moral structure of the Bible." His explorations lead him to the idea of "covenant" as forming this basic structure.[28]

According to Keeling, an ethic rooted in the idea of covenant saves us from a legalistic reading of any particular biblical verse, all of which he is convinced are culturally conditioned. More importantly, however, the covenantal understanding opens the way for us to see that the basic question is not "What should human beings do about sex?" but "How should human beings relate to one another?"[29] And the answer, of course, is "covenantally."

Keeling's ethic of covenant in effect eliminates our need to take seriously the few biblical texts that speak about same-sex behavior. By appealing to the Bible as a whole, we may judge homosexual liaisons as moral insofar as they are "covenantal," that is, based on a mutual covenant.

Love

Perhaps the most widely held suggestion looks beyond the covenant idea to the principle of love. The Christian ethic, proponents argue, is from beginning to end an ethic of love. Victor Furnish, to cite one advocate of this position, views love as forming the heart of the gospel of divine grace. The Christian community receives God's love as saving grace. But the divine love also delineates our task in the world.[30]

If the Christian ethic is fundamentally an ethic of love, then love defines what constitutes an ethical *sexual* relationship as well. Many ethicists take this a step further. They argue that love is not merely the foundational norm, but the *sole* norm in sexual ethics. According to John McNeill, for example, "a general consideration of human sexuality in the Bible leads to only one certain conclusion: those sexual relations can be justified morally which are a true expression of human love." McNeill sees this as the goal of the entire biblical trajectory:

> In the Old Testament an attempt was made to desacralize human sexuality by removing it from the realm of the mysterious and impersonal forces of nature. In the New Testament an attempt was made to resacralize human sexuality by integrating it into the ideal context of free, interpersonal human love.[31]

Walter Wink goes even further. He boldly asserts, *"There is no biblical sex ethic.* The Bible knows only a love ethic, which is constantly being brought to bear on whatever sexual mores are dominant in any given country, or culture, or period."[32]

For many ethicists the application of the love ethic to homosexual relations follows almost automatically. If love is the sole norm for ethical sexual relations, we must look to love—and not sexual orientation—to determine the morality of any such relation. A relation (or an act) is moral insofar as it is characterized by love, regardless of whether it is heterosexual or homosexual.

This, of course, in effect places homosexual and heterosexual relations on the same level. The British process thinker Norman Pittenger forthrightly affirms as much: "I suggest that the 'controls' for homosexual expression of human sexuality are the same as those for its heterosexual expression. They are based upon the centrality and primacy of love—love which is mutuality, sharing, giving-and-receiving, life together in the most radical sense of the phrase."[33]

Some proponents look to love as the hermeneutical key that harmonizes the morality of loving homosexual relations with the biblical texts that appear to condemn such relations. Others, however, simply turn the love hermeneutic against such passages. Victor Furnish, for example, asserts that the answer to the question, "How . . . can Scripture help to inform the mind of the modern church in the matter of homosexuality?" does not lie in "what a few biblical traditions and writers happen to say or imply about same-sex intercourse." Rather,

> New knowledge about the world and new realities within it require the believing community constantly to rethink what actions express God's grace and what actions do not. To accomplish this task in a way that is . . . appropriate to the gospel from which it lives, the church must test every proposed decision and action by the criterion implicit in Paul's appeal, "Let all that you do be done in love" (1 Cor. 16:14). . . . it is, finally, this gospel that must inform the decisions and shape the actions of the believing community in the matter of homosexuality.[34]

Love is undoubtedly the central principle lying at the heart of the Christian ethic.[35] Nevertheless, without further guidelines our attempts to live out a pure ethic of love become fraught with potential pitfalls. Humans are notoriously able to draw erroneous conclusions as to what love might entail in any specific situation. Devoid of guidance as to what love involves, we repeatedly find ourselves distorting genuine love in the name of "love."[36]

What occurs in our attempts to practice an ethic of love appears in our reflections about the nature of love as well. Left on our own, we are susceptible to the temptation of reducing the rich biblical understanding of love to a "shell-word," the content of which quickly finds itself at the mercy of whatever meanings the loudest voices within contemporary culture pour into it. Or we transform "love" into a self-regarding relativistic individualism.[37]

This is an especially irascible pitfall for current attempts to appeal to the ethic of love as a basis for affirming same-sex relations as valid expressions of the Christian ethic. Hence, Joe Dallas's seemingly straightforward observation encompasses a noteworthy insight: "The love between two homosexuals cannot make homosexuality normal or legitimate, any more than the love of two people committing adultery justifies the breaking of marital vows."[38]

Justice

Realizing the potential for problems posed by a focus on the love principle alone, certain ethicists have augmented the Christian ethic of love with additional, informing principles. Christopher Levan, for example, clearly sides with those who find that the elevation of love as the central norm for sexual relations leads to an inclusive stance toward same-sex relations. According to Levan,

> The chief prerequisite for any act to be in conformity with God's will is that it embody the divine intention for self-giving love. Gays and lesbians must ask themselves if their relationships enhance or inhibit

God's purpose of love. . . . Thus, sexuality is not a question of right technique, it is a question of right relationship. Does the practice in question enhance or inhibit the exchange of God's love—the vulnerable giving of self for the empowerment of the other.

But Levan realizes the danger his advice poses: "the discernment and embodiment of God's love is not a simple deed. All of us can so distort what we mean by the word 'love' that it covers practices which are in fact contrary to God's intent." For this reason, he qualifies the concept of love by a second central intention of God—justice.[39]

Liberation

Levan hopes that through the introduction of the idea of justice, sexual relations will not fall away from "God's intent." Hence, his interest lies at the level of interpersonal relationships. The theme of justice takes on a quite different concern in the proposals of gay/lesbian liberationists such as George Edwards.

Building from Rudolf Bultmann's insight that every exegete brings a "preunderstanding" to the text, Edwards argues that the appropriate preunderstanding for our day is "liberation." Our beginning point, he maintains, is the conviction that God is at work in those activities and movements that foster justice and peace. In particular, God is present in the struggle for the liberation of lesbian and gay people from social structures and ideologies that oppress them.[40]

As we might anticipate, Edwards turns this hermeneutical key against the biblical texts that he claims the church has historically used to condemn gays and lesbians. More specifically, he appeals to the theme of liberation as a means to evaluate the view of human sexuality proposed by the one New Testament writer who spoke against homosexual behavior, Paul. Edwards distinguishes the legal aspect from the liberative element in the Pauline texts and gives precedence to the latter.[41] In this manner, Edwards is able to exonerate Paul as a liberation theologian even while setting aside the apostle's negative assessment of homosexual practices, which "current sexology," Edwards asserts (following Victor Furnish), deems "outmoded."[42]

The Bible and the Texts

In advocating a more open stance toward homosexuality, contemporary thinkers like Edwards are drawing from an important hermeneutical principle: The "part" must be understood in the light of the "whole." Hence, the individual texts that deal with homosexuality must be placed in the context of the whole of scripture. Further, the contemporary focus on a hermeneutic of love and justice as providing the foundation for a Christian sex ethic is surely not misguided. Viewed in its entirety, the Bible does teach an ethic of love and does issue a call to justice. But exegetes such as Edwards move beyond sound hermeneutics when their interpretation places the central theme of the Bible as a whole in conflict with the teaching of the texts that censure homosexual behavior.

Implementing the Love Ethic

This problem can be illustrated by returning to the question I posed earlier about the implementation of the love ethic. Given the dangers noted earlier, how can we put such an ethic into operation both in our ethical reflections and in the concrete situations of life? On what basis can we conclude that we are in fact operating in accordance with love (and justice)?

One typical contemporary answer invokes the concept of mutual consent: Love and justice meet whenever two consenting adults voluntarily enter into a sexual relationship (whether it be homosexual or heterosexual).[43] While this proposal holds a certain attraction, its outworking in practice is often quite tricky. The phenomenon of sexual abuse has caused us to realize that even when mutual consent appears to be operative, at a deeper level such consent may in fact be not only lacking but actually impossible.[44]

According to Marie Fortune, meaningful consent "requires full knowledge *and* the power to say 'no.'"[45] Hence, consent can only be given when a certain balance of power exists between the persons involved. In *The Anatomy of Power,* economist John Kenneth Galbraith pinpoints the typical ways in which humans exercise power in relationships.[46] Sometimes a person influences others by threatening adverse consequences (condign power).[47] One also exercises power over others by offering some affirmative reward, that is, something they value (compensatory power). Or a person gains influence by appeal to what others believe to be natural, proper, or right (conditioned power).[48]

Galbraith's taxonomy alerts us to the possibility that one person can readily exercise undue power over another in many ways. Indeed, in many situations, one person enters the relationship at a definite power advantage over the other. This "power differential" works to the detriment of the powerless person in the event that the advantaged party desires to introduce the sexual element into the relationship.[49] Despite appearances to the contrary, the "weaker" person may not be in a position to withhold consent. This person may be so overwhelmed by the power of the other that he or she simply lacks the ability to say no. Cases such as these undermine the viability of "mutual consent" as definitive for measuring the presence of love and justice in a sexual relationship, whether it involves other-sex or same-sex partners.

In addition, mutual consent—even were it always operative—cannot be the only mark of a loving, just relationship. Surely we would not conclude that every sexual liaison or act to which the participants voluntarily consent is ethically proper. This principle would require that we affirm such practices as incest among adults, group sex, and polygamy (which was practiced in the Old Testament) whenever the participants engaged in them voluntarily and consensually.

Another typical contemporary response is to appeal to "long-term commitment." Proponents argue that relations or acts are moral insofar as they involve persons who are committed to each other. But this proposal is likewise problematic, for it begs the question as to what can qualify as a long-term commitment. And like the focus on mutual consent, it erroneously assumes that all acts connected to long-term commitments are ipso facto ethically proper.

Love and Law

The Christian ethic is indeed an ethic of love. Nevertheless, humans stand in need of guidance as to what love entails. It is precisely here that biblical precepts, commands, and prohibitions gain significance. Hence, it is also here that the texts about homosexuality, which must be read in the context of the whole Bible, must inform our understanding of the message of the Bible.

Such texts are, of course, culturally conditioned, insofar as they first arose out of specific historical-cultural situations. Yet as canonical writings, when properly understood within the context of the biblical message, these texts carry implications for the ongoing life of the believing community. This means that we must take seriously the biblical injunctions about same-sex intercourse, expressed as they are in a variety of historical-cultural contexts, in seeking to understand the meaning of Christian sexual love.

This statement introduces the question of the relationship of biblical precepts (i.e., the law) to Christian ethics. Here I can only offer a few preliminary remarks.[50] For Paul and other biblical writers, obedience to the law is not the means toward the ethical life. Even if we could live in perfect conformity to the law, our lives would not thereby correspond to God's intention for us (cf. Matt. 19:16–26), namely, that we develop person-to-person relationships that reflect God's own relationality. In itself the law is powerless to create the kind of godly relationships God wants us to enjoy.[51]

This does not mean, however, that the law is of no importance. Instead, the various biblical imperatives fulfill primarily a somewhat negative function. Scriptural prohibitions and injunctions serve to indicate the parameters within which the relationships

God desires for us can flourish. As believers seek to live within the realm toward which the law points, the indwelling Spirit seeks to create among us the kind of relationships that honor God.

While the Spirit takes us beyond the dictates of the law, this transforming Spirit does not routinely lead us outside the law. The Spirit does not direct us to transgress the law (when the law is properly understood). The connection between Spirit and Word indicates that Christians must test any impulse to act against the law, regardless of what we think our true motivations are. We must realize that such an impulse may be the dictates of an as-of-yet not eradicated sinful disposition, rather than the prompting of the Spirit.

True Liberation

The introduction of the Spirit's role in the ethical life leads us to the theme of liberation proposed by thinkers such as George Edwards. The quest for liberation is, of course, a central biblical concept. But liberation from what? And what exactly is liberation?

Here a person's prior conclusions about the ethical status of homosexuality often determine the answer. Some, like Edwards, approach the discussion with the assumption that homosexuality is positive and good. In their estimation, the problem of our day is not the presence of a homosexual orientation (or preference) in certain people, but the deeply ingrained personal and societal homophobia that prevents gays and lesbians from enjoying acceptance and affirmation. As a result, gay/lesbian liberationists deploy the language of liberation to advocate change in church and society.[52] And they assert that justice for gays and lesbians demands that the church affirm their right to express their sexual preference within same-sex relationships.

Other participants in the debate disagree. Convinced that the homosexual condition is not good, they view liberation as the release of homosexual persons from the dominance of what they see as sinful impulses and aberrant behavior patterns. Thomas Gillespie articulated this perspective well:

because the gospel is 'the power of God unto salvation' (Rom. 1:16), I am faithful to the faces of the people I know and care about when I tell them the gospel truth: that the power of the triune God is at work in and through the good news of Jesus Christ to liberate all from the oppression of sin, whether their particular vices are sexual or nonsexual, and, if the former, whether they are heterosexual or homosexual in kind.

Which of these two visions of liberation ought we embrace? This dilemma takes us back to the question with which I began the chapter, that is, to the fundamental matter of hermeneutics. In the end, we can only determine what vision of liberation ought to inform the contemporary debate by looking to the whole of scripture (and Christian tradition).

Yet, in a certain sense the two visions may not be mutually exclusive. Although calling for personal liberation from sin, Gillespie refuses to limit the liberation motif to the realm of personal salvation. Hence he added, "because 'the justice of God is revealed' in the gospel (Rom. 1:17), I am faithful to those same faces when I seek to overcome every form of systemic injustice that oppresses human life."[53]

In bringing these two seemingly disparate dimensions together, Gillespie is in fact following the example of the Old Testament prophets for whom social justice and personal holiness were intertwined (e.g., Ezek. 18:5–9; 22:6–12; 33:25–29; Amos 2:6–7; 5:24–27). The same principle is evident in the Leviticus Holiness Code, which articulates simultaneously a concern both for creaturely integrity and for the weak and oppressed within society. In fact, for the biblical writers these two concerns are not distinct, but interrelated moments of a single whole—the pursuit of justice. To maintain creatures in their integrity is itself one aspect of upholding justice for them. And in the sexual realm justice entails living in accordance with God's intention for human sexual relationships.

The hermeneutical principle of reading the part in the light of the whole leads us to an ethic of love (and justice), as many proponents of an inclusive stance toward gay and lesbian persons point out. And this principle reminds us that we must understand the significance of the texts that condemn homosexual behavior within the context of the overarching biblical love ethic.

At the same time, however, the concept of love remains nebulous unless it is understood in its own wider biblical context, namely, the context of our human *telos* as intended by God. Consequently, while "just love" lies squarely at the heart of the Christian ethic, this ethic is ultimately teleological. In the end, the ethical life entails living in accordance with God's intention for human existence. To determine this purpose as it relates to our sexuality is the goal of the next chapter.

Homosexuality
and the Christian Sex Ethic

In chapter 4, I inquired about the hermeneutical key that unlocks the significance of the biblical texts that speak about same-sex intercourse for the contemporary debate about homosexuality. I now take up the challenge of responding more directly to this question. My goal in this chapter is to build from the narrative that stood behind the rejection of the various homosexual behaviors found in the scriptural texts. I want to draw out the considerations from the foundational story that motivated biblical writers such as the compiler(s) of the Holiness Code and Paul to declare same-sex intercourse to be "unnatural" and thus unethical.

My assumption is that despite whatever influence other sources had on them, these authors were imbued with the narratives of God acting in human history that lay at the foundation first of the Hebrew and subsequently of the early Christian faith communities. Consequently, the scriptural injunctions against homosexual practices were embedded in a teleological understanding of "natural," an understanding derived fundamentally from an outlook toward God's intention for human life as depicted in the biblical narrative itself. For the biblical writers, then, the "natural" is what is in accordance with God's purpose, goal, or *telos* for human existence. And the divine purpose encompasses human sexual practice.

In keeping with this assumption, I begin the discussion by placing human sexuality in the context of the biblical narrative. My goal is to set forth a summary of Christian theological understanding of sexuality, marriage, and the sex act. The theological understanding of sexuality that emerges from these reflections, in turn, will provide the foundation for an ethical appraisal of same-sex intercourse and homosexuality in general. In this manner, I will be developing a basically teleological approach to the contemporary issue, an approach that draws from considerations of God's *telos*—God's purpose—for human relationships[1] as given in part in the creation narratives.

Human Sexuality in Theological Perspective

An awareness of human sexual distinctions appears almost immediately in the biblical story. Standing at the apex of the first creation narrative is God's fashioning of humankind in the divine image as male and female (Gen. 1:27–28). Sexual differentiation is even more prominent in the second story, which focuses on God's creation of the woman to deliver the man from his solitude (Gen. 2:18–24).

Most participants in the contemporary debate acknowledge the importance of these opening biblical narratives for our discussion of homosexuality. But they differ as to their significance. Traditionalists maintain that the union of male and female depicted in the Genesis accounts is designed to offer the only God-given model for human sexual relationships. Consequently, they argue that heterosexual marriage is the standard by which all human sexual expression is to be judged.[2]

Proponents of a more open stance toward homosexuality readily acknowledge that the narratives leave no place for homosexual persons. But they suggest reasons that heterosexual marriage is central in these texts.

One typical approach asserts that the stories must be understood in the context of the narrator's concern to provide a rationale for the importance of procreation to an ancient agricultural people whose livelihood was dependent on offspring to assist in the tasks associated with food production. Homosexual couples were not mentioned simply because they could not contribute to this goal. Because it was written in a social context quite different from our own, they conclude, we ought not to read the narrative as prescribing what must be true for us today.[3]

Although this understanding of the Genesis accounts is insightful, it nevertheless views the narratives from too narrow an interpretive horizon. This proposal fails to take into account the ongoing role the creation stories play throughout the biblical writings themselves, even in texts that emerged within social contexts that differed from the situation reflected in these stories. Hence, Paul appealed to the Genesis narratives, even though he lived in the more urban, less agrarian culture of the first-century Roman Empire.

Thus, the creation of humankind as male and female is central to the outlook toward human sexuality found within the entire biblical story. This broader creation-based understanding, in turn, lies behind the biblical injunctions that depict homosexual intercourse as "unnatural" and hence unethical.

The Nature of Human Sexuality[4]

Human beings are sexual creatures. But what is the significance of our sexuality?[5] Our first response might be: "for procreation." According to the biblical narrative, procreation is a crucial aspect of our creation as male and female, especially after the Fall (e.g., Gen. 4:1). Yet the begetting of children is not the only purpose for our creation as male and female.

The second creation story suggests that our sexuality is not limited to the physical characteristics and activities associated with male and female reproductive roles. Sexuality encompasses our fundamental existence in the world as embodied persons. It includes our way of being in and relating to the world as male or female. Above all, however, sexuality is connected to our incompleteness as embodied creatures, an incompleteness that biological sex symbolizes. Hence, sexuality lies behind the human quest for completeness. This yearning for wholeness, which we express through our seemingly innate drive to bond with others, forms an important basis for the interpersonal dimension of existence.

The second Genesis narrative highlights the interpersonal aspect of human sexuality. The story presents the creation of the woman as God's solution to Adam's solitude. The man enjoyed a relationship with the animals, yet none of them could provide what he truly needed, a partner with whom he could bond. Cognizant of this situation, God created another—the woman—to deliver Adam from his isolation. The man greeted her with the joyous declaration, she is "bone of my bones and flesh of my flesh" (Gen. 2:23). The episode concludes with the narrator's application of the phenomenon of male-female bonding: "Therefore a man leaves his father and his mother and clings to his wife, and they become one flesh" (v. 24). In this manner, the narrator points out that the drive toward bonding finds expression in the coming together of male and female in the unity of persons we know as marriage.

The interpersonal dynamic is not limited to the sexual bond, however. Our creation as male and female contributes to personal identity development as well. We discover—or construct—who we are in our embodied maleness or femaleness in part through our interaction with the other sex.

This dimension of our sexuality is also evident in the second creation account. Adam first sensed his own maleness when confronted with the woman. That encounter led him to declare joyfully, "She shall be called 'woman,' for she was taken out of man" (Gen. 2:23, NIV). In a sense, this aspect of the story provides an explanation of the first narrative, which links the *imago dei* to our creation as male and female (Gen. 1:27). We discover God's intention for us to be the divine image bearers—and hence our full humanness—through our interaction with one another as male and female. This can occur within marriage, of course, but it is also operative in all male-female relationships.

The Old Testament narrative views the sexual bond of husband and wife as the foundation for human social relationships—family, tribe, and eventually nation. Jesus, however, inaugurated one significant alteration to this pattern. Rather than elevating earthly ancestry, he looked to his heavenly parentage, counting as his true family "whoever does the will of my Father in heaven" (Matt. 12:50). In keeping with his own example, Jesus challenged his followers to place their relationship to him above all familial ties (Matt. 10:37). And he promised them a new spiritual family to compensate for the loss discipleship would exact from them (Mark 10:29–30).

According to Jesus, the primary human bond is not marriage and family, as important as these are, but the company of disciples. In this manner, human sexuality—understood as the quest to forsake our solitude through relations with others—finds ultimate fulfillment through participation in the community of believers who enjoy fellowship with God through Christ. And our innate incompleteness, related as it is to our fundamental sexuality, points toward the consummation of God's activity in the community of God's eternal kingdom.

En route to that future day, humans enter into a variety of personal relationships. Most of these are informal and somewhat fluid. Some people join together in another type of relationship as well, which in contrast to the first is to be permanent and exclusive. Although both are the outworking of the human drive toward bonding and hence are in this sense "sexual," they differ with respect to the type of sexual behavior proper to each, among other differences.

In this manner, the biblical narrative provides the foundation for a rich understanding of human sexuality, one that forms a stark contrast to what the Dutch gay theologian Pim Pronk bemoans as the modern "static-mechanical" model. The model Pronk critiques treats human behavior as divisible into autonomous parts, among which is sexual activity. It draws a sharp distinction between sexual and nonsexual behavior on the basis of whether or not the external sex organs are involved. And it views the link between the sex drive and sexual behavior as being somewhat like the connection between "the wound-up alarm clock and its going off."[6] Pronk concludes that this static-mechanical view suffers from a "one-sided accent on the *private* character of sexual relations," and as a result it "fails to do justice to the social dimension" of human sexuality.[7]

Sexuality and Marriage[8]

Marriage entails the coming together of male and female to form an exclusive sexual bond. The biblical writers connect this human relationship with procreation and child rearing. The second creation narrative and the stories of the Hebrew patriarchs suggest that marriage also serves as a focal point for companionship, as husband and wife share intimacy and friendship.

In scripture, marriage carries an additional crucial meaning. It provides a metaphor of spiritual truth. The bond uniting husband and wife symbolizes certain aspects of the relation between God and God's people. The Old Testament prophets found in marriage an appropriate vehicle for telling the story of Yahweh's faithfulness in the face of Israel's idolatry. The New Testament authors drew from this Old Testament imagery (e.g., Rom. 9:25; 1 Peter 2:9–10). They spoke of marriage as a picture of the great mystery of salvation—the union of Christ and the church. Marriage illustrates Christ's self-sacrifice for the church as well as the submission to Christ (Eph. 5:21–33) of a people who anticipate the future coming of their Lord (Matt. 25:1–13; Rev. 19:7; 21:2; 21:9–10).

In this manner, marriage provides a picture of the exclusive nature of our relationship to God in Christ. Just as marriage is to be an exclusive, inviolate, and hence holy bond, so also our relationship to God must be exclusive and holy, for as God's covenant people we can serve no other gods but the one God (Ex. 20:3). By extension, the exclusive love shared by husband and wife reflects the holiness of the divine love present within the triune God, which in turn overflows from God to creation.

Sexuality and Single Friendship[9]

The ancient Hebrews clearly viewed marriage as the norm. However, the New Testament opened the way for believers to fulfill a divine vocation as single persons as well, as is evidenced by John the Baptist and Jesus. Paul took the matter a step further. He advised that the single life may in certain circumstances be preferable to marriage, for singleness allows for single-minded devotion to the Lord and a certain flexibility for doing the Lord's work (1 Cor. 7:32–35), especially in times of crisis (v. 26).

This dimension of the biblical narrative reminds us that whether married or single we all enter into a variety of informal relationships and friendships with others. These friendships need not be permanent, they are rarely exclusive (that is, limited to only two people), and they are seldom entered through formal covenant. Relationships between single persons provide the clearest example of this nonexclusive, nonmarital friendship bond.

Like marriage, friendship carries theological meaning. In contrast to the marital union, the informal friendship bond is less defined and therefore more open to the inclusion of others. Further, the dynamic of love involved in friendship is generally not contained within exclusive boundaries. For this reason, friendship reflects the open, nonexclusive, expanding aspect of God's love — the divine love that seeks to include within the circle of fellowship those yet outside its boundaries.

Marriage reminds us that God demands holiness and hates idolatry and consequently that the community of God must be characterized by faithfulness. The informal friendship bond, especially as formed by single persons, reminds us of a parallel truth: Because God is always seeking the outsider, rather than being limited to a few, God's community is open to "whosoever will." As the most explicit example of friendship, relationships among single people are the central exemplar of this theological metaphor.

Sexuality and the Sex Act[10]

As several contemporary philosophers have pointed out, events are more than physical happenings, for every event occurs within a context that contributes to its meaning. Similarly, the meaning of a human act is dependent not only on the act itself but also on the context in which it transpires, which includes the actor's intent.[11] As a human act, sexual intercourse is more than a physical occurrence. It is a highly meaningful metaphor. But the meaning of any act of sexual intercourse is dependent on both the physical act itself and the context in which it occurs. The participants pour meaning into the act by the intent that motivates them and by the relationship they bring to it.

The Christian ethic builds from the belief that God intends that the sex act carry specific meanings. Sexual intercourse is not valuable primarily as a means to some other goal, even such good purposes as to experience pleasure or to become pregnant. Rather, the sex act is what the Roman Catholic ethicist James Hanigan calls a symbolic or ritual activity. He writes, "Sex, then, finds its proper value as an act which focuses, celebrates, expresses and enhances the meaning of our substantive activities and relationships."[12]

In part, we may view sexual intercourse as the ritual that celebrates committed, loving relationships. Yet each of us enjoys many such relationships, which we celebrate in various nongenital ways. In fact, sexual intercourse would deeply wound, if not completely destroy, most of these relationships. Consequently, the context in which the sex act occurs is crucial, so much so that in certain contexts the sex act is simply inappropriate. According to the biblical writers the divinely intended meanings of the sex act emerge only when the act occurs within one specific context: marriage.

Practiced within marriage as the sign of the unconditional, covenantal love of husband and wife, sexual intercourse carries several important meanings. It is a beautiful symbol of the exclusive bond between the marriage partners, as through this act wife and husband reaffirm their commitment to each other. Further, it is a beautiful celebration of the mutuality of the relationship, as each partner reaffirms his or her desire to give pleasure to the other. And because of its connection to procreation, the sex act expresses the openness of husband and wife to the new life that may arise from their bond.

Because of the meanings the sex act is intended to carry, the marital bond provides the sole proper context for sexual intercourse. The Old Testament law codified this view (e.g., Ex. 20:14), and Jesus and the New Testament apostles reaffirmed it (e.g., Matt. 19:3–9; 1 Cor. 6:9). As a result, the traditional Christian sex ethic rightly advocates chastity in the form of abstinence in singleness and fidelity in marriage. This ethic, in turn, provides the foundation for a Christian stance toward homosexuality.

The Christian Sex Ethic and Same-Sex Intercourse

Most participants in the contemporary discussion agree that certain homosexual practices—like certain heterosexual practices—are morally wrong. Lists of immoral behaviors commonly include such abuses as prostitution, rape, and pederasty. But does this ethical judgment extend to all homosexual acts? More specifically, is same-sex intercourse morally wrong even when practiced within the context of a loving gay or lesbian relationship?

In dealing with this question, I will avoid the pattern of some advocates of the traditional position who enumerate the purported harmful physical or psychological effects of involvement in various homosexual behaviors.[13] Nor will I deal with the reciprocal argument of those who claim that homosexual liaisons must be affirmed simply because "they harm no one."[14]

Although I acknowledge the propriety of arguing against certain practices on the basis of their potential to cause harm, my central concern lies deeper. I want to probe the ethics of same-sex intercourse viewed apart from any "side effects" it may or may not have. My goal is to determine in what sense the act may be deemed unethical in and of itself. What is it about this practice that makes it morally suspect even when it occurs within the context of a stable homosexual relationship? To anticipate my conclusion: Same-sex intercourse falls short of the Christian ethical ideal, because it is a deficient act occurring in the wrong context.

Same-Sex Intercourse as a Deficient Act

I suggested earlier that the significance of any act arises in part from the context in which it occurs. Now I note the other side of this, namely, the importance of the physical act as an appropriate carrier of intended meaning: A physical act must have the capacity to symbolize the reality it ritualizes and thereby serve as an authentic ritual.[15] Viewed from this perspective, same-sex intercourse falls short. It is deficient as a vehicle for conveying the meaning the sex act is intended to symbolize. Because it cannot ritually enact the reality it symbolizes, it fails to make that reality present.

According to the biblical understanding, sexual intercourse is connected to the coming together of two persons as sexual beings into a one-flesh union. It represents the act of two becoming one at the deepest level of their being (e.g., Gen. 2:23–24; Matt. 19:4–6). As a result, the sex act entails more than the experience of sexual climax. (Indeed, sexual climax can occur apart from sexual intercourse, such as through masturbation or by the manipulation of the genitalia by another.) More crucial than the ability to attain sexual climax is the capability of the sex act to symbolize the uniting of two sexual persons into a new unity. As a ritual act sexual intercourse must be able to represent physically (and thus make present) the two-in-one sexual bond it symbolizes.

This meaning is readily expressed in sexual relations between a man and a woman. Each engages in the sex act through the whole body, of course, but primarily through those body parts (vagina and penis) that most explicitly symbolize their existence as embodied, sexual beings, that most explicitly separate male from female, and that most readily allow male and female to complement the other. In this manner, both their own personal identities and their "otherness" or difference from each other as sexual creatures become the foundation for the expression of the unity of the bond they share. As a result, the sex act itself serves as a ritual act, an appropriate symbol of the union of two who are sexually "other" into a sexual bond.

It is not surprising that male-female intercourse provides such a vivid symbol of the sexual bond. As James Hanigan observes, "The unity ritualized and enacted in sexual behavior is a two-in-one flesh unity, a unity that has its created basis in the physical and biological complementarity of male and female."[16]

The partners in same-sex intercourse also bring to the act the physical features that most deeply represent their existence as sexual beings. But in this act, the specific body part each contributes to the act does not represent what distinguishes each from the other. Nor does it represent the unique contribution each brings to their sexual union, for their roles in the act can be interchanged.

Further, in same-sex intercourse, some other body part (finger or even artificial penis in lesbian acts, mouth or anus in male homosexual acts) routinely substitutes for the sexual organ that neither partner can provide. But whenever this occurs, one or the other partner presses an aspect of his or her anatomy into service of the sex act that, because it is not the definitive mark of the person as a sexual being, is not normally viewed as sexual.

In this manner, same-sex intercourse loses the symbolic dimension of two-becoming-one present in male-female sex. At best, it is only a simulation of the two-becoming-one ritual that the act of sexual intercourse is designed to be. And a homosexual couple can only imitate the unity of two persons joining together as sexual others, so vividly symbolized in male-female coitus. Hence, Hanigan is correct in concluding that homosexual acts are ultimately "only pretense or imaginative simulations of the real thing."[17]

Pastoral theologian John Harvey takes this a step further. He draws out the wider significance of this deficiency. In Harvey's estimation, same-sex intercourse "does not lead to a true union of human persons on the physical genital level. . . . this maladaptation of parts is symbolic of the pseudocomplementarity on the psychological and spiritual levels."[18]

Sexual Intercourse
within the Wrong Context

I noted earlier that acts derive their meaning from the context in which they occur. Same-sex intercourse is also deficient because it occurs within an improper context. That is, the context in which it is practiced—even if this is a stable gay or lesbian relationship—does not confirm the intended meaning of the sex act.

To understand this we must return to the three meanings of the sex act within the context of marriage. At first glance it would appear that when practiced in the context of a stable, monogamous homosexual relationship same-sex intercourse could carry at least two of these meanings. The act could conceivably mark the celebration of the life-long commitment of the two partners to each other, as well as the mutuality of their relationship. Less possible, obviously, is the third meaning. Because children are simply not procreated in this manner, same-sex intercourse cannot express the openness of the couple to new life arising from their bond. At best, the act serves as an imitation of male-female procreative intercourse.

Are we to conclude, then, that ultimately the only basis on which same-sex intercourse can be discounted is its lack of the procreative potential? No. We drew from the biblical narrative the idea that the sex act is the ritual celebration of the exclusive bond of two persons united in a one-flesh union. And we concluded that when viewed from the biblical perspective, the marriage of male and female is the only appropriate expression of that exclusive sexual bond. Of course, this conclusion rules same-sex sexual bonding out of court, even when it involves a mutual, lifelong commitment.

But why privilege heterosexual marriage? Why set up the male-female sexual bond as the standard? Why could we not view same-sex intercourse as the expression of the bond uniting two persons of the same sex, analogous to heterosexual intercourse as the ritual sexual act in marriage?

One response arises from another consideration drawn from the physical aspect of the sex act itself. It is instructive to note that by its very nature, any specific occurrence of male-female sexual intercourse involves—and can only involve—two persons, a male and a female. This characteristic forges a close link between the sex act and the reality it ritualizes, for the sex act provides a vivid symbolic declaration of the monogamous nature of the biblical ideal for marriage. It also connects the sex act as a symbol with the begetting of children, for biologically a child is the union of the contributions of two persons—the biological father and the biological mother.

At this point, however, same-sex intercourse differs fundamentally from heterosexual intercourse. There is nothing inherent in this physical act that would limit involvement to two persons. This observation leads us to ask: On what ritual basis would any homosexual bond necessarily consist of two and only two? If there is no intrinsic aspect of the ritual act that limits its participants to two, why should anyone privilege "monogamous" homosexual relations?

Further, if nothing intrinsic to the act inherently symbolizes the reality of two-becoming-one, then same-sex intercourse, even when practiced within a stable homosexual relationship, is simply unable to ritualize exclusivity. In contrast to heterosexual intercourse, it cannot function as the celebration of an exclusive bond and therefore cannot point to the exclusivity of the relationship God desires to have with us. In this way, same-sex intercourse loses the spiritual meaning of the sex act.

The same conclusion arises from a consideration of the nature of the bond being celebrated in the sex act. When viewed from the perspective we outlined earlier, same-sex intercourse entails a confusing of the bond of informal friendship with the male-female sexual bond of marriage.

We already noted that the otherness of the marital relationship is crucial to its symbolic significance. As Max Stackhouse declared, "the marriage bond is a community of love between those who are 'other.' This means not simply 'an-other' person, but one who is truly 'other.'"[19] Just as homosexual persons cannot ritualize a two-become-one unity in the act of intercourse, so also they cannot become a two-become-one unity in the shared life of unity and difference that typifies the marriage of male and female.[20]

Stackhouse reminds us of one reason that this is crucial: "The marriage of a man to a woman . . . remains the normative physical, social, and moral sign that we are not meant to be isolated individuals or to focus only on relationships with those who are already much like us. We are created for community with the Divine Other and with the human other, and the bonding of sexual otherness is the immediate and obvious evidence of this."[21] Similarly, psychologist Ruth Tiffany Barnhouse appeals to the Song of Songs in declaring that "sexuality itself is a symbol of wholeness, of the reconciliation of opposites, of the loving at-one-ment between God and Creation."[22]

These statements lead us back to the central significance of marriage we noted earlier, namely, its theological symbolism. As the biblical writers themselves suggest, the exclusive bond of husband and wife forms a fitting metaphor of the exclusivity of the divine-human relationship. The sex act, in turn, is the ritual celebration of this exclusive bond. A homosexual relationship is not an appropriate context for the sex act, because in the context of such a relationship sexual intercourse simply cannot express this intended meaning.

This is evident when we realize that every stable same-sex relation is in fact an informal bond between or among friends. As we noted earlier, the friendship bond ought not to find ritualized expression in a sexual act. Several considerations point out why this is so. First, although like marriage friendship includes unity and difference, the difference exemplified between or among friends is not a sexual difference; same-sex friends do not manifest this unity and difference sexually.[23] Further, friendships can wither and die without necessarily incurring moral fault on the part of any of the friends. Although in marriage both friendship and sexual attraction can and do die, the biblical writers suggest that the severing of the marital relationship itself always involves moral fault, however hard it might be to pinpoint that fault. Finally, friendship—which is generally neither an exclusive nor a formalized bond—proclaims the inclusive, rather than the exclusive, love of God. The intent of the sex act, however, is to celebrate exclusivity, not inclusivity.

Same-sex intercourse, then, introduces into the friendship bond the language of exclusivity and permanence that properly belongs solely to marriage. Of course we could back away from the grammar of pair-bonding and conclude that same-sex intercourse intends to say nothing more than "I find you attractive." But mutual attraction is never a sufficient basis for sexual intimacy, regardless of the sexual preference of the persons involved. As ethicist Edward Batchelor pointed out, "love does not always justify sexual union." The implication for homosexual attraction follows: "it is every bit as likely that the love of man for man or woman for woman bids them refrain from sexual intercourse as that it urges them to it."[24]

The Christian Ethic
and Homosexuality

I have looked at the implications of a Christian theology of sexuality for same-sex intercourse. In this process I drew from the divine *telos* for human sexual relationships as indicated in the foundational stories in Genesis and reiterated in the New Testament to indicate why the sex act cannot properly occur within a homosexual relationship. In this sense, same-sex intercourse is "unnatural."

What does all this have to say about the contemporary phenomenon of homosexuality understood as a stable sexual orientation or preference? Specifically, in what sense, if any, is homosexuality sinful? En route to an answer, I will look at the contemporary argument favoring a positive outlook toward homosexuality as a sexual "inversion." Only then can I seek to chart an alternative.

The "Naturalness" of Homosexuality

Many proponents of a more open stance view homosexuality as a stable sexual preference, which properly finds expression in acts such as same-sex intercourse. In effect, the apologetic for this position turns the biblical condemnation of homosexual behavior on its head. In contrast to Paul and others who claim that same-sex acts are "against nature," proponents assert that homosexuality is in fact "natural."

By "natural," some theorists mean nothing more than that homosexuality is a naturally occurring phenomenon among humans. The central foundation for this approach is its purported presence in a variety of societies throughout history.

This approach, however, has been exploded by social constructivists such as David Greenberg,[25] who point out that homosexuality is not a single, identifiable, transcultural human condition. Instead, understandings of same-sex practices vary from culture to culture. These range from the ritualized rites of passage associated with adolescent sexual development found in several tribal societies[26] to the spiritualized pederasty of certain Greek philosophers who downplayed any actual physical content within such relationships.[27]

Other proponents speak of the naturalness of this sexual preference in more individualistic terms. Homosexuality is natural, they assert, in that it is not the product of conscious personal choice. Rather than choosing their sexual orientation, this argument purports, gays and lesbians "discover" their homosexuality as a preexisting reality. As the Christian gay activist and writer Chris Glaser declared, "In my experience, sexual orientation was a given, like race or gender. How I responded in faith to that given was what was spiritually significant to me."[28] Christine Gudorf draws out the erroneous but commonly asserted ethical implication:

The agreement within medical and social science that sexual orientation is not chosen but more commonly discovered absolves homosexual orientation of sinfulness, and calls into question . . . the unnaturalness of homosexual acts for those with homosexual orientation.[29]

Statements such as these are an important reminder that most persons do not consciously set out to develop a specific sexual preference. At the same time, claims about its unchosen nature often harbor an overly simplistic picture of the development of homosexuality. While the jury is still out on what causes any specific instance, most scientists and psychologists agree that a constellation of factors—biological predispositions, personal experiences, and the attitudes and actions of others (including parents)—can contribute to disposing a person to this sexual preference. To this list we ought to add the constellation of social identities and roles that social constructionists like David Greenberg declare are involved in the construction of homosexuality. Yet in this equation we dare not overlook the likelihood of some element of personal choice. As I noted in chapter 1, certain psychologists conclude that homosexuality is a pattern that develops over time, and this conclusion opens the possibly of a limited, yet nevertheless active, role of the person himself or herself. In short, as the designation itself suggests, one's sexual orientation is also in some sense his or her sexual "preference," even if once set that preference "can hardly be abolished by an arbitrary act of will," to cite Greenberg's assessment.[30]

More important, however, is the ethical critique of this perspective. Ethicists remind us that to argue from any supposed natural reality to moral rectitude is to commit the "naturalistic fallacy," that is, to deduce an "ought" from an "is." Ethics, however, is not the condoning of what is natural. Thus, even if homosexuality were indisputably "natural" for certain people, this would not in and of itself justify their engaging in same-sex practices.

Christian ethics takes this critique an additional step: In contrast to those who assert that no one can be held responsible for acting according to his or her nature, the Christian tradition declares that personal responsibility is not limited to matters in which we have full personal choice. Why not? This question leads to the concept of sin. Viewed from the biblical perspective, sin means "missing the mark," that is, failing to live up to God's intention for our lives. Rather than a somewhat localized debilitation, this failure can be felt in all areas of human existence, and its presence predates our conscious choices. This is in part what the Reformers meant by "depravity."

Because of our depravity, we find at work within us desires, impulses, and urges we did not consciously choose but which instead feel quite normal. Yet we dare not entrust ourselves to our natural inclinations, for these are not a sure guide to proper conduct. Jesus himself declared that evil deeds proceed from the human heart (Mark 7:21). Consequently, he instructed his disciples to distrust what they may perceive to be their natural inclinations and follow a radically new ethic.

Caution is necessary as much in our sexual conduct as in any aspect of life. The supposed naturalness of a person's same-sex preference does not set aside the biblical call to engage in genital sexual expression exclusively within monogamous heterosexual marriage. To assert otherwise is to commit the so-called "naturalistic fallacy," that is, to argue from "what is" to "what ought to be."[31] The same fallacy would be at work if I were to set aside the biblical call to marital fidelity on the basis of the claim that as a male I am naturally promiscuous, as contemporary sociobiology suggests.

Rather than excusing us on the basis of the sensed naturalness of our inclinations, the Bible offers divine grace in the midst of the realities of life. This grace brings both forgiveness of our trespasses and power to overcome the workings of our human fallenness in the concrete situations we face.

This cautionary stance toward the appeal to what is natural must be tempered, however, by one additional consideration. Christian ethics does derive an "ought" from an "is";[32] an "is" does determine the Christian moral imperative. But this "is" is ultimately neither what once was, nor what now is. Instead, it is a future "is"—a "will be." Specifically, the "is" that provides the Christian ethical "ought" is the future reality of the new creation. Our calling is to exhibit in our relationships in the here and now God's intentions for human existence, which will be present in their fullness only in the future new community.

While the Christian moral imperative arises out of a future "is," this future does not come as a total contradiction to what is truly natural in the present. As the fullness of God's intention for human relationships, the future community is the completion of what God set forth "in the beginning." And a crucial aspect of what God has intended for human sexual relationships from the beginning is depicted in the biblical creation narratives. This is why reading those stories in the context of the vision of the new creation provides the foundation for our teleological ethical approach to the question of homosexuality.

The "Sin" of Homosexuality

I have asserted that the felt naturalness of a same-sex sexual preference does not in and of itself provide a sufficient rationale for accepting homosexual behavior. But the question remains as to whether or not the preference itself is sinful.

Sin, Judgment, Acts, and Disposition

The search for an answer leads once again to the biblical understanding of sin. Christian theology maintains that the present world is fallen, that is, creation does not yet correspond to the fullness of God's intention. What can be said about humankind as a whole—and even the universe itself (see Rom. 8:20–22)—is true of each person as well. Each of us is fallen. This fallenness extends beyond our specific actions. It encompasses every aspect of our existence, including what might be called our moral disposition (which one day will be conformed to the character of Christ [1 John 3:1–3]) and even the body itself in its mortality (which will be transformed at the resurrection [e.g., Rom. 8:11, 23]). Is this human fallenness "sin"?

In its widest sense "sin" refers to every aspect of human life that fails to reflect the design of God. Viewed from this perspective, fallenness means that we are sinful in the totality of our existence. At the same time, we generally use the word more narrowly; thus, we speak about "sins," that is, specific actions, even transgressions.

The word "sin" immediately conjures up another idea that likewise carries two related yet distinct meanings: "judgment." On the one hand, insofar as God will one day transform every dimension of creaturely fallenness, human fallenness comes under divine judgment. On the other hand, the biblical writers consistently reserve the idea of a divine judgment leading to condemnation for sinful acts (e.g., Rom. 2:3; 2 Cor. 5:10; Rev. 20:12).

Putting the two together leads to the conclusion that as the great physician, God will heal our fallen sinfulness in the new creation, and as our judge, God will condemn our sinful actions. Hence, our fallen disposition is sinful in that it is foundational to our sinning. But it is our sinful acts—which bring God's condemnation upon us—that are what marks us as guilty before God.[33]

Sexual Desire and Lust

These observations have important implications for the discussion of homosexuality. To draw these out, I must reframe the conclusions about human sexuality I outlined earlier in this chapter.

God created us as sexual beings. Within us is the drive to leave our isolation and enter into relationships with others and ultimately with God. We might term this drive "sexual desire," because it arises out of our fundamental embodied existence as sexual creatures. One aspect of this drive is the "desire for sex," that is, the urge to form a genital sexual bond with another person.[34] Certain people find at work in their psyche a desire for sex with persons of the other sex. For other people the desire for sex is largely, if not exclusively, targeted toward persons of the same sex. At what point does sin enter into the picture? When does what belongs to the goodness of our creaturely existence run counter to God's intention?

It seems that the clearest answer the biblical writers and the

Christian tradition offer is "at the point of lust," that is, at the point when a person harbors the desire for sex with someone who is not his or her spouse (e.g., Matt. 5:27–28). Thus, the presence in us of both sexual desire and the desire for sex are the manifestation of the goodness of our creaturely sexuality. But these good gifts can come under the power of sin.

With the incursion of sin the desire for sex gives birth to lust. Lust involves allowing the desire for sex to control us so that the goal of sexual satisfaction has become in that moment our god. Lust entails as well the harboring of the desire to engage in inappropriate sexual expressions, including the urge to introduce a genital sexual dimension into relationships in which this dimension would be improper.

What we said earlier suggests that all same-sex relationships are an example of one such improper context. To understand this, we must keep in mind that sexual desire in the sense outlined above not only lies behind the drive to enter into the bond of marriage but also gives rise to the desire to enter into friendship bonds—even close, intimate friendships. Such friendships may be formed with persons of either sex.

Because of the close connection between sexual desire and the desire for sex, we readily confuse the two, even within the context of our intimate friendships. Sin enters the picture whenever this confusion results in lust, that is, when we harbor the thought of introducing inappropriate sexual conduct into the friendship relationship. The desire to bring genital sexual behavior into a same-sex relationship is ethically problematic, because it involves treating a friendship like the marital bond.

But what about the situation of those persons for whom homo-eroticism has become an ongoing, seemingly stable personal disposition? A proper response requires that I note where the ethical problem actually lies. The presence within the person's psyche of either sexual desire or the desire for sex is not ethically problematic. Instead, the moral difficulty emerges when the person involved harbors—and thus creates—an ongoing urge to express the desire for sex in acts that are inappropriate, in that the "targets" of these desires are potential or actual friends. Ultimately, it is lust and its outworking in overt acts—not the sex of those toward whom a person might feel drawn (i.e., a person's disposition)—that incur divine condemnation. Consequently, it is lust and its outworking that are ethically problematic.

Homosexuality as an Orientation?

One additional question remains to be treated. What about the language of "homosexual orientation" itself? Can we properly talk about "sexual orientation" as separable from sexual acts?

Many evangelical traditionalists find themselves in agreement with proponents of a more open stance at this important point. Both distinguish between a homosexual orientation (or propensity) and homosexual practices.[35] But they do so for quite different reasons. Gay/lesbian theologians often claim that one's sexual orientation is always good, because it is a gift from God. Consequently, the task of the homosexual person is to accept his or her sexual orientation, and this includes acting on the basis of it.

Evangelical traditionalists, in contrast, generally assert that while the Bible condemns homosexual acts, it does not mention the orientation.[36] On this basis, they treat homosexual feelings, attractions, urges, desires, and longings as temptations to be mastered, rather than as sins to be confessed. Sin, they add, emerges only when a person acts (whether physically or merely mentally) on these urges.

The goal of this approach, of course, is to encourage believers who admit to the ongoing presence of homosexual inclinations but who are able to resist acting them out.[37] Hence, Michael R. Saia asserts that:

> when people do not keep the matter of preference (which, *functionally* is in the realm of metaphysics) and sin (which is moral) separate, a heavy load of false guilt and condemnation is laid on hurting people who are already having a hard enough time feeling good about God and themselves.

He then adds,

> As one man put it, "I feel as if God is always breathing down my neck." If, no matter how pure his life is, he has to feel guilty for his

attractions, then there is never any relief from guilt. "How would you feel," another man said, "if you had to feel guilty every time you become hungry?" Hunger is not gluttony, and preference is not homosexual sin. But the confused Church has often equated preference and homosexual acts (sin) and held people responsible for something that is not actually a moral issue.[38]

In a sense, the separation of orientation from behavior is appropriate. It offers a handy way of differentiating between what truly requires ethical scrutiny (lust and overt acts) and what does not (the desire for sex as a dimension of human existence). To this end, my argument in the previous section drew from a similar distinction, that of disposition versus conduct. Likewise, the pastoral goal of this separation is surely correct. Feeling guilty about what does not incur guilt is simply not justifiable ethically, and it can actually be counterproductive in the journey of discipleship.

While cautiously affirming its utility, we dare not overlook the dangers that lurk in the use of the contemporary language of sexual orientation. I have noted already that social constructivists object to the idea of homosexuality as a transcultural phenomenon. They point out that the idea of a given, stable same-sex sexual orientation that is somehow natural to a certain percentage of people is more the product of a contemporary social construction than an actual essential reality that can be sociologically or historically documented. By using the language of orientation, we risk transposing a construction of contemporary society into indelible scientific fact.

Further, using this language may encourage a significant group of people to construct, perhaps prematurely, their personal identity (the self) on the basis of these socially based cognitive tools. One important potential group is today's adolescents. Research in the human sciences suggests that adolescents often move through a stage in their development in which certain same-sex activities are present. The grammar of sexual orientation may lead certain youths to assume on the basis of such experiences that they are constitutionally homosexual. Ruth Tiffany Barnhouse indicates how such an assumption may work to their detriment:

Adolescence is a period which requires the utmost of young people in working their way through the enormously difficult transition from childhood to adulthood. . . . the anxieties surrounding the psychosexual maturation process are severe, and the temptation to opt for less than one is capable of is very great. While it is probably true that one cannot proselytize the invulnerable, there are a great many youngsters whose childhoods have been sufficiently problematic so that homosexuality presented to them as an acceptable alternative would be convincingly attractive.[39]

The "threat," however, is not limited to young people. The widespread use of the language of sexual orientation tempts each of us in a potentially detrimental direction. It may lead us to place our sense of having a sexual orientation, and with it our desire for sex, at the center of our understanding of ourselves and others. But as certain radical lesbian theologians have asked rhetorically, Why should the sex of those who we desire to sleep with be the determining characteristic of our identity?[40] Indeed, just as "one's life does not consist in the abundance of possessions" (Luke 12:15), so also there is more to human existence than the desire for sex.

There is yet a deeper theological issue at stake here. The uncritical use of the language of sexual orientation may lead us to accept blindly the therapeutic focus rampant in our society. As I noted in chapter 1, traditional psychologists routinely assert that homosexual practices are in the end the outworking of a psychological maladjustment or a "disorientation."[41] To do so, however, is to replace the moral discussion by a disease model, and to turn a debate about ethics into a discussion of cures for a psychological illness. David Greenberg offered this sobering reminder:

Though the Renaissance sodomite was depicted as a monster whose vice signified a repudiation of God and nature, no one suggested that he suffered from a disease and required therapy. . . . His repudiation of God and morality was considered volitional; it was his acts, not his physiology or psychology that made him monstrous.[42]

While Greenberg's choice of the word "monstrous" is unfortunate, his main point is well taken.

The potential problems of "sexual orientation" language ought to give us pause before we too quickly adopt it. Nevertheless, being able to distinguish between homoeroticism and its outworking in thought and overt act—that is, between disposition and conduct—has certain positive benefit in discussing the ethics of homosexuality. Perhaps the best designation, given these considerations, is "sexual preference."

Homosexual Persons and Sexual Expression

These conclusions raise one final ethical question: What viable options are there for homoerotic persons to express their sexuality? And does the stance argued in this chapter mean that a same-sex sexual preference "condemns" a person to a life devoid of sexuality?

Sexual Chastity

The position taken in these pages leads to only two ethically feasible options for homosexual persons: fidelity within (heterosexual) marriage or abstinent singleness. Invariably, proponents of a more open stance toward homosexuality find this proposal uncharitably narrow. They claim that such a narrowing of the options for gays and lesbians is simply unfair.

The fairness critique would carry weight if the call for a life characterized by fidelity in marriage or abstinent singleness were directed solely toward homosexual persons. The fact is, however, that the elevation of marriage and abstinent singleness is merely the outworking of an ethic of sexual chastity intended for all persons without exception.

Some critics do not find this answer at all compelling. They argue that it is far easier for heterosexual than for homosexual persons to live out such an ethical proposal. James Nelson, for example, claims that this stance "demonstrates lack of sensitivity to the gay person's socially-imposed dilemma." Why? Nelson explains: "The heterosexual's abstinence is either freely chosen for a lifetime or it is temporary until marriage. But the celibacy some Christians would impose on the gay person would be involuntary and unending."[43]

Other critics add that this proposal erroneously assumes that every homosexual person is automatically called to celibacy. Pamela Dickey Young writes, "in making celibacy mandatory for homosexual persons we violate the traditional Protestant emphasis on celibacy as individual calling."[44]

These objections, however, are wide of the mark. The fact that some persons may find it easier to live out an ethical ideal does not militate against the ideal itself. Each of us could point to dimensions of the Christian ethic that we find ourselves disadvantaged to follow in comparison with other persons. But this does not mean that those who uphold the ideal are treating us unjustly.

Further, proponents of a more open stance toward homosexuality are often overly optimistic about the viability of the marriage option for heterosexuals. In contrast to such optimism, many single people attest to the fact that despite their good intentions and personal willingness they are simply unable to find a suitable marriage partner.

Likewise, such objections often confuse celibacy and abstinence.[45] Pamela Dickey Young correctly pointed out that only certain Christians sense a divine call to celibacy, understood as forgoing marriage and genital sexual intimacy for the purpose of a special service to God and others.[46] But this is not the same as my proposal that unmarried homosexual persons commit themselves to abstinence. Unlike celibacy, abstinence in singleness is not a particular calling for certain persons, but an ethical ideal for all who are not married. And unlike celibacy, which is a chosen, permanent (or semi-permanent) response to a sensed call from

God, the commitment to abstinence in singleness is a particular, and for many people temporary, outworking of the overarching call to a life of sexual chastity that comes to all. This general call to chastity, while remaining the same call, demands a quite different response from married persons than it does from single people.

Finally, the objection that this proposal is unfair rests on a highly questionable emphasis on rights. John McNeill, for example, defends homosexual behavior on the basis that "every human being has a God-given right to sexual love and intimacy."[47] This claim, however, displays a faulty understanding of what a right entails. Love is a relational reality, and sexual love in particular requires a partner (a lover). For this reason, no one can claim a personal right to sexual love. Such a right would demand that a lover exist somewhere for every person, but no one is entitled to, or can be guaranteed, a sexual partner. Further, such a right would place on someone else the corresponding obligation to enter into a sexual relationship with the person who possesses the right. But no one can require that someone else love, let alone become sexually intimate with, him or her.

James Hanigan draws out the implications of these considerations for same-sex relations:

> Since, strictly speaking, there is no positive right to sexual satisfaction, sexual fulfillment and sexual happiness, the human desire for such things and the pursuit of these goods, even the natural human orientation to these goods, cannot itself be a justification for doing just anything to achieve them. . . .
>
> Therefore, just because a homosexual relationship may possibly be the only way some people can find, or think they can find, a satisfying degree of humanity in their lives does not make such a relationship morally right by that very fact.[48]

In contrast to contemporary proposals such as McNeill's, the New Testament writers do not build their ethic on an appeal to personal rights. Instead, the early Christian leaders were convinced that discipleship entails a call to follow the example of Jesus, who freely laid aside his personal prerogatives for the sake of a higher good (Phil. 2:5–8; 1 Peter 2:18–25). This Jesus calls his disciples to give expression to their fundamental human sexuality in ways that bring glory to the God he himself served. As the New Testament writers concluded, his call requires chastity of all persons, a chastity that acknowledges the God-given boundaries of genital sexual expression.[49]

But can we truly expect unmarried people to commit themselves to abstinence? Jesus himself noted that certain persons would willingly set aside the sex act for the sake of God's kingdom (Matt. 19:12). The human sciences confirm that sexual activity is not a human necessity, thereby holding open the possibility of abstinence. In the words of Jones and Workman, "There is no basis in behavioral science . . . to suggest that abstinence is detrimental to human welfare, or that expression of genital eroticism is necessary for wholeness."[50] Abstinent single Christians stand as living examples of this possibility.

Homosexual Persons and Sexual Expression

To commit oneself to abstinence outside of marriage does not mean that as a single homosexual person one is "condemned" to a life devoid of sexual expression. On the contrary, those who are not "sexually active" still experience dimensions of affective sexual expression.

The differentiation between sexual desire and the desire for sex I made earlier suggests how this is so. As the basis for our innate drive toward bonding, sexuality is operative in the lives of all humans. Hence, our sensed needs to bond with other humans, to live in community with others, and even to find God are all aspects of human sexual desire. But as most of our day-to-day relationships indicate, sexual desire does not require that we fulfill the desire for sex, that is, that we engage in sexual intercourse. Rather, as I have argued already, the only context in which the desire for sex can be properly expressed is marriage.

At the same time, we all form nonmarital friendship bonds with others. Whenever such bonding occurs, our fundamental sexuality—sexual desire—comes to expression. And as I noted earlier, friendship bonds know no gender boundaries. Hence, our fundamental sexuality readily leads persons of the same sex to develop close, even intimate friendships, albeit ones that exclude sexual intimacy in the form of genital relations.

To conclude: A question commonly asked today is, Does God really care about whom I sleep with? We dare not answer this question in the negative, for to do so is to banish God from our sex lives. Rather, Christians seek to understand every aspect of life, including the sexual dimension, within the context of Christian discipleship. Christians seek to place life itself—and hence sexual expression—under the lordship of Christ.

Viewed from this perspective, Christians are convinced that God does care about our sexual conduct. And by taking care to live in appropriate sexual chastity, the choice we make as to who we do—and do not—sleep with becomes a powerful theological statement. This choice speaks loudly about our understanding of ourselves, about our view of the nature of life, and ultimately about our deepest convictions as to what God is like.

Homosexuality and the Church

The contemporary discussion of homosexuality leads inevitably to the central practical issue needing resolution today, the place of homosexual persons in the church. Some Christians strive to deal with this question by appeal to what they perceive to be the most "pastoral" response. Yet in the end the gospel is not advanced if the church reaches conclusions about its life and ministry solely on the basis of pragmatic, or even what appear to be solid, pastoral considerations. Rather, the church's ministry is best served through genuine ethical reflection on the pressing issues it faces. For this reason, I now attempt to tackle this question in a manner consistent with, and arising out of, the ethical point of view I developed in the preceding chapters.

Is there a place for homosexual persons in the church? A wide range of views is found among contemporary Christians. Yet the spectrum of opinion coalesces into four basic positions.[1]

Some Christians advocate what we might call "unqualified openness." They are convinced that the way forward is to place homosexuality on equal footing with heterosexuality. Thus, they argue that homosexual persons should participate fully in all dimensions of church life. Gays and lesbians should serve in any role—including the ordained office—to which they sense the requisite call and gifting of the Spirit. Further, the church should sanction significant times in the lives of gay and lesbian persons. Above all, clergy ought to bless same-sex unions in a manner similar to heterosexual marriages.

A second group of Christians offer a more "qualified

acceptance." They gladly accept lesbians and gays as members of the church. But they cannot support the ordination of practicing homosexual persons. Nor do they believe that the church should sanction same-sex marriages.

Somewhat similar to this position is a third, which we may term "differentiated acceptance." Proponents differentiate between homosexual acts, which they deem sinful, and the same-sex preference, which they believe is not. On the basis of this distinction, proponents urge the church to focus on behavior and to treat homosexual practices as one type of sin among many. Further, not only ordination but even church membership (at least ongoing status in the church) ought to be limited to those homosexual persons who are sexually abstinent.

Finally, some Christians advocate undifferentiated rejection. They find no warrant for distinguishing between sexual orientation and sexual behavior. As a result, they believe that no admittedly homosexual person can be a member in good standing in the church. Some proponents even suggest that the church support civil laws against same-sex behaviors including "sodomy."

As this delineation suggests, the question "Is there a place for homosexual persons in the church?" encompasses several issues. My task in this chapter is to look at four of these: church membership, same-sex unions, ordination, and civil rights. The goal of my deliberations is to reach some clarity as to what a Christian ethical response to these issues might entail.

Homosexual Persons and Church Membership

Should the church welcome gay and lesbian believers into membership? If no homosexual behavior is sinful, our response could only be an unambiguous yes. However, few Christians today would offer unqualified approval of all same-sex acts, just as no one would condone every form of heterosexual behavior.

Rather, the point of contention among Christians lies with the moral status of persons living in stable same-sex relationships. Can such persons be members in good standing of the church?

Even if we find such liaisons questionable, we might nevertheless assert that the church ought to minister to, and even provide a spiritual home for, homosexual persons. Regardless of the moral status of homosexual behavior, lesbians and gays are people whom God values, for whom Jesus died, and to whom the gospel must come.

Further, the church is composed of sinners—redeemed sinners to be sure—but sinners nonetheless. It consists of people who are seeking to do God's will in the midst of the brokenness of life. The church can only assist people to overcome sin and live in obedience to God if they receive the ministry of, and perhaps even participate in, the believing community. This is as true for gays and lesbians as for anyone else.

In addition, homosexual persons have an important contribution to make to the life of the community. Richard Hays put it well:

> We live, then, in a community that embraces sinners as Jesus did, without waiving God's righteousness. We live confessing that God's grace claims us out of confusion and alienation and sets about making us whole. We live knowing that wholeness remains a hope rather than an attainment in this life. The homosexual Christians in our midst may teach us something about our true condition as people living between the cross and the final redemption of our bodies.[2]

Consequently, the church and its ministry are poorer if it ostracizes homosexual believers.

The church, therefore, ought not only to minister to all but also to welcome all into membership on the same basis. And this basis consists of personal reception of salvation by faith through Jesus Christ together with personal commitment to discipleship.

At the same time, participation in the faith community involves a give-and-take. Discipleship demands that each member understand that he or she is accountable to the community in all dimensions of life, including the sexual. As one homosexual believer wrote to Richard Hays, "Anyone who joins such a community should know that it is a place of transformation, of discipline, of learning, and not merely a place to be comforted or indulged."[3] Because it is a community of discipleship, the church in turn has a responsibility both to nurture and also to admonish and discipline the wayward in its midst, including those who are not living in sexual chastity, whatever the exact nature of the unchaste behavior may be.

But what form should this nurturing and disciplining responsibility take in the case of homosexual persons? Here Christians differ. At one end of the spectrum of opinion are those who argue that the focus of the church's ministry ought to be that of fostering a transformation in the sexual orientation of homosexual persons in its midst.

Others advocate a diametrically opposite approach. They see the church's task as assisting lesbians and gays to accept their homosexuality. John McNeill, for example, suggests that one dimension of such self-acceptance is coping with anger. Thus, in his estimation, the church ought to help gays and lesbians overcome their ill feelings toward God by bringing them to see that God does not condemn them or their behavior:

> For many gay people there is also the issue of anger at God. Since we do not usually choose our sexual orientation, we experience it as a given, an objective fact that is part of God's creation. Insofar as our experience of our sexual orientation is negative, as long as we see it as sinful, sick, or evil, we experience a deep crisis in our relationship with God and real anger at God. Only a sadistic God would create millions of humans as gay with no choice in the matter and no hope of changing and then deny them the right to express their gayness in a loving relationship for the rest of their lives under threat of eternal damnation. . . .
>
> Once again, the only way to forgive someone we see as having wounded us is to heal the wound. We gay people must risk believing that God is not homophobic even though the human church is.

We must learn to accept our gayness as a gift from God and live it out joyfully in a way that is compatible with God's law. In that process of self-acceptance and in our new awareness of God's love for us, we can then let go of our anger.[4]

Neither of these opposing viewpoints is totally misguided. The church must hold out the possibility of change, albeit in a realistic manner. At the same time, Christians ought to help their homosexual brothers and sisters overcome whatever anger, ill will, and negative feelings may be eating at their souls, albeit without compromising biblical teaching about what behavior pleases God, which I have argued includes sexual chastity (fidelity in heterosexual marriage and abstinence in singleness).

While each of these proposals is helpful in its own way, neither of them captures the focus of the church's ministry. God's grace is never content to leave us merely as we are. Yet God's primary goal is not the transformation of one's sexual preference, even though many homosexual persons do experience varying degrees of transformation. Rather, God is primarily concerned about how we live in the midst of the fallenness of this present age.

Specifically, God calls each of us to personal holiness, purity in conduct, and sexual chastity. God is at work in the midst of our brokenness and woundedness. This God walks with us on the journey to wholeness, although the exact pathway along which God leads may differ from person to person. For some homosexual believers, the journey toward sexual chastity may actually be quite smooth. They may experience a marvelous, perhaps even nearly instantaneous transformation. For others, in contrast, commitment to holiness in sexual conduct may demand lifelong vigilance (just as is the case for many heterosexual believers).

At the heart of the church's mandate, therefore, is the task of ministering to all persons—including gays and lesbians—in the midst of their brokenness and the difficulties they face. Ministering to others requires that we create a climate of acceptance that looks beyond their faults to see their needs. Actually, the gospel offers persons struggling with their sexuality a level of acceptance found nowhere else. While not approving acts the biblical writers declare sinful, the church must be concerned about and care for gays and lesbians as persons whom God loves. Martin Hoffman makes this penetrating statement about the attitude prevalent in the world many homosexual persons inhabit: "Since large sections of the gay world view the homosexual as a commodity and judge him by his cosmetic qualities, he soon begins to develop that same view of himself."[5] By mediating God's own love and compassion, Christians hold out a healthy, healing alternative to the widespread outlook that accepts others only insofar as they have something to offer in return.

Further, the church ministers to lesbians and gays by extending assistance. Many homosexual persons are convinced that the kind of self-acceptance McNeill and others advocate is simply not helpful. These people long for release from behavior patterns and relationships they sense have entrapped them. Christians must lend a sympathetic hand to aid and support such persons through the struggles associated with unlearning deep-seated behavior patterns and moving out of unwholesome relationships. By standing with them during the difficult periods of the process, Christians who extend unqualified, noncondemnatory support, coupled with the assurance of divine assistance, can provide the boost needed for such persons to gain full liberation from the behaviors and relationships that now bind them. Part of this process may well involve assisting brothers and sisters who are seeking liberation from homosexual behavior patterns in finding places of ministry within the church and accepting the ministry these persons can offer to the community of Christ.

Gay and Lesbian Unions

Writing in the *New Republic,* Andrew Sullivan indicated why civil marriage is so important for gay and lesbian people: "Marriage is not simply a private contract; it is a social and public recognition of a private commitment. As such it is the highest public recognition of our personal integrity. Denying it to gay people is the most public affront possible to their civil equality."[6] What Sullivan stated about the civil context is equally significant for the ecclesiastical. If the church were formally to "bless" same-sex relationships in a manner similar to heterosexual marriages, this would mark the ultimate recognition of homosexual unions. Should the church do so? Opinions vary.

Gay/Lesbian Marriage and the Bible

Some Christians insist that a move to recognize homosexual relationships is long overdue.[7] In support of this claim, they look to the Bible. Certain proponents point out that scripture nowhere explicitly condemns such unions. The idea of homosexual marriage was simply unknown in the ancient world, they argue, and therefore the biblical authors never spoke to the issue.

This claim, however, fails to take into consideration the presence of homosexual marriages in ancient Greek and Roman culture. In Greece, same-sex unions were sometimes formalized through wedding ceremonies.[8] Likewise, homosexual marriages may have been in vogue in first-century Rome, especially among young males of well-to-do families. Emperor Nero himself was supposedly involved in two homosexual weddings, once as the groom and the other occasion as the bride.[9] In addition, a love story written by the first-century C.E. novelist Iamblichus included the intimate relations between a prominent Egyptian princess and another woman, as well as the war the liaison provoked.[10] This is not to suggest that homosexual marriages were the accepted social pattern, but to point out that they were not as unknown in the ancient world as some contemporary theorists suggest.

Paul, therefore, was likely aware of the possibility of same-sex marriage. Yet he nowhere advocates that Christians be participants in homosexual wedding celebrations. Nor does he exempt "married" same-sex couples from his blanket condemnation of the homosexual practices he knew.

All participants in the contemporary debate acknowledge that from Genesis to Revelation, the biblical writers speak of marriage as a covenant between a man and a woman. Opinions differ, however, as to whether heterosexual marriage is the only sexual covenant explicitly mentioned in the Bible.

Proponents of same-sex marriage sometimes cite David and Jonathan, Naomi and Ruth, and even Jesus and the beloved disciple as examples of the same-sex unions the Bible condones. Chris Glaser, for example, writes, "No scholarly analysis is required for a reader of Scripture to see that same-gender covenants are lifted up as models for relationships in the Bible." He then concludes, "If the covenants between Ruth and Naomi and David and Jonathan were validated and blessed and heralded in Scripture, what prevents the church from validating and blessing and heralding same-gender covenants today?"[11]

Glaser is surely correct in pointing out that these narratives caution us against seeing marriage as the only significant human relationship. Yet the texts he cites do not support his claim that the biblical writers condone explicitly sexual unions between persons of the same sex. Although the Old Testament stories narrate the sealing of some type of covenant between two persons of the same sex, nowhere in the texts do we read that these covenants were officially "blessed," as Glaser suggests. Rather than being a public, community event, each of the covenants was a private declaration of loyal, committed friendship between the persons involved.

Further, unlike the sexual unions Glaser wants the biblical stories to authenticate, the relationships to which he appeals were not exclusive sexual bonds. Both David and Jonathan were married. And rather than suggesting that their covenant precluded marriage, Naomi actually encouraged Ruth to marry Boaz. In fact, as I noted in chapter 2, it is unlikely that any of the covenantal relationships between persons of the same sex found in the biblical narratives involved genital sexual relations.

Rather than supporting his theory, therefore, the biblical materials to which Glaser appeals lead to a different conclusion. In both testaments, the biblical writers celebrate the loyalty and devotion that can arise between two people of the same sex. Yet nowhere does scripture endorse genital sexual expression within such relationships. Consequently, Christian gay or lesbian persons might well enjoy caring, loving, supporting, and affirming friendships; nevertheless, in that these are in fact friendship bonds, their commitment to each other is not to be expressed through genital sexual acts. For this reason, it would be inappropriate for the church to bless such relationships with language befitting marriage.

Gay/Lesbian Marriage and the Nature of Marriage

Some Christian ethicists advocate recognition of same-sex unions less by direct appeal to the Bible than by more pragmatic considerations. The church's official blessing, they argue, would serve to strengthen loving, committed homosexual relationships. The sanctioning of same-sex marriages would help combat homosexual promiscuity, as well as the instability that critics declare typifies gay and lesbian relationships.[12] The church's blessing would also promote important values, such as self-giving love and mutual acceptance, within homosexual relationships. Considerations such as these have led even certain traditionalists to view church sanctioning as the best way of dealing with homosexuality.[13]

In the end, however, the specifically ethical case for homosexual marriage presupposes that same-sex intercourse is proper for those persons who sense they are naturally homoerotic. If the sex act is a proper expression within the context of stable gay or lesbian relationships, there may be no moral grounds for the church to refuse to bless gay and lesbian unions as marriages. In chapter 5, however, I precluded this argument, for I asserted that same-sex intercourse is in fact morally problematic. I must now take that discussion a step further, determining in what sense homosexual unions are not marriages.

In this process, I will avoid invoking the typical arguments against homosexual marriage: the purported instability of same-sex unions,[14] the seemingly inherent promiscuity of homosexual persons (especially males),[15] and the supposed inability of gay men to form thoroughly monogamous relationships.[16] Instead, I will look at same-sex unions themselves. My goal is to set forth why such relationships are inherently problematic. What is it about a homosexual union that disqualifies it from being marriage?

The obvious reason that such a relationship is not marriage arises from the fact that the partners are of the same sex. A homosexual union does not bring male and female together in an exclusive sexual bond. But why is this crucial? Why should we privilege heterosexual marriage? One answer is: because such a union lies at the heart of marriage. The presence of male and female is required by the very nature of marriage, so that marriage is by definition the sexual bond between a man and a woman.

To understand this we must remind ourselves of what marriage is and how the nature of marriage lends symbolic significance to it as a sexual bond. As I noted in chapter 5, marriage involves the coming together of two people as sexual "others" to form a new unity, a union that is appropriately depicted in the sex act. Of course, to a certain degree a same-sex union also entails the uniting of two who are "other." (Actually this dynamic is present in all human bonding.) However, in a same-sex relationship the two partners do not contribute to the union what is uniquely theirs to bring, namely, their *sexual* otherness. Because our sexuality is central to our essential personhood, a homosexual union can never fully be a uniting of the persons as two who are "other."

Marriage entails two becoming one at the deepest level of their existence, namely, in the sexual dimension. This essential nature of the marital bond provides, in turn, the foundation for its profound theological meaning. The inability of a same-sex union to be a coming together of two who are sexually "other," in contrast, impedes such a relationship from symbolizing what marriage is intended to convey: the reconciliation of otherness on the deepest level. Hence, because a homosexual relationship does not entail the uniting of the two foundational ways of being human, that is, as male or female, it does not appropriately symbolize human reconciliation. Nor can it connote the reconciliation of God and creation, who likewise are profoundly "other" to each other.

Marriage differs from a same-sex union in another way as well. As I noted in chapter 5, marriage is intended to be inviolate in a manner that homosexual relationships could never be. Even if same-sex unions attained legal status and received ecclesiastical blessing, we would still not need to treat them with the same degree of moral seriousness inherent in marriage.

To cite one example, the breakup of a homosexual relationship cannot carry the deep sense of moral failure that divorce involves. Were the parties to a homosexual union to go their separate ways, they would have at most breached a legal contract. The breakup of a marriage, in contrast, always entails the effacing of the picture of the relationship between God and God's people (or Christ and the church) that God intends each marriage to depict. Therefore, treating same-sex relationships as marriage devalues marriage, for it reduces the significance of the marital union as an inviolate moral commitment.

A same-sex union is likewise not a marriage because it cannot be sealed with the sex act understood in its fullest sense. As I noted in chapter 5, some type of genital sexual activity can occur between members of the same sex. Nevertheless, same-sex intercourse is not a complete expression of the sex act.

I would readily admit that sexual intercourse is not necessary for the ongoing existence of a marriage; persons who for various reasons cannot engage in the sex act remain married. However, same-sex unions are quite distinct from exceptional heterosexual cases. In the latter, true sexual intercourse is precluded by some militating circumstance, whereas in the former it is inherently impossible.

This leads to a final consideration. I acknowledged in chapter 5 that procreation is not definitive for sexual union. But this does not mean that the potential to beget children is inconsequential for marriage. The Genesis narratives suggest that the creation of humankind as male and female serves both procreation and companionship. In marriage these two aspects become closely linked—to the point of being present simultaneously.[17] Ideally companionship precedes and creates the context in which procreation may occur. In such a situation, the birth of children does not suddenly dissolve the link between the two aspects. On the contrary, the companionship of husband and wife provides a nurturing environment for the rearing of whatever children are born from their sexual union.

A same-sex relationship can never combine the procreative potential with the aspect of companionship found in marriage. The companionship same-sex couples enjoy can provide a nurturing context for rearing children (albeit not children created from their union). But the sexual expression of their companionship (i.e., same-sex intercourse) cannot symbolize the potential procreative aspect of their relationship, for same-sex unions are inherently devoid of that potential. Therefore, the same-sex intercourse they share lacks any connection—even symbolically—to the presence of children in their midst.

Reflections such as these preclude our treating same-sex relationships as marriage. But could we not establish an ecclesiastical ceremony for gay and lesbian unions that loosely parallels marriage? Three considerations militate against this suggestion.

First, it would be difficult to maintain a clear distinction between the blessing of same-sex unions and marriage. Second, we have repeatedly asserted that same-sex relationships are friendships. Establishing a ceremony to celebrate gay and lesbian relationships would raise the question as to why these friendships are being singled out: What is it about this particular friendship covenant that warrants a formal, public acknowledgment and blessing by the faith community?

Third, ultimately gays and lesbians are seeking church recognition for same-sex relationships not as friendship covenants but as sexual unions. Catherine Clark Kroeger has pinpointed the central question at stake in the drive for church recognition of homosexual relationships: "Should the church, the visible Body of Jesus Christ in this world, countenance an overtly *sexual* union as being ordained and blessed of God?"[18] Put in this manner, the answer can only be no. The sexual aspect is precisely the dimension of same-sex relationships that the church cannot bless without sanctioning sinful conduct.

Homosexual Persons and the Ordained Office

According to the ecumenical document *Baptism, Eucharist and Ministry,* "The chief responsibility of the ordained ministry is to assemble and build up the body of Christ by proclaiming and teaching the Word of God, by celebrating the sacraments, and by guiding the life of the community in its worship, its mission and its caring ministry."[19] Is this office open to homosexual persons?

Almost no one today articulates an unqualified yes to this question. Nearly all participants in the contemporary debate agree that certain sexual practices disqualify a gay or lesbian person from church office, just as some heterosexual behaviors preclude ordination for those who engage in them. While advocating the ordination of practicing homosexual persons, Tex Sample, for example, declared, "let it be clear that I am no more suggesting that the church approve all homosexual behaviors than I am heterosexual ones. Promiscuity, whatever the orientation, makes one unready for ordination,"[20] as does "the exploitative use of young boys by older men."[21]

The question, therefore, is not whether or not the church must be discriminating in its ordination practices. The issue that divides Christians today is whether persons in committed same-sex relationships ought on this basis alone to be barred from ordination. Our search for an answer to this question leads us to consider what forms the ethical basis for ordination.

Several operative understandings of what it means to be clergy can be found within the family of Christian churches. Yet despite the differences, most denominations view the ordained office as in some sense carrying exemplary significance. Clergy ought to exemplify what "graced living" looks like. This does not suggest that clergy are sinless, of course, but that they are seekers after God's heart (1 Sam. 13:14; Ps. 119:10). Exemplary disciples strive for holiness and are repentant in the face of failure.

For this reason, the requirements for ordination in most churches do not stop with cognitive credentials, such as biblical understanding and theological expertise, or with the relational and pastoral skills necessary for performing the duties of the office. Rather, ordaining churches also inquire as to whether or not the candidate is known to be morally upright.

The exemplary dimension of the ordained ministry finds its basis in the Bible itself. The New Testament writers admonished first-century church leaders to be "examples to the flock" (1 Peter 5:3), not only in knowledge of theology but also "in speech and conduct, in love, in faith, in purity" (1 Tim. 4:12). As Dennis Campbell noted, "These leaders were to articulate the gospel of Jesus Christ, to teach the faith, to help others practice the faith in daily life, and to be exemplars of the faith representing Christ to church and world."[22] In keeping with this understanding of the office, the New Testament prescribed that every candidate for ordination be "above reproach" (1 Tim. 3:2).

The exemplary aspect of the ordained office extends to a person's sexual conduct as well. But what does it mean to be "above reproach" in sexual behavior? More specifically, are gays and lesbians in stable, loving sexual relationships "above reproach" and hence fit candidates? Here the lines are quickly drawn.

Some Christians are convinced that practicing homosexual persons are appropriate candidates for ordination. Advocates assert that rather than negatively affecting their ministry, being gay or lesbian could actually enhance it. Placing practicing homosexual persons in authority positions, they argue, would allow such persons to experience greater self-actualization. Hence, Gary Comstock asserted, "Churches and denominations need to be reminded that when they ask lesbians/bisexual/gay clergy to be celibate, to refrain from practicing or expressing their sexual preference/orientation, they are telling people what they want them to do and are not listening to what people need to do."[23] Further, homosexual clergy would serve as role models for others, thereby assisting homosexual congregants in their own struggles with self-esteem and acceptance.

Rather than merely defending their position, proponents sometimes launch an attack against their opponents. One criticism asserts that the opposition to the ordination of gays and lesbians is ultimately due more to psychological hang-ups than to solid theological reflection. Pamela Dickey Young provides an articulate example: "My own sense is that one of the reasons many male clergy object vociferously to the ordination of gay men is a fear of the clergy being further marginalized (feminized?) and an accompanying furthering of ambiguity around their own sexual identities."[24]

Although arguments such as these may at first glance appear weighty, they in fact skirt the central ethical issue. In the end, the fitness of practicing homosexual persons for ordination does not rise or fall with pragmatic concerns or even their giftedness for ministry, but with the moral status of same-sex intercourse and hence with the propriety of homosexual unions. If sexual behavior within the context of a stable gay or lesbian relationship is proper, and if it is appropriate for the church to treat such sexual unions as marriages, there may in the end be no inherent moral impediment to the ordination of persons in such relationships. The deliberations in these chapters, however, have led to quite different conclusions: Same-sex intercourse is ethically problematic, and same-sex relationships are not appropriate sexual unions.

Some might argue that even these conclusions do not necessitate barring practicing homosexual persons from ordination. All clergy are sinners, and all sins are the same in God's sight. Therefore, they surmise, it is arbitrary and uncharitable to focus on homosexuality. Even Richard Hays, who upholds the traditional view on the ethics of same-sex unions, warns, "It is arbitrary to single out homosexuality as a special sin that precludes ordination. The Church has no analogous special rules to exclude from ordination the greedy or the self-righteous."[25]

This argument, however, fails to take seriously exactly what about a candidate's morality can potentially bar him or her from ordination. We are, of course, all sinful—even clergy. Therefore, the exemplary disciple is not marked by perfection (for no one is perfect), but by a sense of humility that leads to confession of personal sin (1 John 1:9) and the earnest desire to forsake sin. A person who willfully continues in sinful practices—whatever these may be—is not fit for ordained leadership, not because clergy are perfect but because willful sin casts doubt on one's spiritual vitality (1 John 3:4–10). This suggests that the church ought not to ordain a practicing homosexual person for the same reason we dare not place an immoral heterosexual person—or anyone who deliberately continues in any sin, including greed and self-righteousness—in office. Such persons simply cannot serve Christ's people as examples of Christian integrity.

While Hays and others offer an important caution against elevating homosexual behavior above other sins, there is something unique about sexual failure. I have argued earlier that both marriage and the informal friendship bond are theological metaphors picturing aspects of God and God's intended relationship to humans. Consequently, to transgress the biblical ethic of chastity is to efface what God has ordained to be a powerful theological symbol. For this reason, the church is surely not misguided in instinctively expecting—even demanding—of all ordained persons as "examples to the flock" exemplary conduct in the realm of sexuality, whether they are married or single. With good reason, therefore, the ordination guidelines of the United Methodist Church (1992) and the Book of Order of the Presbyterian Church (U.S.A.) (1997) specify that persons set apart for ordained ministry are "required to maintain the highest standards represented by the practice of fidelity in marriage and celibacy [i.e., sexual abstinence] in singleness."[26] The requirement of abstinence for homosexual persons is one aspect of this wider stipulation.

But what about persons who continue to struggle with homosexual feelings? Some Christians declare that a homosexual candidate must first lose all same-sex desires, perhaps even become heterosexual. To require this, however, is tantamount to setting up perfection as the prerequisite for ordination. The moral basis for ordination does not consist in the candidate experiencing a complete change in disposition, for no one's sinful disposition is eradicated in this life. Nor does being an exemplary Christian necessitate complete freedom from temptation and struggle. Instead, the moral test for fitness for ordination lies with the candidate's ongoing conduct, and exemplary Christian integrity entails leading a chaste life in the midst of the experience of the brokenness of our desires. Sexual chastity involves forsaking sinful practices, whether these be same-sex behaviors or licentious relations with persons of the other sex.

The Church's Public Stance

In the 1990s, "gay rights" emerged as the most divisive political and social issue in North American society.[27] Christians have not stood on the sidelines of the wider public debate. Nor have they spoken with one voice on the pressing questions of the day. On the contrary, the church has been as divided over public policy issues as it has been racked with division about such internal matters as the ordination of homosexual Christians.

My intent in this section is not to engage in the impossible task of dealing with all the various particular issues currently debated, for the status of such questions is in constant flux. Rather, I want to take a step back and look at what ought to be at the heart of the church's stance on the central dimensions of the current public debate. To this end, I will concentrate on the implications of the ethical point of view developed in the previous chapters for the church's stand on the treatment of homosexual persons and on society's understanding of marriage.

The Treatment of Homosexual Persons

In 1984, Charlie Howard, a twenty-three-year-old homosexual man, was attacked by a gang of taunting gay bashers in Bangor, Maine. During his ordeal, Howard pleaded for his life—but to no avail. The incident ended when the group threw their hapless victim from a bridge, an act that resulted in Howard's death.

Throughout the Bible, a crucial test for the genuineness of a person's faith is his or her treatment of the needy, as well as the social outcasts of the day (e.g., Ex. 22:21–27; Matt. 25:31–46; James 1:27). One important aspect of this "test" is one's attitude toward persons whose conduct does not square with Christian moral convictions. Taking this seriously means that we never allow the conclusion that homosexual behavior is immoral to provide fodder for physical or psychological attacks on persons who engage in such conduct. Nor can we condone the practice of painting homosexual persons in the worst possible light as a means to raise funds for Christian organizations.[28]

Yet simply avoiding such abuses is not sufficient. The New Testament writers instruct Jesus' disciples to pattern themselves after his own example. Our Lord was able to extend nonjudgmental, compassionate grace without moral compromise to all persons (e.g., John 8:1–11; Luke 7:36–50). Consequently, Christians ought to be known as a people who come alongside, and minister to, those with whom they disagree.

This includes ministering as persons to persons, of course. Christians ought to help homosexual persons and their families cope with their situation in constructive, God-honoring ways.[29] Unfortunately, however, Darlene Bogle's pointed observation about her conservative coreligionists is too often true: "Many well-meaning Christians want to protest and 'out-legislate' pro-gay bills in the state senate. Not as many want to cultivate a friendship that will help change the heart of a person struggling with homosexuality [i.e., someone who desires to overcome personal homosexual tendencies]."[30]

Another significant way of coming alongside gays and lesbians is promoting wholesome attempts to combat homophobia in the church and in society. A first step toward this goal involves gaining a clear understanding as to what homophobia actually is. In contrast to what the term itself suggests, homophobia is in fact not a phobia at all; it is not an irrational fear, similar to claustrophobia or agoraphobia. The current widespread use of the word as a pejorative designation for anyone who questions the morality of homosexual relationships and same-sex intercourse is nonproductive.

Rightly understood, homophobia is a prejudice. In certain respects it is somewhat akin to racism and anti-Semitism.[31] Hence, the homophobia Christians ought to combat is hatred or devaluing of persons for no other reason than because they are sexually aroused by persons of the same sex. As we noted earlier, Christians simply cannot countenance such attitudes. Instead, patterning our lives after Jesus leads us to love and value all persons—including gays and lesbians—as persons whom God loves and values.

Unfortunately, an improper prejudice against homosexual persons is prevalent in the church. In the stirring story of the journey of a homosexual member of his congregation, Don Baker, pastor of the Hinson Memorial Baptist Church of Portland, Oregon, offers a striking example. Baker reports how upon hearing "Jerry" confess his struggle with homosexual feelings despite being married to "Rosie," the pastor confessed his own sin of homophobia. Baker describes the scene in these vivid words:

> I came out from behind my desk, took Jerry's and Rosie's hands in mine, knelt down beside their chairs, and asked God for forgiveness and for grace for the three of us, each caught in a trap. . . . It was no longer just a homosexual who craved freedom from his habit or a wife who sought deliverance for her husband. It was also

a pastor who sought freedom from a fear and from a revulsion that had invaded his soul and had made a redemptive ministry to this imprisoned group an impossibility.[32]

Patterning our lives after Jesus' example includes adamant support of fair treatment for all persons in our society, including gays and lesbians. But what exactly does this entail? More specifically, ought concern for fair treatment translate into support for human rights legislation that singles out "sexual preference" for legal protection? Here Christians find themselves divided.

According to trial lawyer and Christian activist Roger J. Magnuson, the addition of any new category to human rights codes requires a demonstrable pattern of discrimination that is based on criteria that are arbitrary and irrational, and that causes substantial injury to a class of people with an unchangeable or immutable status which has no element of moral fault.[33] He is convinced that homosexual persons do not qualify under these guidelines. Other Christians, in contrast, are strong advocates for such legislative and judicial initiatives. The answers to this question are far from clear-cut. Nor can we offer a blanket response apart from looking at specific proposals offered in specific situations.

The Status of Marriage

A central concern of this book has been to evaluate same-sex unions by comparison to heterosexual marriage. Although my deliberations have focused on the specifically moral status of such relationships, the connection between gay/lesbian partnerships and heterosexual marriage has emerged as a major social and political issue as well. Whereas activists have been intent on gaining legal status for homosexual unions on an equal basis with heterosexual marriage, other voices have articulated the fear that marriage is becoming a casualty in the process.

This negative appraisal is not limited to conservative Christians. Even some homosexual persons argue that it is not in society's best interest to treat same-sex relationships on a par with marriage. Ca-

nadian cultural critic Paul Nathanson, to cite one example, purportedly believes that enduring heterosexual relationships need to
be encouraged and nurtured.[34] To this end, he argues that marriage
should enjoy a privileged status in society, including legal recognition as well as certain social and economic advantages.

Proponents of a special status for marriage base their argument
on recent statistics confirming that heterosexual marriage is indis-
pensable to the ongoing health of society because it is the best
environment for raising children. Studies indicate that ideally children should live in households that include one parent of each sex
united in a long-term, committed relationship. This is one reason
that society has steadfastly refused to view group "marriage"
arrangements as marital bonds, in contrast to its treatment of co-
habiting couples (who are deemed as being married "common-
law").

But where does this leave gay and lesbian couples? A Christian
response to this question requires that we seek to understand some
of the reasons that persons in same-sex relationships desire marital status. The benefits enjoyed by married persons include participation in each other's insurance and pension plans; favorable tax
treatment; an orderly distribution of property should divorce occur; "next of kin rights" for the spouse in the event of hospitaliza-
tion, medical emergency, or death; and child custody rights in the
case of death or divorce.[35] Craig Dean poignantly contrasted the
situation of heterosexual and homosexual couples: "Heterosexuals
can meet each other tonight in a bar, and have more rights through
marriage in five days than [homosexual couples] are able to obtain
after five years of being together."[36]

As a way forward in this situation, some theorists today propose
the establishment of a new legal entity: "registered domestic partnerships." This category opens the door to legal status for the
variety of living arrangements present in our society without
changing the traditional definitions of "marriage" and "spouse."

What is the role of the church in this discussion? Considerations
I developed earlier would lead Christians to voice an ongoing

concern that society differentiate marriage, which intrinsically entails a sexual bond between male and female, from whatever other living arrangements gain legal status. Thus, the conferring of legal standing on "domestic partnerships" ought not to be based on the presence of sexual relationships between or among the parties to the relationship nor even the number of persons involved. Rather, whether or not the participants are engaging in sexual intercourse must be viewed as irrelevant to the legal status of any alternative living arrangement.

Further, Christians' chief interest must always be the maintenance of justice in every type of human relationship. Thus, our concern in such arrangements as domestic partnerships is that all parties act justly toward each other at all stages in the life of the relationship. Ensuring justice becomes especially crucial in the event of the breakup of the living arrangement. It is here that legislation guaranteeing that all parties treat each other equitably might be most necessary.

This concern for justice within a relationship does not allow us to ignore the question of social and economic benefits to various types of living arrangements. Determining which benefits these ought to be is no easy matter. Nevertheless, a first step involves differentiating between benefits society affords to married couples as spouses themselves and benefits that have as their purpose the support of marriage as a nurturing environment for children (and by extension grandchildren).[37] The principles I espouse in this book would suggest that Christians might well support extending the former to participants in a variety of living arrangements, so long as the latter are reserved for marriage.

Epilogue

The Welcoming but Not Affirming Community

The North American church has come to a fork in the road in its understanding of sexuality and of the sex ethic it proclaims. Perhaps the single most significant issue that has been responsible for leading the church to this fork is the stormy question of homosexuality. The church today appears to be faced with two seemingly contrary alternatives: Do we maintain the traditional ecclesiastical opposition to same-sex intercourse and to homosexual unions? Or do we conclude that the time has come to revise our stance on this moral issue?

The debate over homosexuality is important not only because it affects the church's ministry but also because it brings to the surface a deeper question of ecclesiastical identity. The contemporary discussion of this moral issue has launched the church on a process of rethinking and possibly even reconstructing our communal identity. Through the ethical debate that is now raging, we are determining what kind of community we will be.

Several visions of the Christian community are currently vying for attention. Each of these seeks to preserve a dimension of the foundational, biblical narrative we share. And each has the power to shape the church in the immediate, if not long-term, future.

Proponents of an open stance toward homosexuality articulate one such vision. Their goal is to construct a community that is truly inclusive and that stands firmly on the side of the oppressed and marginalized of society.

The architects of this vision are certain that the current battle for liberation is being waged by persons who are outcasts due to their sexual preference. Because they are convinced this is where God is now at work in our world, proponents are attempting to mobilize the church to engage in this battle in solidarity with gay and lesbian persons. But because the front line of the battle runs directly through the church, it is the church itself that must be reformed, proponents argue. Consequently, advocates envision a new, liberated, and liberating church. They hope to foster a community in which homosexual and heterosexual persons stand together as equals and as equal partners.

Proponents cite several scriptural narratives as paradigms for the inclusive community they desire. But one story is particularly poignant—the narrative of the conversion of Cornelius (Acts 10:1–11:18). Jeffrey Siker, who identifies himself as a repentant heterosexist, articulates the significance of this story in the context of his own "faith journey":

> Before I came to know various Christians who are also homosexual in their sexual orientation, I was like the hard-nosed, doctrinaire, circumcised Jewish Christians who denied that Gentiles could receive the Spirit of Christ as Gentiles. But just as Peter's experience of Cornelius in Acts 10 led him to realize that even Gentiles were receiving God's Spirit, so my experience of various gay and lesbian Christians has led me to realize that these Christians have received God's Spirit as gays and lesbians, and that the reception of the Spirit has nothing to do with sexual orientation.[1]

Without a doubt, Siker has chosen well. The Cornelius story carries strong emotive appeal. Yet on closer inspection, we discover that Siker's reading of the text, as well as of our situation, is wide of the mark.

Despite Siker's take on our situation, the question at issue in the contemporary debate is not, Can gays and lesbians be Christians, or have homosexual persons received the Spirit? Few participants in the current discussion deny that homosexual persons can be Christians. Nor are many voices today asserting that gay and lesbian believers have not received the Holy Spirit. The point of contention is not the spiritual status of this particular group, but the moral status of certain acts and relationships. The question that divides the discussion participants is: Is it proper for Christians to respond to homosexual urges by forming same-sex sexual unions?

Siker likewise misses the point of the narrative he cites, at least when read in its original context. In the first-century world in which Cornelius lived, Gentiles were excluded from the Old Testament covenant people solely on the basis of their birth to non-Jewish parents. The point of the story is that in Christ the old racial distinction, based as it was on physical birth, has been eradicated. Because the covenant people form a spiritual family whose Parent is God, the door to participation in this people is now open to all regardless of human parentage.

Based as it is on a misreading of the text and a misunderstanding of the issue at stake in the contemporary debate, Siker's analogy is a misappropriation of the Cornelius narrative. The connections he draws from "then" to "now" are erroneous. Traditionalists do not stand in the position of the first-century Jewish Christians. Nor are gays and lesbians modern-day Corneliuses. Unlike the misguided believers of an earlier day, traditionalists are not claiming that the doorway to the church is closed to homosexual persons. Their concern has to do with the kind of conduct that befits disciples within the covenant community.

This leads to another difficulty with Siker's analogy. The first-century inclusion of the Gentiles did not occur on "Gentile terms." The apostles did not urge the new converts to bring their old Gentile ideas and ways with them into the church. Thus, for example, in the opening chapter of his letter to the Romans, Paul does not affirm the preferences of Gentiles on the basis of their inclusion into the people of God. Instead the apostle penned a stinging critique of pagan ways. The early church leaders instructed Gentile converts to leave behind their former "ignorance." They were to park their pagan religious practices and immoral activities outside the door of the church. All Christians—whether Jew or Gentile—were to live out the same ethical calling, namely, to be holy (1 Peter 1:13–16).

This same calling is ours today. Like the earliest Christians, we must struggle with the questions: What kind of sexual behavior befits persons within the believing community? What constitutes holiness in life and relationships? Yet the issue at stake here is larger than merely the morality of same-sex relationships. As gay activist Chris Glaser correctly pointed out in his autobiography, "I knew the church needed to address other issues for heterosexual and homosexual alike: singleness without celibacy, sexual intimacy outside covenant relationships, bisexuality."[2] Traditionalists find in the biblical writings clear direction on these matters. The standard of sexual morality for all Christians is chastity, that is, sexual abstinence in singleness and fidelity in marriage.

Other voices, however, are seeking to undercut this traditional view in the name of becoming an inclusive community. This suggests that a more appropriate biblical analogy for our situation today might well be Paul's interaction with the Corinthian church in the face of sexual immorality within their ranks.

The Corinthians were radical inclusivists—so much so that they even prided themselves over their tolerance of a case of incest among them. Perhaps this even involved a loving, consensual relationship between a believer and his father's wife. Yet Paul rebuked the community for their tolerant, inclusive spirit (1 Cor. 5:1–2). In admonishing them to take action, the apostle was not revealing his own "incestophobia." Rather, he was concerned for the offender's salvation (v. 5) as well as for the purity of the church (vv. 6–13). He prescribed disciplinary action in the hope that the offender would repent and on the basis of his repentance be welcomed back into the community. In fact, Paul later chided the church for not embracing a formerly wayward member (2 Cor. 2:5–11).

Siker rightly proposes that we build our communal identity on the foundational, biblical narratives. And he helpfully suggests that we view our situation in the light of the Cornelius story. Our Christian calling is to acknowledge every person as a recipient of God's compassion, concern, and love. Like Peter we are to accept without prejudice all who seek the God of Israel by looking on the face of Jesus. Hence, the narrative leads us to be a welcoming community.

But reading the Cornelius story within the context of the entire biblical narrative directs us to realize that all who would become the Lord's disciples and hence join the discipleship community must do so on God's terms, not their own. This entails being willing to leave behind old sinful practices—including unchaste sexual behaviors—so that together we might become a holy people.

For this reason, the welcoming community that the narrative calls us to construct cannot always be an affirming one. Christ's community welcomes all sinners, affirming them as persons of value in God's sight. But like the Master who boldly commanded the adulterous woman the Jewish leaders brought to him, "from now on do not sin again" (John 8:11), the welcoming community of Christ's disciples steadfastly refuses to affirm any type of sinful behavior.

The current discussion about homosexuality poses a grave challenge to the church. At the same time, it is a moment of great opportunity. The current debate offers us an opportunity to think through the Christian sexual ethic clearly and carefully. More importantly, it calls us back once again to God's bountiful grace. The divine call to live out our sexuality in ways that bring honor to God is a difficult challenge, especially in our permissive society. Yet the resources of the Holy Spirit are greater than the obstacles that would thwart us. And because the challenge is one we all face, whether "straight" or "gay," we face it best together. For the sake of the gospel in the world, therefore, we need to assist each other and rely on each other, so that by the power of the Spirit working through us, we might live in true biblical chastity to the glory of God. In the end, this is what it means to be a welcoming, yet not always affirming, community.

NOTES

INTRODUCTION

1. One such mainline denomination that the debate over homosexuality brought to the brink of schism is the United Church of Canada. For a biased account of the events leading up to the historic 1990 decision, see Michael Riordon, *The First Stone: Homosexuality and the United Church* (Toronto: McClelland & Stewart, 1990).
2. See, for example, Richard Cleaver, *Know My Name: A Gay Christian Liberation* (Louisville, Ky.: Westminster John Knox Press, 1995), 24; Gary David Comstock, *Gay Theology without Apology* (Cleveland: Pilgrim Press, 1993), 124.
3. Suzanne Pharr, *Homophobia: A Weapon of Sexism* (Inverness, Calif.: Chardon Press, 1988), 45.
4. Early examples include the mainline Protestant James B. Nelson, *Embodiment* (Minneapolis: Augsburg, 1978), the Roman Catholic John J. McNeill, *The Church and the Homosexual* (Kansas City: Sheed, Andrews & McMeel, 1976), and evangelicals Letha D. Scanzoni and Virginia R. Mollenkott, *Is the Homosexual My Neighbor? A Positive Christian Response* (San Francisco: Harper & Row, 1978).
5. For a discussion of the problem of defining homosexuality, see Pim Pronk, *Against Nature? Types of Moral Argumentation regarding Homosexuality,* trans. John Vriend (Grand Rapids: Eerdmans, 1993), 113–26.
6. George A. Kanoti and Anthony R. Kosnik, "Homosexuality: Ethical Aspects," in *Encyclopedia of Bioethics,* ed. Warren T. Reich (New York: Free Press, 1978), 2:671.
7. Perhaps 90 percent of children develop a core gender identity consistent with their biologic sex by age three. See Gerald D. Coleman, *Homosexuality: Catholic Teaching and Pastoral Practice* (New York: Paulist Press, 1995), 18.
8. Alfred C. Kinsey, Wardell B. Pomeroy, and Clyde E. Martin, *Sexual Behavior in the Human Male* (Philadelphia: W. B. Saunders, 1948), 623, 650.
9. Kinsey et al., *Sexual Behavior in the Human Male,* 651.

10. See, for example, Judith A. Reisman and Edward W. Eichel, *Kinsey, Sex and Fraud: The Indoctrination of a People* (Lafayette, La.: Lochinvar-Huntington House Publications, 1990), esp. chapter 6. See also Robert T. Michael et al., *Sex in America: A Definitive Survey* (Boston: Little, Brown & Co., 1994), 172–74. See also Milton Diamond and Arno Karlen, *Sexual Decisions* (Boston: Little, Brown & Co., 1980), 219–22.

11. John M. Livingood, ed., *National Institute of Mental Health Task Force on Homosexuality: Final Report and Background Papers* (Rockville, Md.: National Institute of Mental Health, 1972), 27.

12. See Felicity Barringer, "Sex Survey of American Men Finds 1 Percent Are Gay," *New York Times,* 14 April 1993, Section A, p. 1. Barringer reported these figures as being in line with other surveys in the early 1990s. Cf. the slightly higher figures in the 1994 survey reported in Tamar Lewin, "Sex in America: Faithfulness in Marriage Thrives after All," *New York Times,* 7 October 1994, Section A, p. 1.

13. Joseph Nicolosi, "What Does Science Teach about Human Sexuality?" in *Caught in the Crossfire: Helping Christians Debate Homosexuality,* ed. Sally B. Geis and Donald E. Messer (Nashville: Abingdon Press, 1994), 71.

14. Stanton L. Jones, "Homosexuality According to Science," in *The Crisis of Homosexuality,* ed. J. Isamu Yamamoto (Wheaton, Ill.: Victor Books, 1990), 105. For a list of recent research findings, see Stanton L. Jones, "Addendum," in *Homosexuality in the Church: Both Sides of the Debate,* ed. Jeffrey S. Siker (Louisville, Ky.: Westminster John Knox Press, 1994), 107–12. See also Michael et al., *Sex in America,* 172–74.

15. See, for example, Eric Marcus, *Is It a Choice? Answers to Three Hundred of the Most Frequently Asked Questions about Gays and Lesbians* (San Francisco: HarperSanFrancisco, 1993), 6.

16. Stanton L. Jones and Don E. Workman, "Homosexuality: The Behavioral Sciences and the Church," *Journal of Psychology and Theology* 17/3 (Fall 1989): 214.

17. James G. Wolf, ed., *Gay Priests* (San Francisco: Harper & Row, 1989), 162–63.

18. Mary E. Hunt, "Lovingly Lesbian: Toward a Feminist Theology of Friendship," reprinted in *Sexuality and the Sacred: Sources for Theological Reflection,* ed. James B. Nelson and Sandra P. Longfellow (Louisville, Ky.: Westminster John Knox Press, 1994), 170.

19. Jerry Bartram, "A Sacred Gift from God," *Globe and Mail,* 11 June 1994, D5.

20. "The Silver Lake Challenge," 29 April 1995.

21. Larry Witham, "Episcopal Bishops Divided on Sexuality," *Wash-*

ington Times, 10 September 1994, A13; Richard Vara, "Uneasy Peace Reigns over Episcopal Convention," *Houston Chronicle,* 3 September 1994, Religion section, p. 1. See also John W. Kennedy, "Episcopalians Tone Down Sexuality Statement," *Christianity Today,* 3 October 1994, 70; Julie A. Wortman, "Sex—Getting It Straight?" *Witness* 77/10 (October 1994): 21; Louie Crew, "Cracks in the Wall of Opposition to Lesbians and Gays," *Witness* 77/11 (November 1994): 24.

22. Jerry R. Kirk, *The Homosexual Crisis in the Mainline Church* (Nashville: Thomas Nelson, 1978), 73.
23. Don Williams, *The Bond That Breaks: Will Homosexuality Split the Church?* (Los Angeles: BIM, 1978), 128.
24. Choon-Leong Seow, in his Introduction to *Homosexuality and Christian Community,* ed. Choon-Leong Seow (Louisville, Ky.: Westminster John Knox Press, 1996), viii–ix.
25. Peter Coleman, *Gay Christians: A Moral Dilemma* (London: SCM Press, 1989), 13.
26. *The New Shorter Oxford English Dictionary* (Oxford: Clarendon Press, 1993), s.v. "homophobia." See also Richard Isay, *Being Homosexual* (New York: Farrar, Straus & Giroux, 1989), 145.
27. George Weinberg, *Society and the Healthy Homosexual* (New York: St. Martin's Press, 1972), 8, 19–21.
28. For this characterization, see Joseph Nicolosi, *Reparative Therapy of Male Homosexuality: A New Clinical Approach* (Northvale, N.J.: Jason Aronson, 1991), 137–38. See also Marshall Forstein, "Homophobia," *Psychiatric Annals* 18/1 (January 1988): 33–36.

Chapter One
HOMOSEXUALITY AND CHRISTIAN SEXUAL ETHICS

1. See, for example, David F. Greenberg, *The Construction of Homosexuality* (Chicago: University of Chicago Press, 1988), 25–298.
2. Manfred Herzer, "Kertbeny and the Nameless Love," *Journal of Homosexuality* 12/1 (Fall 1986): 1–26; Peter Coleman, *Christian Attitudes to Homosexuality* (London: SPCK, 1980), 2, 4. David M. Halperin, *One Hundred Years of Homosexuality and Other Essays on Greek Love* (New York: Routledge, 1990), 155n2.

The idea that homosexuality is innate came somewhat earlier. This view was introduced into the medical community in Hanover, Germany, by Karl Heinrich Ulrichs, who spoke of homosexual persons as constituting a "third sex" but who coined the word "Uranians" to refer to male homosexual persons. See Greenberg, *Construction of Homosexuality,* 408. See also Richard Cleaver, *Know My Name: A Gay Liberation Theology* (Louisville, Ky.: Westminster John Knox Press, 1995), 21.

3. Maggie Gallagher, *Enemies of Eros: How the Sexual Revolution Is Killing Family, Marriage, and Sex and What We Can Do about It* (Chicago: Bonus, 1989), 256–57. See also Camille Paglia, *Sexual Personae: Art and Decadence* (New Haven, Conn.: Yale University Press, 1990), 234: "The sexual revolution [Rousseau] wrought is evident in the emergence of homosexuality as a formal category. From antiquity, there were homosexual acts, honorable or dissolute depending upon culture and time. Since the late nineteenth century, there is homosexuality, a condition of being entered into after searching or 'questioning,' a Rousseauist identity crisis."

4. See, for example, John P. DeCecco, "Homosexuality's Brief Recovery: From Sickness to Health and Back Again," *Journal of Sex Research* 23/1 (February 1987): 106–14; Wendell Ricketts, "Biological Research on Homosexuality: Ansell's Cow or Occam's Razor?" *Journal of Homosexuality* 9/4 (Summer 1984): 65–93.

5. For Freud's theory, see Sigmund Freud, "Three Essays on the Theory of Sexuality," in *The Standard Edition of the Complete Psychological Works of Sigmund Freud,* vol. 7, ed. James Strachey (London: Hogarth Press, 1953), esp. 144–47n, 181–83, 225–30. See also Sigmund Freud, "The Disposition to Obsessional Neurosis," in *The Standard Edition of the Complete Psychological Works of Sigmund Freud,* vol. 12, ed. James Strachey (London: Hogarth Press, 1958), 311–26.

6. George Grant and Mark A. Horne, *Legislating Immorality: The Homosexual Movement Comes Out of the Closet* (Chicago: Moody, 1993), 114.

7. See, for example, his advice to a mother of a homosexual son in Sigmund Freud, Letter 277, known as "Letter to an American Mother," 9 April 1935, in *Letters of Sigmund Freud,* ed. Ernst L. Freud, trans. Tania and James Stern (New York: Basic Books, 1960), 423–24.

8. Freud, "Letter to an American Mother," 423–24.

9. Ronald Bayer, *Homosexuality and American Psychiatry: The Politics of Diagnosis* (New York: Basic Books, 1981), 167. Robert Kronemeyer, *Overcoming Homosexuality* (New York: Macmillan, 1980), 4–6.

10. Elizabeth R. Moberly, *Homosexuality: A New Christian Ethic* (Cambridge, Eng.: James Clarke & Co., 1983), 30.

11. Irving Bieber, "A Discussion of 'Homosexuality: The Ethical Challenge,'" *Journal of Consulting and Clinical Psychology* 44/2 (1976): 164. For a summary of Bieber's findings and their

significance, see Stanton L. Jones and Don E. Workman, "Homosexuality: The Behavioral Sciences and the Church," *Journal of Psychology and Theology* 17/3 (Fall 1989): 219. See also Vance Packard, *The Sexual Wilderness* (New York: David McKay Co., 1968), 129–30.

12. Moberly, *Homosexuality,* 2.
13. Moberly, *Homosexuality,* 17–18.
14. Michael R. Saia, *Counseling the Homosexual* (Minneapolis: Bethany House, 1988), 56.
15. Moberly, *Homosexuality,* 28.
16. Lawrence J. Hatterer, *Changing Homosexuality in the Male: Treatment for Men Troubled by Homosexuality* (New York: McGraw-Hill, 1970), 38.
17. Joseph Nicolosi, *Reparative Therapy of Male Homosexuality: A New Clinical Approach* (Northvale, N.J.: Jason Aronson, 1991), 25–29.
18. Hence, evangelical counselors often presuppose that homosexuality "primarily develops out of the early childhood experience of a poorly established love-bonding relationship with the parent of the same gender" (William Consiglio, *Homosexual No More* [Wheaton, Ill.: Victor, 1991], 58). See also Mario Bergner, *Setting Love in Order: Hope and Healing for the Homosexual* (Grand Rapids, Mich.: Baker Book House, 1995).
19. William H. Masters and Virginia E. Johnson, *Homosexuality in Perspective* (New York: Bantam Books, 1982), 271.
20. Richard Green, *The "Sissy Boy Syndrome" and the Development of Homosexuality* (New Haven, Conn.: Yale University Press, 1987), 5, 99, 370–78.
21. Jerome Kagan, "Psychology of Sex Differences," in *Human Sexuality in Four Perspectives,* ed. Frank A. Beach (Baltimore: Johns Hopkins University Press, 1977), 103.
22. C. A. Tripp, *The Homosexual Matrix* (New York: McGraw-Hill Book Co., 1975), 20–21. A second edition of the book was published by New American Library in 1987.
23. Tripp, *Homosexual Matrix,* 15–16.
24. Tripp, *Homosexual Matrix,* 74–75.
25. Tripp, *Homosexual Matrix,* 80–82.
26. Tripp, *Homosexual Matrix,* 100.
27. Richard F. Hettlinger, *Living with Sex: The Student's Dilemma* (New York: Seabury Press, 1966), 111. In *Human Sexuality: A Christian View* (Kansas City, Mo.: Sheed & Ward, 1987) Roman Catholic ethicist John Dwyer echoes this conclusion. He declares that homosexuality is "the result of an early fixation on one parent" (68). And again, "Male homosexuality seems to be the result of a definite pattern of child-rearing and acculturation" (69).

28. Hatterer, *Changing Homosexuality in the Male,* 47.
29. Alan P. Bell, Martin S. Weinberg, and Sue Kiefer Hammersmith, *Sexual Preference: Its Development in Men and Women* (Bloomington, Ind.: Indiana University Press, 1981), 191–92.
30. Gerald D. Coleman, *Homosexuality: Catholic Teaching and Pastoral Practice* (New York: Paulist Press, 1995), 48.
31. See, for example, Bell et al., *Sexual Preference,* 3.
32. For summaries of the more recent research, see G. Coleman, *Homosexuality: Catholic Teaching,* 38–47; Chandler Burr, "Homosexuality and Biology," in *Homosexuality in the Church: Both Sides of the Debate,* ed. Jeffrey S. Siker (Louisville, Ky.: Westminster John Knox Press, 1994), 116–34; Sherwood O. Cole, "The Biological Basis of Homosexuality: A Christian Assessment," *Journal of Psychology and Theology* 23/2 (1995): 89–100. For an older study, see Milton Diamond, "Human Sexual Development: Biological Foundations for Social Development," in *Human Sexuality in Four Perspectives,* ed. Frank A. Beach (Baltimore: Johns Hopkins University Press, 1977), 40–42.
33. Richard C. Pillard and James D. Weinrich, "Evidence of Familial Nature of Male Homosexuality," *Archives of General Psychiatry* 43/8 (August 1986): 808–12; J. Michael Bailey and Deana S. Benishay, "Family Aggregation of Female Sexual Orientation," *American Journal of Psychiatry* 150/2 (February 1993): 272–77.
34. J. Michael Bailey and Richard C. Pillard, "A Genetic Study of Male Sexual Orientation," *Archives of General Psychiatry* 48/12 (December 1991): 1089–96; J. Michael Bailey et al., "Heritable Factors Influence Sexual Orientation," *Archives of General Psychiatry* 50/3 (March 1993): 217–23.
35. Michael King and Elizabeth McDonald, "Homosexuals Who Are Twins: A Study of Forty-Six Probands," *British Journal of Psychiatry* 160 (March 1992): 407–9.
36. Dean H. Hamer et al., "Linkage between DNA Markers on the X Chromosome and Male Sexual Orientation," *Science* 261 (1993): 321–27.
37. Cheryl M. McCormick and Sandra F. Witelson, "Functional Cerebral Asymmetry and Sexual Orientation in Men and Women," *Behavioral Neuroscience* 108/3 (June 1994): 525–31.
38. For a discussion of this direction of research, see Marcia Barinaga, "Is Homosexuality Biological?" *Science* 253 (1991): 956–57.
39. S. LeVay, "A Difference in Hypothalamic Structure between Heterosexual and Homosexual Men," *Science* 253 (1991): 1034–37.
40. D. F. Swaab and M. A. Hofman, "An Enlarged Suprachiasmatic Nucleus in Homosexual Men," *Brain Research* 537 (1990): 141–48.

41. One biological theory is articulated in John Shelby Spong, *Living in Sin? A Bishop Rethinks Human Sexuality* (San Francisco: Harper & Row, 1988), 71–74. Spong cites recent studies in Berlin that point to prenatal hormonal processes as the source of homosexuality. For a summary of the prenatal versus developmental discussion, see Milton Diamond and Arno Karlen, *Sexual Decisions* (Boston: Little, Brown & Co., 1980), 228–30.

42. For a discussion of the shortcomings of the various theories of hereditary causes, see Jones and Workman, "Homosexuality: Behavioral Sciences," 218–19.

43. Joseph Nicolosi, "What Does Science Teach about Human Sexuality?" in *Caught in the Crossfire: Helping Christians Debate Homosexuality,* ed. Sally B. Geis and Donald E. Messer (Nashville: Abingdon Press, 1994), 70.

44. S. Marc Breedlove, "Sex on the Brain," *Nature* 389 (23 October 1997): 801.

45. See William Byne and Bruce Parsons, "Human Sexual Orientation," *Archives of General Psychiatry* 50/3 (March 1993): 236–37; William Byne and Bruce Parsons, "In Reply," *Archives of General Psychiatry* 51/5 (May 1994): 432–33.

46. Byne and Parsons, "Human Sexual Orientation," 228.

47. This conclusion finds support among certain Christian psychologists as well. See, for example, Cole, "Biological Basis," 96.

48. Nicolosi, "What Does Science Teach about Human Sexuality?" 67.

49. G. Coleman, *Homosexuality: Catholic Teaching,* 54.

50. Irving Bieber, *Homosexuality: A Psychoanalytic Study* (New York: Basic Books, 1962), 318–19.

51. Irving Bieber and Toby B. Bieber, "Male Homosexuality," *Canadian Journal of Psychiatry* 24/5 (August 1979): 416.

52. For a critique of this study, see Douglas C. Haldeman, "Sexual Orientation Conversion Therapy for Gay Men and Lesbians: A Scientific Examination," in *Homosexuality: Research Implications for Public Policy,* ed. John C. Gonsiorek and James D. Weinrich (Newbury Park, Calif.: Sage Publications, 1991), 154–56.

53. Masters and Johnson, *Homosexuality in Perspective,* 401.

54. For a short summary, see Jones and Workman, "Homosexuality: Behavioral Sciences," 221. See also Ruth Tiffany Barnhouse, *Homosexuality: A Symbolic Confusion* (New York: Seabury Press, 1977), 109. Diamond and Karlen report a one-third success rate with an additional one-third changing to "a partly heterosexual pattern," 231. For a review of treatments and statistics since the 1960s, see Louis Diamant, "The Therapies," in *Male and Female Homosexuality: Psychological Approaches,* ed. Louis Diamant (Washington, D.C.: Hemisphere

Publishing, 1987), 199–217; Fred S. Berlin, "Media Distortion of the Public's Perception of Recidivism and Psychiatric Rehabilitation," *American Journal of Psychiatry* 148/11 (November 1991): 1572–76.

55. For an optimistic presentation of outcomes, see Jeffrey Satinover, *Homosexuality and the Politics of Truth* (Grand Rapids, Mich.: Baker Book House, 1996), 186–87.

56. Martin Hoffman, "Homosexuality," in *Human Sexuality in Four Perspectives,* ed. Frank A. Beach (Baltimore: Johns Hopkins University Press, 1977), 186–88.

57. Consiglio, *Homosexual No More,* 85.

58. Moberly, *Homosexuality,* 18–19.

59. Paul D. Meier, "Counseling Homosexuals," *Fundamentalist Journal* 4/3 (March 1985): 21.

60. Participants in the various organizations have produced a flood of books recounting their activities, setting forth the principles they employ and recounting the stories of persons whom they have treated successfully. See, for example, Bob Davies and Lori Rentzel, *Coming Out of Homosexuality: New Freedom for Men and Women* (Downers Grove, Ill.: InterVarsity Press, 1993).

61. See, for example, the gripping autobiography of a former "ghost writer" for many leading figures in the Christian Right, by Mel White (*Stranger at the Gate: To Be Gay and Christian in America* [New York: Simon & Schuster, 1994]).

62. Tim Stafford, "Coming Out," *Christianity Today,* 18 August 1989, 21.

63. Jones and Workman, "Homosexuality: Behavioral Sciences," 221.

64. George Weinberg, *Society and the Healthy Homosexual* (New York: St. Martin's Press, 1972), 64–66.

65. For a discussion and critique of the social constructivist approach to homosexuality, see Pim Pronk, *Against Nature? Types of Moral Argumentation Regarding Homosexuality,* trans. John Vriend (Grand Rapids, Mich.: Eerdmans, 1993), 193–209.

66. Greenberg, *Construction of Homosexuality,* 487.

67. Weinberg, *Society and the Healthy Homosexual,* 72–73.

68. Don Clark, *Loving Someone Gay* (New York: New American Library, 1978), 3. Revised editions were published in 1987 and 1997 by Celestial Arts, Berkeley, Calif.

69. Clark, *Loving Someone Gay,* 73–74.

70. Clark, *Loving Someone Gay,* 55.

71. For this descriptor, see Ekman P. C. Tam, "Counseling with Gay

Men and Lesbians: An Integrative Approach," *Pastoral Sciences* 16 (1997): 172.

72. Richard A. Isay, "Psychoanalytic Theory and the Therapy of Gay Men," in *Homosexuality/Heterosexuality: Concepts of Sexual Orientation,* ed. David P. McWhirter, Stephanie A. Sanders, and June Machover Reinisch (New York: Oxford University Press, 1990), 283–303.

73. Charles W. Socarides, and Benjamin Kaufman, "Reparative Therapy" (letter to the editors with replies by Fred Gottlieb and Richard A. Isay), *American Journal of Psychiatry* 151/1 (January 1994): 157–59. See also Fred Gottlieb, "The Council on National Affairs," *American Journal of Psychiatry* 150/2 (February 1993): 376–77.

Chapter 2
THE BIBLE AND HOMOSEXUALITY

1. See, for example, John Shelby Spong, *Living in Sin? A Bishop Rethinks Human Sexuality* (San Francisco: Harper & Row, 1988), 139–40.

2. A succinct summary of the newer exegesis of the New Testament texts and the relevant literature is provided in Joseph J. Kotva, "Scripture, Ethics, and the Local Church: Homosexuality as a Case Study," *Conrad Grebel Review* 7/1 (Winter 1989): 56–57.

3. Davies and Rentzel, for example, declare, "So this incident was only a final confirmation of the homosexual activities already occurring. Certainly not all the previous homosexual behavior in the city was characterized by forcible rape." (Bob Davies and Lori Rentzel, *Coming Out of Homosexuality: New Freedom for Men and Women* [Downers Grove, Ill.: InterVarsity Press, 1993], 184).

4. Derrick Sherwin Bailey, *Homosexuality and the Western Christian Tradition* (London: Longmans, Green & Co., 1955), 5. For Bailey's parallel interpretation of the Judges story, see pp. 54–55.

5. John Boswell, *Christianity, Social Tolerance and Homosexuality: Gay People in Western Europe from the Beginning of the Christian Era to the Fourteenth Century* (Chicago: University of Chicago Press, 1980), 95.

6. Bailey, *Homosexuality,* 6.

7. Victor Paul Furnish, "What Does the Bible Say about Homosexuality?" in *Caught in the Crossfire: Helping Christians Debate Homosexuality,* ed. Sally B. Geis and Donald E. Messer (Nashville: Abingdon Press, 1994), 60.

8. Bailey, *Homosexuality*, 31.
9. H. Darrell Lance, "The Bible and Homosexuality," *American Baptist Quarterly* 8/2 (June 1989): 143.
10. Bailey, *Homosexuality*, 16.
11. George R. Edwards, *Gay/Lesbian Liberation: A Biblical Perspective* (New York: Pilgrim Press, 1984), 64–69.
12. See, for example, Letha Dawson Scanzoni and Virginia Ramey Mollenkott, *Is the Homosexual My Neighbor? A Positive Christian Response*, rev. ed. (San Francisco: HarperSanFrancisco, 1994), 63–66.
13. For this opinion, see H. Kimball Jones, *Toward a Christian Understanding of the Homosexual* (New York: Association Press, 1966), 69.
14. Peter Coleman, *Gay Christians: A Moral Dilemma* (London: SCM Press, 1989), 54.
15. P. Coleman, *Gay Christians*, 52.
16. Thomas E. Schmidt, *Straight and Narrow? Compassion and Clarity in the Homosexuality Debate* (Downers Grove, Ill.: Inter-Varsity Press, 1995), 92–93.
17. For what appears to be perhaps the most plausible suggestion, see Tom Horner, *Jonathan Loved David: Homosexuality in Biblical Times* (Philadelphia: Westminster Press, 1978), 65–67.
18. Bailey, *Homosexuality*, 36.
19. Boswell, *Christianity*, 100–1.
20. Furnish, "What Does the Bible Say?" 60–61. See also Victor Paul Furnish, "The Bible and Homosexuality: Reading the Texts in Context," in *Homosexuality in the Church: Both Sides of the Debate*, ed. Jeffrey S. Siker (Louisville, Ky.: Westminster John Knox Press, 1994), 20.
21. William Morrow, "Sexual Ethics and Biblical Principles: A Response to *Dirt, Greed and Sex*," in *Theological Reflections on Ministry and Sexual Orientation*, ed. Pamela Dickey Young (Burlington, Ont.: Trinity Press, 1990), 37.
22. Lynne C. Boughton, "Biblical Texts and Homosexuality: A Response to John Boswell," *Irish Theological Quarterly* 58/2 (1992): 145.
23. David F. Greenberg, *The Construction of Homosexuality* (Chicago: University of Chicago Press, 1988), 195.
24. Greenberg, *Construction of Homosexuality*, 196.
25. G. J. Wenham, "The Old Testament Attitude to Homosexuality," *Expository Times* 102/12 (September 1991): 360.
26. P. Coleman, *Gay Christians*, 53.
27. Bailey, *Homosexuality*, 58.
28. P. Coleman, *Gay Christians*, 54.
29. Bailey, *Homosexuality*, 60.

30. Lance, "The Bible and Homosexuality," 145. See also Joseph Jenson, "Human Sexuality in the Scriptures," in *Human Sexuality and Personhood* (Chicago: Franciscan Herald Press, 1981), 23.
31. P. Coleman, *Gay Christians*, 55.
32. Scanzoni and Mollenkott, *Is the Homosexual My Neighbor?* 64, 132–34.
33. L. William Countryman, *Dirt, Greed and Sex* (Philadelphia: Fortress Press, 1988), 32.
34. P. Michael Ukleja, "Homosexuality and the Old Testament," *Bibliotheca Sacra* 140/559 (July–September 1983): 265.
35. Furnish, "What Does the Bible Say?" 62.
36. Margaret Davies, "New Testament Ethics and Ours: Homosexuality and Sexuality in Romans 1:26–27," *Biblical Interpretation* 3/3 (1995): 318.
37. Robin Scroggs, *The New Testament and Homosexuality: Contextual Background for Contemporary Debate* (Philadelphia: Fortress Press, 1983), 115–18.
38. Plato, *Laws*, 836c, trans. R. G. Bury, in Loeb Classical Library, ed. G. P. Wood (Cambridge, Mass.: Harvard University Press, 1926), 2:151.
39. Greenberg, *Construction of Homosexuality*, 214–15.
40. P. Coleman, *Gay Christians*, 77; Bailey, *Homosexuality*, 41.
41. Boswell, *Christianity*, 108–14
42. This is the judgment even of some who support a more open stance toward homosexuality. See, for example, Bailey, *Homosexuality*, 38.
43. Jerry R. Kirk, *The Homosexual Crisis in the Mainline Church* (Nashville: Thomas Nelson, 1978), 86–87. See also Helmut Thielicke, *Ethics of Sex*, trans. John W. Doberstein (New York: Harper & Row, 1964), 279–83. Thielicke, however, advocates monogamous relationships for "constitutional homosexual persons" (284–86).
44. Michael R. Saia, *Counseling the Homosexual* (Minneapolis: Bethany House, 1988), 71–72.
45. P. Coleman, *Gay Christians*, 77.
46. See Richard B. Hays, "Relations Natural and Unnatural: A Response to John Boswell's Exegesis of Romans 1," *Journal of Religious Ethics* 14/1 (Spring 1986): 200.
47. Countryman, *Dirt, Greed and Sex*, 110.
48. Edwards, *Gay/Lesbian Liberation*, 85–102.
49. Countryman, *Dirt, Greed and Sex*, 109–23.
50. For a sustained critique of Countryman's thesis, see Schmidt, *Straight and Narrow?* 64–85.
51. Greenberg, *Construction of Homosexuality*, 215.
52. For a discussion of Paul's use of the term "natural," see James B.

DeYoung, "The Meaning of 'Nature' in Romans 1 and Its Implications for Biblical Proscriptions of Homosexual Behavior," *Journal of the Evangelical Theological Society* 31/4 (1988): 429–41.

53. Boswell, *Christianity,* 110n63.
54. Furnish, "What Does the Bible Say?" 62. See also the longer discussion in Furnish, "Bible and Homosexuality," 26–27. See also Bernadette J. Brooten, *Love between Women: Early Christian Responses to Female Homoeroticism* (Chicago: University of Chicago Press, 1996).
55. Actually, there is some question as to whether Roman culture shared the active/passive differential typical of the understanding of roles in the sex act prevalent among certain other ancient societies. See Roy Bowen Ward, "Why Unnatural? The Tradition behind Romans 1:26–27," *Harvard Theological Review* 90/3 (July 1997): 282–83.
56. For a discussion of the Stoic writings see, for example, Hays, "Relations Natural and Unnatural," 192–93.
57. Furnish, "Bible and Homosexuality," 29–30.
58. P. Coleman, *Gay Christians,* 77.
59. Dale B. Martin, "Heterosexism and the Interpretation of Romans 1:18–32," *Biblical Interpretation* 3/3 (October 1995): 334–35.
60. Martin, "Heterosexism," 338.
61. For the importance of this, see David E. Malick, "The Condemnation of Homosexuality in Romans 1:26–27," *Bibliotheca Sacra* 150 (July–September 1993): 332.
62. Hays, "Relations Natural and Unnatural," 196.
63. Wolfgang Schrage, *The Ethics of the New Testament,* trans. David E. Green (Philadelphia: Fortress Press, 1988), 202.
64. Greenberg, *Construction of Homosexuality,* 182–83.
65. Furnish, "Bible and Homosexuality," 24.
66. Boswell, *Christianity,* 353.
67. Boswell, *Christianity,* 341–53.
68. See, for example, Peter Zaas, "1 Cor. 6:9ff.: Was Homosexuality Condoned in the Corinthian Church?" in *Society of Biblical Literature 1979 Seminar Papers,* ed. Paul J. Achtemeier (Missoula, Mont.: Scholars Press, 1979), 2:205–12.
69. For a counterargument, see Boughton, "Biblical Texts and Homosexuality," 150–51.
70. Furnish, "What Does the Bible Say?" 61.
71. Boswell, *Christianity,* 338–53; Countryman, *Dirt, Greed and Sex,* 119–20.
72. Bailey, *Homosexuality,* 38.
73. Furnish, "Bible and Homosexuality," 24.
74. *A Greek-English Lexicon of the New Testament,* ed. Walter Bauer, William F. Arndt, and F. Wilbur Gingrich (Chicago: University of

Chicago Press, 1957), s.v. "malakos." See also Gordon Fee, *The First Epistle to the Corinthians* (Grand Rapids: Eerdmans, 1987), 243–44.

75. *Greek-English Lexicon of the NT,* s.v. "koite." See also Fee, *1 Corinthians,* 244.

76. See, for example, Boughton, "Biblical Texts and Homosexuality," 150.

77. Victor Paul Furnish, *The Moral Teaching of Paul: Selected Issues,* 2d ed. (Nashville: Abingdon Press, 1985), 69.

78. Scroggs, *The New Testament and Homosexuality,* 62–65, 83, 106–9. For a dissenting opinion, see Countryman, *Dirt, Greed and Sex,* 128, 202.

79. David F. Wright, "Homosexuals or Prostitutes? The Meaning of *Arsenokoitai* (1 Cor. 6:9, 1 Tim. 1:10)," *Vigiliae Christianae* 38/2 (June 1984): 125–53.

80. Gerald D. Coleman, *Homosexuality: Catholic Teaching and Pastoral Practice* (New York: Paulist Press, 1995), 65. See also Kotva, "Scripture, Ethics, and the Local Church," 57. The claim that the term refers to active male prostitutes is rebutted in William L. Petersen, "On the Study of 'Homosexuality' in Patristic Sources," *Studia Patristica 20,* ed. Elizabeth A. Livingstone (Louvain: Peeters, 1989), 284–85.

81. Scroggs, *The New Testament and Homosexuality,* 120 (Material in brackets is Scroggs's).

82. Wright, "Homosexuals or Prostitutes?" 146.

83. P. Coleman, *Gay Christians,* 85.

84. See, for example, Horner, *Jonathan Loved David,* 40–46.

85. For the most compelling discussion of this possibility, see Horner, *Jonathan Loved David,* 26–39.

86. See especially Horner, *Jonathan Loved David,* 15–39.

87. Greenberg, *Construction of Homosexuality,* 114.

88. See, for example, Horner, *Jonathan Loved David,* 33–36.

89. Greenberg, *Construction of Homosexuality,* 114.

90. Horner argues that the bisexuality of the leading characters of the story is in keeping with the ideals of ancient culture. See *Jonathan Loved David,* 37–39.

91. G. Coleman, *Homosexuality: Catholic Teaching,* 69.

92. Horner, *Jonathan Loved David,* 125.

93. Horner, *Jonathan Loved David,* 125.

94. Horner, *Jonathan Loved David,* 122–24. See also John J. McNeill, *Church and the Homosexual,* 3d ed. (Boston: Beacon Press, 1988), 64–65.

95. Bailey, *Homosexuality,* 22–27.

96. Robert Lane Fox, *Pagans and Christians* (New York: Alfred A. Knopf, 1987), 352.

Chapter 3

HOMOSEXUALITY AND CHURCH TEACHING

1. For this conclusion, see, for example, Richard B. Hays, "Relations Natural and Unnatural: A Response to John Boswell's Exegesis of Romans 1," *Journal of Religious Ethics* 14/1 (Spring 1986): 202.

2. Derrick Sherwin Bailey, *Homosexuality and the Western Christian Tradition* (London: Longmans, Green & Co., 1955), 85.

3. "Epistle of Barnabas," trans. James A. Kleist, in *Ancient Christian Writers,* vol. 6, ed. Johannes Quasten and Joseph C. Plumpe (New York: Paulist Press, 1948), 19.4. See also "Epistle of Barnabas," 10.6.

4. "Didache," II.2, trans. James A. Kleist, in *Ancient Christian Writers,* vol. 6, ed. Johannes Quasten and Joseph C. Plumpe (New York: Paulist Press, 1948), 16.

5. "Constitutions of the Holy Apostles," VII.2, in *The Ante-Nicene Fathers of the Christian Church,* vol. 7, ed. Alexander Roberts and James Donaldson, rev. A. Cleveland Coxe (Grand Rapids: Eerdmans, 1975), 466.

6. Council of Elvira, Canon 71, in *The Faith of the Early Fathers,* ed. and trans. W. A. Jurgens (Collegeville, Minn.: Liturgical Press, 1970), 257. See also John Boswell, *Christianity, Social Tolerance and Homosexuality: Gay People in Western Europe from the Beginning of the Christian Era to the Fourteenth Century* (Chicago: University of Chicago Press, 1980), 179.

7. For a fuller description, see Bailey, *Homosexuality,* 101–10.

8. The Irish Penitentials proscribed homosexual actions. See, for instance, "Penitential of St. Columbanus," A.3, B.3, 15, pp. 97, 101, 103; "The So-called Bigotian Penitential," II.2, p. 211; "Penitential of Cummean," II.8–10, X.2, 3, 6–9, 14–16, pp. 115, 127, 129; "Sinodus Luci Victorie," 8, p. 69; in *The Irish Penitentials,* ed. Ludwig Bieler (Dublin: Dublin Institute for Advanced Studies, 1963). See also "The Penitential of Theodore," I.2, 4–8, 11–12, 15, 19, p. 185–86; "Penitential Ascribed to Albers," V.1, p. 226; "The Burgundian Penitential," 4, p. 274; "The So-called Roman Penitential," 6, 13, pp. 302–3; in *Medieval Handbooks of Penance,* ed. and trans. John T. McNeill and Helena M. Gamer (New York: Octagon Books, 1965).

Canon law also denounced homosexual actions. See Council of Elvira, Canon 71; Third Lateran Council (1179), 11, in *Decrees of the Ecumenical Councils,* vol. 1, ed. Norman P. Tanner (London: Sheed & Ward, 1990), 217. For discussions of canon law, see James A. Brundage, "Sex and Canon Law," pp. 33–50;

Warren Johansson and William A. Percy, "Homosexuality," pp. 155–89; and Jacqueline Murray, "Twice Marginal and Twice Invisible: Lesbians in the Middle Ages," pp. 191–222; in *Handbook of Medieval Sexuality,* ed. Vern L. Bullough and James A. Brundage (New York: Garland Publishing, 1996). See also Bailey, *Homosexuality,* 82–120. For a broader discussion of sex and law, including homosexual acts, see James A. Brundage, *Law, Sex, and Christian Society in Medieval Europe* (Chicago: University of Chicago Press, 1987).

9. Boswell, *Christianity,* 28–30.

10. Bailey, *Homosexuality,* 86.

11. See, for example, John Chrysostom, *On the Epistle to the Romans,* Homily 4, trans. J. B. Morris and W. H. Simcox, rev. George B. Stevens, in *Saint Chrysostom: Homilies on the Acts of the Apostles and the Epistle to the Romans, Nicene and Post-Nicene Fathers,* vol. 11, ed. Philip Schaff (Grand Rapids: Eerdmans, 1975), 355–56; Tertullian, "On the Pallium," IV, trans. S. Thelwall, in *The Ante-Nicene Fathers of the Christian Church,* vol. 4, ed. Alexander Roberts and James Donaldson, rev. A. Cleveland Coxe (Grand Rapids: Eerdmans, 1976), 10; Tertullian, "The Chaplet," VI, in *Tertullian: Disciplinary, Moral, and Ascetical Works,* trans. Edwin A. Quain, *The Fathers of the Church,* vol. 40 (Washington, D.C.: Catholic University of America Press, 1959), 242–43; Tatian, *Oratio ad Graecos and Fragments,* trans. Molly Whittaker (Oxford: Clarendon Press, 1982), XXXIII, pp. 61, 63. See also Bernadette J. Brooten, "Patristic Interpretations of Romans 1:26," in *Studia Patristica 18,* vol. 1, ed. Elizabeth A. Livingstone (Kalamazoo, Mich.: Cistercian Publications, 1985), 287–91.

12. See, for example, "Apocalypse of Peter," I.23, 31, trans. Andrew Rutherfurd, in *The Ante-Nicene Fathers of the Christian Church,* vol. 10, ed. Allan Mazies (Grand Rapids: Eerdmans, 1974), 146. For pederasty, see "Didache," II.2, p. 16.

13. St. Basil, Letter 217.58, 59, 62, 63, pp. 109–10, and Letter 188.7, pp. 16–17, in *St. Basil: Letters 186–368,* trans. Agnes Clare Way, Fathers of the Church, vol. 28, ed. Roy Joseph Deferrari et al. (Washington, D.C.: Catholic University of America Press, 1955).

14. Gregory of Nyssa, "Canonical Epistle to Letoius, Bishop of Melitene," IV, in *The Seven Ecumenical Councils of the Undivided Church,* ed. Henry R. Percival, *The Nicene and Post-Nicene Fathers,* vol. 14, ed. Philip Schaff and Henry Wace (Grand Rapids: Eerdmans, 1974), 611.

15. See, for example, St. Basil, "On the Renunciation of the World," trans. M. Monica Wagner, in *St. Basil: Ascetical Works, The Fathers*

of the Church, vol. 9, ed. Bernard M. Peebles et al. (Washington, D.C.: Catholic University of America Press, 1950), 23–24.

16. Hence, Augustine, Letter 211.14, trans. J. G. Cunningham, *The Nicene and Post-Nicene Fathers of the Christian Church,* first series, vol. 1, ed. Philip Schaff (Grand Rapids: Eerdmans, 1974), 568. See also the Epistle of the sixth-century abbot of Elusa Paul Helladicus cited in J. B. Bury, *History of the Later Roman Empire* (London: Macmillan, 1923), 412n5.

17. Romans 1:26–27 was quoted by such church fathers as Clement of Alexandria and John Chrysostom. See Clement of Alexandria, *Christ the Educator,* II.10, trans. Simon P. Wood, Fathers of the Church, vol. 23, ed. Roy Joseph Deferrari, et al. (Washington, D.C.: Catholic University of America Press, 1953), 166–67. See also Chrysostom, *Romans,* Homily 4, pp. 355–59.

18. Tertullian, "The Five Books against Marcion," I.29, trans. Peter Holmes, *The Ante-Nicene Fathers of the Christian Church,* vol. 3, ed. Alexander Roberts and James Donaldson, rev. A. Cleveland Coxe (Grand Rapids: Eerdmans, 1976), 294.

19. Origen, *Commentarii in epistulam ad Romanos,* IV.4.9–22. The Latin text with German translation is available in Origenes, *Römerbriefkommentar,* trans. Theresia Heither Osb, in Fontes Christiani (Frieburg in Breisgau: Herder, 1992), 2/2: 202–3.

20. Clement of Alexandria, *Christ the Educator,* II.10, pp. 169–70.

21. Eusebius, *The Proof of the Gospel* (*Demonstratio Evangelica*), ed. and trans. W. J. Ferrar (Grand Rapids: Baker Book House, 1981), 4.10.161–2, p. 181. Eusebius, *Preparation for the Gospel* (*Praeparatio Evangelica*), trans. Edwin Hamilton Gifford, vol. 2 (Grand Rapids: Baker Book House, 1981), 13.19.709b–710d.

22. See David F. Wright, "Homosexuals or Prostitutes? The Meaning of *Arsenokoitai* (1 Cor. 6:9, 1 Tim. 1:10)," *Vigiliae Christianae* 38/2 (June 1984): 127–28.

23. E.g., Chrysostom, *Romans,* Homily 4, p. 355.

24. For a discussion of Augustine, see, for example, Boswell, *Christianity,* 150–51.

25. Augustine, *Confessions,* III.8, trans. Vernon J. Bourke, Fathers of the Church, vol. 21, ed. Roy Joseph Deferrari et al. (Washington, D.C.: Catholic University of America Press, 1953), 63–64.

26. Clement of Alexandria, *Christ the Educator,* II.10.83–115, esp. 86–93, pp. 166–72.

27. John Chrystostom, "Discourse on Blessed Babylas and against the Greeks," XLIX, in *Saint John Chrystostom: Apologist,* Fathers of the Church, vol. 73, trans. Margaret A. Schatkin and Paul W. Harkins, ed. Thomas P. Halton et al. (Washington, D.C.: Catholic University of America Press, 1985), 103.

28. Reay Tannahill, *Sex in History* (London: Hamish Hamiton, 1980), 136–37, 155–56.
29. Peter Coleman, *Gay Christians: A Moral Dilemma* (London: SCM Press, 1989), 97.
30. Clyde Pharr, trans., *The Theodosian Code and Novels and the Sirmondian Constitutions* (Princeton, N.J.: Princeton University Press, 1952), 9.7.6, p. 232.
31. For the text of the Justinian edicts, see Bailey, *Homosexuality,* 73–75.
32. Bailey, *Homosexuality,* 79–80.
33. Bailey, *Homosexuality,* 80.
34. This conclusion is in basic agreement with the assessment of Boswell, *Christianity,* 179. Greenberg rightly concluded, "As in the early church, homosexuality was not the primary category for distinguishing acceptable sex from unacceptable." He is, however, incorrect in adding, "the principal distinction had to do with the potential for conception. As applied to sexual acts, homosexuality was a subsidiary category of nonreproductive sex." David F. Greenberg, *The Construction of Homosexuality* (Chicago: University of Chicago Press, 1988), 265.
35. Boswell, *Christianity,* 177–78.
36. Boswell, *Christianity,* 172–74.
37. Bailey, *Homosexuality,* 99.
38. Third Lateran Council (1179), XI, in Tanner, *Decrees of the Ecumenical Councils,* 217.
39. Bailey, *Homosexuality,* 132.
40. Greenberg, *Construction of Homosexuality,* 280–92.
41. Boswell, *Christianity,* 301.
42. The reign of Alfonso the Wise in the thirteenth century provides a typical example. See Boswell, *Christianity,* 289–91.
43. Boswell, *Christianity,* 203–5.
44. Bailey, *Homosexuality,* 136.
45. Greenberg, *Construction of Homosexuality,* 278.
46. Thomas Aquinas, *Summa Theologica,* trans. Fathers of the English Dominican Province (Westminster, Md.: Christian Classics, 1981), II–IIQQ: 153.2–3, 154.1, 154.11.
47. P. Coleman, *Gay Christians,* 106.
48. For Luther's view, see, for example, Martin Luther, *Lectures on Genesis: Chapters 15—20,* Luther's Works, vol. 3, ed. Jaroslav Pelikan, trans. George V. Schick (St. Louis: Concordia, 1961), 3:225 where he writes, "The heinous conduct of the people of Sodom is extraordinary, inasmuch as they departed from the natural passion and longing of the male for the female, which was implanted into nature by God, and desired what is altogether contrary to nature."

49. See, for example, John Cotton, *An Abstract or* [*sic*] *the Laws of New England* (1641), 11.
50. Bailey, *Homosexuality,* 147–50.
51. Peter Gay, *The Enlightenment: An Interpretation* (New York: Alfred A. Knopf, 1969), 2:431.
52. P. Coleman, *Gay Christians,* 2–3, 126–28.
53. Greenberg, *Construction of Homosexuality,* 347.
54. For France under Louis XIV, see Arno Karlen, *Homosexuality: A New View* (New York: W. W. Norton, 1971), 134–38. For Enlightenment France, see Bryant T. Ragan, "The Enlightenment Confronts Homosexuality," in *Homosexuality in Modern France,* ed. Jeffrey Merrick and Bryant T. Ragan (New York: Oxford University Press, 1996), 8–29. In Russia, Peter the Great—who was given to bisexuality—instituted military laws against homosexual acts in 1706. Within a decade he reduced the punishment from death to permanent exile. See Igor S. Kon, *The Sexual Revolution in Russia from the Age of the Czars to Today,* trans. James Riordan (New York: Free Press, 1995), 16.
55. Greenberg, *Construction of Homosexuality,* 337.
56. Bailey, *Homosexuality,* 162.
57. Bailey, *Homosexuality,* 163.
58. Even some proponents of a more open stance toward homosexuality do not find this argument compelling. Tom Horner, for example, finds no evidence in the Old Testament of a long-standing aversion to willful destruction of male seed nor that the Jews believed that only the male seed was important in conception. See Horner, *Jonathan Loved David: Homosexuality in Biblical Times* (Philadelphia: Westminster Press, 1978), 83–84.
59. Greenberg, *Construction of Homosexuality,* 306.
60. Greenberg, *Construction of Homosexuality,* 222–24.
61. Robert Lane Fox, *Pagans and Christians* (New York: Alfred A. Knopf, 1987), 341–42.
62. John Chrysostom, "Against the Opponents of the Monastic Life," III.8, in *A Comparison Between a King and a Monk/Against the Opponents of the Monastic Life: Two Treatises by John Chrysostom,* trans. David G. Hunter (Lampeter, Wales: Edwin Mellen Press, 1988), 142.
63. Boswell, *Christianity,* 134–35. See also pp. 188–94.
64. John F. Harvey, review of Boswell, *Christianity, Social Tolerance, and Homosexuality,* in *Linacre Quarterly* 48/3 (August 1981): 273–74; Bruce A. Williams, "Homosexuality and Christianity: A Review Discussion," *The Thomist* 46/4 (October 1982): 617.

Chapter 4

HOMOSEXUALITY AND BIBLICAL AUTHORITY

1. John J. McNeill, *Church and the Homosexual,* 3d ed. (Boston: Beacon Press, 1988), 59–60.
2. Robin Scroggs, *The New Testament and Homosexuality: Contextual Background for Contemporary Debate* (Philadelphia: Fortress Press, 1983), 126–28.
3. See, for example, the succinct statement of this view in Jeffrey S. Siker, "Homosexual Christians, the Bible, and Gentile Inclusion: Confessions of a Repenting Heterosexist," in *Homosexuality in the Church: Both Sides of the Debate,* ed. Jeffrey S. Siker (Louisville, Ky.: Westminster John Knox Press, 1994), 185.
4. For examples of the use of this argument, see Roger E. Biery, *Understanding Homosexuality: The Pride and the Prejudice* (Austin, Tex.: Edward William Publishing Co., 1990), 146; Mel White, *Stranger at the Gate: To Be Gay and Christian in America* (New York: Simon & Schuster, 1994), 305. Letha Dawson Scanzoni and Virginia Ramey Mollenkott, *Is the Homosexual My Neighbor? A Positive Christian Response* (San Francisco: HarperSanFrancisco, 1994), 74, 83.
5. Marilyn Bennett Alexander and James Preston, *We Were Baptized Too: Claiming God's Grace for Lesbians and Gays* (Louisville, Ky.: Westminster John Knox Press, 1996), xvii.
6. For examples of this argument, see Richard Woods, *Another Kind of Love: Homosexuality and Spirituality* (Chicago: Thomas Moore Press, 1977), 102–6, 135–37; McNeill, *Church and the Homosexual,* 41–42; John Boswell, *Christianity, Social Tolerance and Homosexuality: Gay People in Western Europe from the Beginning of the Christian Era to the Fourteenth Century* (Chicago: University of Chicago Press, 1980), 100–2.
7. James B. Nelson, "Are Christianity and Homosexuality Incompatible?" in *Caught in the Crossfire: Helping Christians Debate Homosexuality,* ed. Sally B. Geis and Donald E. Messer (Nashville: Abingdon, 1994), 102.
8. See, for example, John Gray, *The Legacy of Canaan: The Ras Shamra Texts and Their Relevance to the Old Testament,* 2d ed. (Leiden: E. J. Brill, 1965), 192ff.
9. Ptolemy, *Tetrabiblos,* III.14, trans. F. E. Robbins, Loeb Classical Library (Cambridge, Mass.: Harvard University Press, 1940), pp. 363–72.
10. Phaedrus, *The Fables of Phaedrus,* 4.15, trans. P. F. Widdows (Austin, Tex.: University of Texas Press, 1992), 102.
11. Plato, *Symposium,* 189d–193d, trans. W. R. M. Lamb, Loeb

Classical Library, ed. G. P. Goold (Cambridge, Mass.: Harvard University Press, 1925), 135–47.

12. See Wayne A. Meeks, "The Image of the Androgyne: Some Uses of a Symbol in Earliest Christianity," *History of Religions* 13 (1974): 185–86. Recently certain scholars have sought to re-vamp this explanation. See, for example, Phyllis Trible, *God and the Rhetoric of Sexuality* (Philadelphia: Fortress Press, 1978), 80, 97–99. Although Trible argues that the first creation narrative "disallows an androgynous interpretation of *ha-'adam*" (p. 18), she avers that in the second story the "earth creature" is initially "sexually undifferentiated." The creation of the woman serves as well to transform the original creature into a male (p. 98).

13. Boswell, *Christianity,* 109.

14. Christopher Levan, "Homosexuality and Sin," in *Theological Reflections on Ministry and Sexual Orientation,* ed. Pamela Dickey Young (Burlington, Ont.: Trinity Press, 1990), 66.

15. Walter Wink, "Biblical Perspectives on Homosexuality," *Christian Century* 96/36 (7 Nov. 1979): 1085.

16. James B. Nelson, *Embodiment* (Minneapolis: Augsburg, 1978), 188. See also Tom Horner, *Jonathan Loved David: Homosexuality in Biblical Times* (Philadelphia: Westminster Press, 1978), 98.

17. Gary David Comstock, *Gay Theology without Apology* (Cleveland: Pilgrim Press, 1993), 43.

18. For example, Levan, "Homosexuality and Sin," 66.

19. John J. McNeill, *Taking a Chance on God: Liberating Theology for Gays, Lesbians, and Their Lovers, Families, and Friends* (Boston: Beacon Press, 1988), 21.

20. McNeill, *Taking a Chance,* 22.

21. Comstock, *Gay Theology,* 131.

22. Comstock, *Gay Theology,* 108.

23. See, for example, George R. Edwards, *Gay/Lesbian Liberation: A Biblical Perspective* (New York: Pilgrim Press, 1984), 86–89, 100–1. See also Victor Paul Furnish, *The Moral Teaching of Paul: Selected Issues,* 2d ed. (Nashville: Abingdon Press, 1985), 78–81.

24. Victor Paul Furnish, "What Does the Bible Say about Homosexuality?" in *Caught in the Crossfire: Helping Christians Debate Homosexuality,* ed. Sally B. Geis and Donald E. Messer (Nashville: Abingdon Press, 1994), 63.

25. Comstock, *Gay Theology,* 37–38.

26. Marion L. Soards, *Scripture and Homosexuality: Biblical Authority and the Church Today* (Louisville, Ky.: Westminster John Knox Press, 1995), 73.

27. Nelson, "Are Christianity and Homosexuality Incompatible?" 102.

28. Michael Keeling, "A Christian Basis for Gay Relationships," in *To-*

wards a Theology of Gay Liberation, ed. Malcolm Macourt (London: SCM Press, 1977), 101.

29. Keeling, "Christian Basis," 102–3.
30. Furnish, "What Does the Bible Say?" 63.
31. McNeill, *Church and the Homosexual,* 66.
32. Wink, "Biblical Perspectives on Homosexuality," 1085.
33. Norman Pittenger, "What It Means to Be Human," in *Towards a Theology of Gay Liberation,* ed. Malcolm Macourt (London: SCM Press, 1977), 88.
34. Furnish, "What Does the Bible Say?" 64.
35. For my own development of the love ethic, see Stanley J. Grenz, *The Moral Quest: Foundations of Christian Ethics* (Downers Grove, Ill.: InterVarsity Press, 1997), 276–97.
36. This is stated, for example, in Marva J. Dawn, "Are Christianity and Homosexuality Incompatible?" in *Caught in the Crossfire: Helping Christians Debate Homosexuality,* ed. Sally B. Geis and Donald E. Messer (Nashville: Abingdon Press, 1994), 94.
37. Donald L. Faris, *Trojan Horse: The Homosexual Ideology and the Christian Church* (Burlington, Ont.: Welch, 1990), 29.
38. Joe Dallas, *A Strong Delusion: Confronting the "Gay Christian" Movement* (Eugene, Oreg.: Harvest House, 1996), 174.
39. Levan, "Homosexuality and Sin," 78–79.
40. Edwards, *Gay/Lesbian Liberation,* 4–13.
41. Edwards, *Gay/Lesbian Liberation,* 75, 97, 99, 101.
42. See Edwards's summation of Furnish's *Moral Teaching of Paul* in *Gay/Lesbian Liberation,* 73. See also Edwards's discussion of sexology on pp. 13–23.
43. Marie Marshall Fortune offers a typical example. A strong advocate of mutual consent, she writes, "The only rule that should guide one's sexual decision-making and behavior is 'thou shalt not sexually manipulate, abuse, or take advantage of another at any time.'" Fortune warns that any relationship—including marriage—can be exploitive, and therefore that even marital partners must acknowledge that principle of mutual consent (Fortune, *Sexual Violence: The Unmentionable Sin* [New York: Pilgrim Press, 1983]), 100.
44. Fortune herself admits that "Freely chosen, fully informed, and mutually agreed upon sexual activity with another might in fact be a rare experience." Fortune, *Sexual Violence,* 101.
45. Fortune, *Sexual Violence,* 110.
46. John Kenneth Galbraith, *Anatomy of Power* (Boston: Houghton Mifflin, 1983), 4–6, 14–37.
47. Galbraith, *Anatomy of Power,* 3.
48. Galbraith, *Anatomy of Power,* 5–6.
49. This power differential is prevalent in many human relationships.

For a discussion of one example of such a differential, namely, within clergy-congregant relationships, see Stanley J. Grenz and Roy D. Bell, *Betrayal of Trust: Sexual Misconduct in the Pastorate* (Downers Grove, Ill: InterVarsity Press, 1995), 84–106.

50. For a further discussion, see Grenz, *The Moral Quest,* 123, 241–57.
51. This Reformation emphasis remains a central emphasis even among nonevangelical Protestant ethicists. See, for example, Paul Tillich's statement of this principle in *Morality and Beyond* (New York: Harper & Row, 1963), 49.
52. See, for example, Richard Cleaver, *Know My Name: A Gay Liberation Theology* (Louisville, Ky.: Westminster John Knox Press, 1995), 29–37.
53. Thomas W. Gillespie, "Pastoral Dilemma," in *Homosexuality and Christian Community,* ed. Choon-Leong Seow (Louisville, Ky.: Westminster John Knox Press, 1996), 121.

Chapter 5

HOMOSEXUALITY AND THE CHRISTIAN SEX ETHIC

1. This focus on teleology is also present among proponents of an open stance. See, for example, John J. McNeill, *The Church and the Homosexual,* 3d ed. (Boston: Beacon Press, 1988), 130–31.
2. See, for example, Joe Dallas, *A Strong Delusion: Confronting the "Gay Christian" Movement* (Eugene, Oreg.: Harvest House, 1996), 187–88.
3. See John Boswell, *Christianity, Social Tolerance and Homosexuality: Gay People in Western Europe from the Beginning of the Christian Era to the Fourteenth Century* (Chicago: University of Chicago Press, 1980), 31–34, 105; McNeill, *Church and the Homosexual,* 58–66; Victor Paul Furnish, "The Bible and Homosexuality: Reading the Texts in Context," in *Homosexuality in the Church: Both Sides of the Debate,* ed. Jeffrey S. Siker (Louisville, Ky.: Westminster John Knox Press, 1994), 21–23.
4. For a fuller explication of human sexuality from the author's point of view, see Stanley J. Grenz, *Sexual Ethics: An Evangelical Perspective,* 2d ed. (Louisville, Ky.: Westminster John Knox Press, 1997), 15–54.
5. For several contemporary answers to this question, see, for example, the taxonomy and discussion in Peter Coleman, *Gay Christians: A Moral Dilemma* (London: SCM Press, 1989), 191–96, 198–200.
6. Pim Pronk, *Against Nature? Types of Moral Argumentation Regarding Homosexuality* (Grand Rapids: Eerdmans, 1993), 63–64.
7. Pronk, *Against Nature?* 65–66.

8. For a more detailed discussion reflecting the author's perspective, see Grenz, *Sexual Ethics,* 57–77.

9. See also Grenz, *Sexual Ethics,* 181–222.

10. See also Grenz, *Sexual Ethics,* 78–97.

11. Maslow notes the implications of this understanding: "It would appear that no single sexual act can per se be called abnormal or perverted. It is only abnormal or perverted individuals who can commit abnormal or perverted acts. That is, the dynamic meaning of the act is far more important than the act itself" (Abraham Maslow, "Self-Esteem [Dominance-Feeling] and Sexuality in Women," in *Sexual Behavior and Personality Characteristics,* ed. Manfred F. DeMartino [New York: Citadel Press, 1963], 103).

12. James P. Hanigan, *Homosexuality: The Test Case for Christian Sexual Ethics* (Mahwah, N.J.: Paulist Press, 1988), 77.

13. For a discussion of such harmful effects, see Jeffrey Satinover, *Homosexuality and the Politics of Truth* (Grand Rapids: Baker Book House, 1996), 49–70; Thomas E. Schmidt, *Straight and Narrow? Compassion and Clarity in the Homosexuality Debate* (Downers Grove, Ill.: InterVarsity Press, 1995), 100–30.

14. For an example of a slightly more academically credible version of this reasoning, see Michael Keeling, "A Christian Basis for Gay Relationships," in *Towards a Theology of Gay Liberation,* ed. Malcolm Macourt (London: SCM Press, 1977), 104.

15. For a helpful discussion, see Hanigan, *Homosexuality,* 100.

16. Hanigan, *Homosexuality,* 101–2.

17. Hanigan, *Homosexuality,* 102.

18. John Harvey, "The Traditional View of Homosexuality as Related to the Pastoral Situation of Homosexual Persons," as quoted by Eileen Flynn, *AIDS: A Catholic Call for Compassion* (Kansas City: Sheed & Ward, 1985), 71.

19. Max L. Stackhouse, "The Heterosexual Norm," in *Homosexuality and Christian Community,* ed. Choon-Leong Seow (Louisville, Ky.: Westminster John Knox Press, 1996), 141.

20. Hanigan, *Homosexuality,* 99.

21. Stackhouse, "Heterosexual Norm," 141.

22. Ruth Tiffany Barnhouse, *Homosexuality: A Symbolic Confusion* (New York: Seabury Press, 1977), 172.

23. Hanigan, *Homosexuality,* 100.

24. Edward Batchelor Jr., *Homosexuality and Ethics* (New York: Pilgrim Press, 1980), 76.

25. David F. Greenberg, *The Construction of Homosexuality* (Chicago: University of Chicago Press, 1988).

26. See William H. Davenport, "Sex in Cross-Cultural Perspective," in *Human Sexuality in Four Perspectives,* ed. Frank A. Beach (Baltimore: Johns Hopkins University Press, 1977), 156. See

also Milton Diamond and Arno Karlen, *Sexual Decisions* (Boston: Little, Brown & Co., 1980), 228.

27. Michel Foucault, *The History of Sexuality: The Use of Pleasure,* vol. 2 (New York: Pantheon Books: 1985), 245.

28. Chris Glaser, *Uncommon Calling: A Gay Christian's Struggle to Serve the Church* (Louisville, Ky.: Westminster John Knox Press, 1996), 181.

29. Christine E. Gudorf, *Body, Sex, and Pleasure: Reconstructing Christian Sexual Ethics* (Cleveland: Pilgrim Press, 1994), 16.

30. Greenberg, *Construction of Homosexuality,* 492.

31. For a discussion, see Stanley J. Grenz, *The Moral Quest: Foundations of Christian Ethics* (Downers Grove, Ill.: InterVarsity Press, 1997), 46–47, 76–77.

32. For the author's fuller discussion of this idea, see Grenz, *Moral Quest,* 223–27.

33. For a more extensive discussion from the author's viewpoint, see Stanley J. Grenz, *Theology for the Community of God* (Nashville: Broadman & Holman, 1995), 257–68.

34. For a similar distinction between sexual desire and the desire for sex, see Hanigan, *Homosexuality,* 143.

35. For an evangelical statement, see, for example, Ronald M. Enroth and Gerald E. Jamison, *The Gay Church* (Grand Rapids: Eerdmans, 1974), 137.

36. Hence, Alex Davidson, *The Returns of Love: Letters of a Christian Homosexual* (London: InterVarsity Press, 1970), 38, 41.

37. See, for example, William Consiglio, *Homosexual No More* (Wheaton, Ill.: Victor, 1991), 36.

38. Michael R. Saia, *Counseling the Homosexual* (Minneapolis: Bethany House, 1988), 23.

39. Barnhouse, *Homosexuality,* 152–53.

40. See, for example, Mary E. Hunt, "Lovingly Lesbian: Toward a Feminist Theology of Friendship," in *Sexuality and the Sacred: Sources for Theological Reflection,* ed. James B. Nelson and Sandra P. Longfellow (Louisville, Ky.: Westminster John Knox Press, 1994), 170.

41. For this designation, see Consiglio, *Homosexual No More,* 36.

42. Greenberg, *Construction of Homosexuality,* 335.

43. James B. Nelson, *Embodiment* (Minneapolis: Augsburg, 1978), 208.

44. Pamela Dickey Young, "Homosexuality and Ministry: Some Feminist Reflections," in *Theological Reflections on Ministry and Sexual Orientation,* ed. Pamela Dickey Young (Burlington, Ont.: Trinity Press, 1990), 104.

45. For the author's perspective on this distinction, see Grenz, *Sexual Ethics,* 182–85, 196–99.

46. For insight into the positive significance of celibacy, see Jim Cotter, "The Gay Challenge to Traditional Notions of Human Sexuality," in *Towards a Theology of Gay Liberation,* ed. Malcolm Macourt (London: SCM Press, 1977), 67–68.

47. John J. McNeill, "Homosexuality: Challenging the Church to Grow," *Christian Century* 104/8 (11 March 1987): 243. This position was also articulated in McNeill's important work, *The Church and the Homosexual.*

48. Hanigan, *Homosexuality,* 72.

49. A similar understanding of chastity is developed in Donald Goergen, *The Sexual Celibate* (New York: Seabury Press, 1974), 101–3.

50. Stanton L. Jones and Don E. Workman, "Homosexuality: The Behavioral Sciences and the Church," *Journal of Psychology and Theology* 17/3 (Fall 1989): 224.

Chapter 6
HOMOSEXUALITY AND THE CHURCH

1. For a somewhat similar taxonomy, see James B. Nelson, *Embodiment* (Minneapolis: Augsburg, 1978), 188–99.

2. Richard B. Hays, "Awaiting the Redemption of Our Bodies: Drawing on Scripture and Tradition in the Church Debate on Homosexuality," *Latimer* 110 (June 1992): 29–30.

3. As quoted in Hays, "Awaiting the Redemption," 30.

4. John J. McNeill, *Taking a Chance on God: Liberating Theology for Gays, Lesbians, and Their Lovers, Families, and Friends* (Boston: Beacon Press, 1988), 38.

5. Martin Hoffman, "Homosexuality," in *Human Sexuality in Four Perspectives,* ed. Frank A. Beach (Baltimore: Johns Hopkins University Press, 1977), 182.

6. Andrew Sullivan, "The Politics of Homosexuality," *The New Republic* 208/19 (10 May 1993): 37.

7. A few suggest that there is even precedence for this in the Christian tradition. See John Boswell, *Same-Sex Unions in Premodern Europe* (New York: Villard Books, 1994), esp. 178ff., 199ff., and 218ff. Boswell's thesis, however, has not been widely accepted among historians.

8. Lucian, "Dialogues of Courtesans," V.3, in *Lucian in Eight Volumes,* vol. 7, trans. M. D. MacLeod, Loeb Classical Library (Cambridge, Mass.: Harvard University Press, 1961), 383; Ovid, *Metamorphoses,* IX.762–64, trans. Frank Justus Miller, Loeb Classical Library (Cambridge, Mass.: Harvard University Press, 1916), 2:57–59. See also Ptolemy, *Tetrabiblos,* III.14.172, trans. F. E. Robbins, Loeb Classical Library (Cambridge, Mass.: Harvard University Press, 1940), 369–71.

9. Catherine Clark Kroeger, "Are Gay Unions Christian Covenants?" in *Caught in the Crossfire: Helping Christians Debate Homosexuality,* ed. Sally B. Geis and Donald E. Messer (Nashville: Abingdon Press, 1994), 136.

10. Iamblichus, as summed up in Photius, *Bibliotheca,* 94.77a–77b, trans. N. G. Wilson (London: Duckworth, 1994), 109–10.

11. Chris Glaser, "Are Gay Unions Christian Covenants?" in *Caught in the Crossfire: Helping Christians Debate Homosexuality,* ed. Sally B. Geis and Donald E. Messer (Nashville: Abingdon Press, 1994), 144.

12. Some proponents of homosexual marriage suggest that homosexual promiscuity is the product of social repression on the part of the wider society. The implication is that a change in societal attitude, brought about in part by sanctioning homosexual unions, would result in a decrease in homosexual instability. For example, see Hoffman, "Homosexuality," 182–85.

13. See, for example, Lewis B. Smedes, *Sex for Christians: The Limits and Liberties of Sexual Living,* rev. ed. (Grand Rapids: Eerdmans, 1994), 48–59, 239.

14. Richard F. Hettlinger goes so far as to claim that gay relationships are inherently unstable; see *Living with Sex: The Student's Dilemma* (New York: Seabury Press, 1966), 105.

15. This view often borrows from the work of psychiatrists, such as Charles Socarides, who purportedly concluded that only about 2 percent of homosexual males are able to live in a committed relationship. As quoted by Michael McManus, "Homosexuals Anonymous Gives Gay Christians a Way Out," *Sioux Falls (S.D.) Argus Leader,* 7 March 1987, Section A, p. 9.

16. Proponents of this argument appeal to studies such as that by Bell and Weinberg, who concluded from their research that only 10 percent of male homosexual respondents could be classified as existing in "close couple" relationships. And even these relationships could only be characterized as "relatively monogamous" or "relatively less promiscuous" (Alan P. Bell and Martin S. Weinberg, *Homosexualities: A Study of Diversity among Men and Women* [New York: Simon & Schuster, 1978], 346). For an analysis of Bell and Weinberg's research, see Stanton L. Jones and Don E. Workman, "Homosexuality: The Behavioral Sciences and the Church," *Journal of Psychology and Theology* 17/3 (Fall 1989): 216.

17. For a helpful discussion of this from a Roman Catholic perspective, see Gerald D. Coleman, *Homosexuality: Catholic Teaching and Pastoral Practice* (New York: Paulist Press, 1995), 121–22.

18. Kroeger, "Are Gay Unions Christian Covenants?" 133.

19. *Baptism, Eucharist and Ministry,* Faith and Order Paper 111 (Geneva: World Council of Churches, 1982), 22.

20. Tex Sample, "Should Gays and Lesbians Be Ordained?" in *Caught in the Crossfire: Helping Christians Debate Homosexuality,* ed. Sally B. Geis and Donald E. Messer (Nashville: Abingdon Press, 1994), 128–29.
21. Sample, "Should Gays and Lesbians Be Ordained?" 123–24.
22. Dennis M. Campbell, *The Yoke of Obedience* (Nashville: Abingdon Press, 1988), 28.
23. Gary David Comstock, *Gay Theology without Apology* (Cleveland: Pilgrim Press, 1993), 131.
24. Pamela Dickey Young, "Homosexuality and Ministry: Some Feminist Reflections," in *Theological Reflections on Ministry and Sexual Orientation,* ed. Pamela Dickey Young (Burlington, Ont.: Trinity, 1990), 109.
25. Richard B. Hays, *The Moral Vision of the New Testament* (San Francisco: Harper, 1996), 403.
26. *The Book of Discipline of the United Methodist Church* (Nashville: United Methodist Publishing House, 1992), par. 402, p. 202; see also par. 71, p. 92. See also *The Constitution of the Presbyterian Church (USA): Part II, Book of Order* (Louisville, Ky.: Office of the General Assembly, 1997–98), G-6.0106.b, W-4.9001.
27. For this judgment, see, for example, John Gallagher and Chris Bull, *Perfect Enemies: The Religious Right, the Gay Movement, and the Politics of the 1990s* (New York: Crown Publishers, 1996), xi.
28. For recent examples, see Gallagher and Bull, *Perfect Enemies,* 265–81.
29. For an example of such advice from an evangelical perspective, see Anita Worthen and Bob Davies, *Someone I Love Is Gay* (Downers Grove, Ill.: InterVarsity Press, 1996).
30. Darlene Bogle, *Strangers in a Christian Land: Reaching Out with Hope to the Homosexual* (Old Tappan, N.J.: Chosen Books, 1990), 106.
31. G. Coleman, *Homosexuality: Catholic Teaching,* 136.
32. Don Baker, *Beyond Rejection* (Portland, Oreg.: Multnomah, 1986), 56.
33. Roger J. Magnuson, *Are Gay Rights Right? Making Sense of the Controversy,* rev. ed. (Portland, Oreg.: Multnomah, 1990), 83.
34. As noted in J. Fraser Field, "Social Consequences of Gay Rights Laws Can't Be Ignored," *Vancouver Sun,* 28 August 1997, Section A, p. 15.
35. See, for example, Eric Marcus, *Is It a Choice? Answers to Three Hundred of the Most Frequently Asked Questions about Gays and Lesbians* (San Francisco: HarperSanFrancisco, 1993), 83–84. For a comprehensive look at same-sex marriages, see Andrew Sullivan, ed., *Same-Sex Marriage: Pro and Con, A Reader* (New York: Vintage Books, 1997).

36. Craig R. Dean, "Legalizing Gay Marriage Would Help Homosexuals," in *Homosexuality: Opposing Viewpoints,* ed. William Dudley (San Diego: Greenhaven, 1993), 174.
37. See, for example, G. Coleman, *Homosexuality: Catholic Teaching,* 123–24.

EPILOGUE

1. Jeffrey S. Siker, "Homosexual Christians, the Bible, and Gentile Inclusion: Confessions of a Repenting Heterosexist," in *Homosexuality in the Church: Both Sides of the Debate,* ed. Jeffrey S. Siker (Louisville, Ky.: Westminster John Knox Press, 1994), 188.
2. Chris Glaser, *Uncommon Calling: A Gay Christian's Struggle to Serve the Church* (Louisville, Ky.: Westminster John Knox Press, 1996), 174.

FOR FURTHER READING

Achtemeier, Paul J., ed. *Society of Biblical Literature 1979 Seminar Papers*. Missoula, Mont.: Scholars Press, 1979.

Alexander, Marilyn Bennett, and James Preston, *We Were Baptized Too: Claiming God's Grace for Lesbians and Gays*. Louisville, Ky.: Westminster John Knox Press, 1996.

"Apocalypse of Peter." Trans. Andrew Rutherfurd. In vol. 10 of *The Ante-Nicene Fathers of the Christian Church,* ed. Allan Mazies, 139–47. Grand Rapids: Eerdmans, 1974.

Aquinas, Thomas. *Summa Theologica.* Trans. Fathers of the English Dominican Province. Westminster, Md.: Christian Classics, 1981.

Augustine. *Confessions.* Trans. Vernon J. Bourke. Vol. 21 of *Fathers of the Church,* ed. Roy Joseph Deferrari, et al. Washington, D.C.: Catholic University of America Press, 1953.

———. "Letter 211." Trans. J. G. Cunningham. In vol. 1 of *The Nicene and Post-Nicene Fathers of the Christian Church,* first series, ed. Philip Schaff, 563–68. Grand Rapids: Eerdmans, 1974.

Bailey, Derrick Sherwin. *Homosexuality and the Western Christian Tradition.* London: Longmans, Green & Co., 1955.

Bailey, J. Michael, and Deana S. Benishay. "Family Aggregation of Female Sexual Orientation." *American Journal of Psychiatry* 150/2 (February 1993): 272–77.

Bailey, J. Michael, and Richard C. Pillard. "A Genetic Study of Male Sexual Orientation." *Archives of General Psychiatry* 48/12 (December 1991): 1089–96.

Bailey, J. Michael; Richard C. Pillard; Michael C. Neale; and Yvonne Agyei. "Heritable Factors Influence Sexual Orientation." *Archives of General Psychiatry* 50/3 (March 1993): 217 23.

Baker, Don. *Beyond Rejection.* Portland, Oreg.: Multnomah, 1986.

Baptism, Eucharist and Ministry, Faith and Order Paper 111. Geneva: World Council of Churches, 1982.

Barinaga, Marcia. "Is Homosexuality Biological?" *Science* 253 (30 August 1991): 956–57.

Barnhouse, Ruth Tiffany. *Homosexuality: A Symbolic Confusion.* New York: Seabury Press, 1977.

Barringer, Felicity. "Sex Survey of American Men Finds 1 Percent Are Gay." *New York Times,* 14 April 1993, Section A, p.1.

Bartram, Jerry. "A Sacred Gift from God." *Globe and Mail,* 11 June 1994, Section D, p. 5.

Basil, St. "Letter 188" and "Letter 217." In *Letters 186–368,* trans. Agnes Clare Way. Vol. 28 of *Fathers of the Church,* ed. Roy Joseph Deferrari, et al., 4–24; 105–17. Washington, D.C.: Catholic University of America Press, 1955.

———. "On the Renunciation of the World." Trans. M. Monica Wagner. In vol. 9 of *Fathers of the Church,* ed. Bernard M. Peebles, et al., 15–31. Washington, D.C.: Catholic University of America Press, 1950.

Batchelor, Edward Jr. *Homosexuality and Ethics.* New York: Pilgrim Press, 1980.

Bayer, Ronald. *Homosexuality and American Psychiatry: The Politics of Diagnosis.* New York: Basic Books, 1981.

Beach, Frank A., ed. *Human Sexuality in Four Perspectives.* Baltimore: Johns Hopkins University Press, 1977.

Bell, Alan P., and Martin S. Weinberg, *Homosexualities: A Study of Diversity among Men and Women.* New York: Simon & Schuster, 1978.

Bell, Alan P.; Martin S. Weinberg; and Sue Kiefer Hammersmith. *Sexual Preference: Its Development in Men and Women.* Bloomington, Ind.: Indiana University Press, 1981.

Bergner, Mario. *Setting Love in Order: Hope and Healing for the Homosexual.* Grand Rapids: Baker Book House, 1995.

Berlin, Fred S. "Media Distortion of the Public's Perception of Recidivism and Psychiatric Rehabilitation." *American Journal of Psychiatry* 148/11 (November 1991): 1572–76.

Bieber, Irving. *Homosexuality: A Psychoanalytic Study.* New York: Basic Books, 1962.

———. "A Discussion of 'Homosexuality: The Ethical Challenge.'" *Journal of Consulting and Clinical Psychology,* 44/2 (1976): 163–66.

Bieber, Irving, and Toby B. Bieber. "Male Homosexuality," *Canadian Journal of Psychiatry* 24/5 (August 1979): 409–21.

Bieler, Ludwig, ed. *The Irish Penitentials.* Dublin: Dublin Institute for Advanced Studies, 1963.

Biery, Roger E. *Understanding Homosexuality: The Pride and the Prejudice.* Austin, Tex.: Edward William Publishing Co., 1990.

Bogle, Darlene. *Strangers in a Christian Land: Reaching Out with Hope to the Homosexual.* Old Tappan, N.J.: Chosen Books, 1990.

The Book of Discipline of the United Methodist Church. Nashville: United Methodist Publishing House, 1992.

Boswell, John. *Christianity, Social Tolerance and Homosexuality: Gay People in Western Europe from the Beginning of the Christian Era* to the Fourteenth Century. Chicago: University of Chicago Press, 1980.

———. Same-Sex Unions in Premodern Europe. New York; Villard Books, 1994.

Boughton, Lynne C. "Biblical Texts and Homosexuality: A Response to John Boswell." Irish Theological Quarterly 58/2 (1992): 141–53.

Bowen Ward, Roy. "Why Unnatural? The Tradition Behind Romans 1:26–27." Harvard Theological Review 90/3 (July 1997): 263–84.

Breedlove, S. Marc. "Sex on the Brain." Nature 389/6653 (23 October 1997): 801.

Brooten, Bernadette J. "Patristic Interpretations of Romans 1:26." In Studia Patristica 18, vol. 1, ed. Elizabeth A. Livingstone, 287–91. Kalamazoo, Mich.: Cistercian Publications, 1985.

———. Love between Women: Early Christian Responses to Female Homoeroticism. Chicago: University of Chicago Press, 1996.

Brundage, James A. "Sex and Canon Law." In Handbook of Medieval Sexuality, ed. Vern L. Bullough and James A. Brundage, 33–50. New York: Garland Publishing, 1996.

———. Law, Sex, and Christian Society in Medieval Europe. Chicago: University of Chicago Press, 1987.

Bullough, Vern L., and James A. Brundage, eds. Handbook of Medieval Sexuality. New York: Garland Publishing, 1996.

Burr, Chandler. "Homosexuality and Biology." In Homosexuality in the Church: Both Sides of the Debate, ed. Jeffrey S. Siker, 116–34. Louisville, Ky.: Westminster John Knox Press, 1994.

Bury, J. B. History of the Later Roman Empire. London: Macmillan, 1923.

Byne, William, and Bruce Parsons. "Human Sexual Orientation." Archives of General Psychiatry 50/3 (March 1993): 228–39.

———. "In Reply." Archives of General Psychiatry 51/5 (May 1994): 432–33.

Campbell, Dennis M. The Yoke of Obedience. Nashville: Abingdon Press, 1988.

Chrysostom, John. On the Epistle to the Romans, trans. J. B. Morris and W. H. Simcox, rev. George B. Stevens. In Saint Chrysostom: Homilies on the Acts of the Apostles and the Epistle to the Romans. Vol. 11 of Nicene and Post-Nicene Fathers, ed. Philip Schaff. Grand Rapids: Eerdmans, 1975.

———. "Against the Opponents of the Monastic Life." In A Comparison between a King and a Monk/Against the Opponents of the Monastic Life: Two Treatises by John Chrysostom, ed. and trans. David G. Hunter, 77–176. Lampeter, Wales: Edwin Mellen Press, 1988.

———. "Discourse on Blessed Babylas and against the Greeks." In vol. 73 of *Fathers of the Church,* trans. Margaret A. Schatkin and Paul W. Harkins, ed. Thomas P. Halton, et al., 1–152. Washington, D.C.: Catholic University of America Press, 1985.

Clark, Don. *Loving Someone Gay.* New York: New American Library, Signet, 1978. Revised editions: Celestial Arts, Berkeley, Calif., 1987 and 1997.

Cleaver, Richard. *Know My Name: A Gay Christian Liberation.* Louisville, Ky.: Westminster John Knox Press, 1995.

Clement of Alexandria. *Christ the Educator.* Trans. Simon P. Wood. Vol. 23 of *Fathers of the Church,* ed. Roy Joseph Deferrari, et al. Washington, D.C.: Catholic University of America Press, 1953.

Cole, Sherwood O. "The Biological Basis of Homosexuality: A Christian Assessment." *Journal of Psychology and Theology* 23/2 (1995): 89–100.

Coleman, Gerald D. *Homosexuality: Catholic Teaching and Pastoral Practice.* New York: Paulist Press, 1995.

Coleman, Peter. *Christian Attitudes to Homosexuality.* London: SPCK, 1980.

———. *Gay Christians: A Moral Dilemma.* London: SCM Press, 1989.

Comstock, Gary David. *Gay Theology without Apology.* Cleveland: Pilgrim Press, 1993.

Consiglio, William. *Homosexual No More.* Wheaton, Ill.: Victor, 1991.

The Constitution of the Presbyterian Church (USA): Part II, Book of Order. Louisville, Ky.: Office of the General Assembly, 1997–98.

"Constitutions of the Holy Apostles." In vol. 7 of *The Ante-Nicene Fathers of the Christian Church,* ed. Alexander Roberts and James Donaldson, rev. A. Cleveland Coxe, 385–508. Grand Rapids: Eerdmans, 1975.

Cotter, Jim. "The Gay Challenge to Traditional Notions of Human Sexuality." In *Towards a Theology of Gay Liberation,* ed. Malcolm Macourt, 63–80. London: SCM Press, 1977.

Cotton, John. *An Abstract or [sic] the Laws of New England* (1641).

Countryman, L. William. *Dirt, Greed and Sex.* Philadelphia: Fortress Press, 1988.

Crew, Louie. "Cracks in the Wall of Opposition to Lesbians and Gays." *Witness* 77/11 (November 1994): 24.

Dallas, Joe. *A Strong Delusion: Confronting the "Gay Christian" Movement.* Eugene, Oreg.: Harvest House, 1996.

Davenport, William H. "Sex in Cross-Cultural Perspective." In *Human Sexuality in Four Perspectives,* ed. Frank A. Beach, 115–63. Baltimore: Johns Hopkins University Press, 1977.

Davidson, Alex. *The Returns of Love: Letters of a Christian Homosexual.* London: InterVarsity Press, 1970.

Davies, Bob, and Lori Rentzel. *Coming Out of Homosexuality: New Freedom for Men and Women.* Downers Grove, Ill.: InterVarsity Press, 1993.

Davies, Margaret. "New Testament Ethics and Ours: Homosexuality and Sexuality in Romans 1:26–27." *Biblical Interpretation* 3/3 (1995): 315–31.

Dawn, Marva J. "Are Christianity and Homosexuality Incompatible?" In *Caught in the Crossfire: Helping Christians Debate Homosexuality,* ed. Sally B. Geis and Donald E. Messer, 89–98. Nashville: Abingdon Press, 1994.

Dean, Craig R. "Legalizing Gay Marriage Would Help Homosexuals." In *Homosexuality: Opposing Viewpoints,* ed. William Dudley, 172–76. San Diego: Greenhaven, 1993.

DeCecco, John P. "Homosexuality's Brief Recovery: From Sickness to Health and Back Again." *Journal of Sex Research* 23/1 (February 1987): 106–14.

DeYoung, James B. "The Meaning of 'Nature' in Romans 1 and Its Implications for Biblical Proscriptions of Homosexual Behavior." *Journal of the Evangelical Theological Society* 31/4 (1988): 429–41.

Diamant, Louis. "The Therapies." In *Male and Female Homosexuality: Psychological Approaches,* ed. Louis Diamant, 199–217. Washington, D.C.: Hemisphere Publishing, 1987.

Diamant, Louis, ed. *Male and Female Homosexuality: Psychological Approaches.* Washington, D.C.: Hemisphere Publishing, 1987.

Diamond, Milton. "Human Sexual Development: Biological Foundations for Social Development." In *Human Sexuality in Four Perspectives,* ed. Frank A. Beach, 22–61. Baltimore: Johns Hopkins University Press, 1977.

Diamond, Milton, and Arno Karlen. *Sexual Decisions.* Boston: Little, Brown & Co., 1980.

Dickey Young, Pamela. "Homosexuality and Ministry: Some Feminist Reflections." In *Theological Reflections on Ministry and Sexual Orientation,* ed. Pamela Dickey Young, 99–110. Burlington, Ont.: Trinity Press, 1990.

Dickey Young, Pamela, ed. *Theological Reflections on Ministry and Sexual Orientation.* Burlington, Ont.: Trinity, 1990.

"Didache." Trans. James A. Kleist. In vol. 6 of *Ancient Christian Writers,* ed. Johannes Quasten and Joseph C. Plumpe, 1–25. New York: Paulist Press, 1948.

Dudley, William, ed. *Homosexuality: Opposing Viewpoints.* San Diego: Greenhaven, 1993.

Dwyer, John. *Human Sexuality: A Christian View.* Kansas City, Mo.: Sheed & Ward, 1987.

Edwards, George R. *Gay/Lesbian Liberation: A Biblical Perspective.* New York: Pilgrim Press, 1984.

Enroth, Ronald M., and Gerald E. Jamison. *The Gay Church.* Grand Rapids: Eerdmans, 1974.

"Epistle of Barnabas." Trans. James A. Kleist. In vol. 6 of *Ancient Christian Writers,* ed. Johannes Quasten and Joseph C. Plumpe, 27–65. New York: Paulist Press, 1948.

Eusebius. *Preparation for the Gospel (Praeparatio Evangelica).* Trans. Edwin Hamilton Gifford. Grand Rapids: Baker Book House, 1981.

————. *The Proof of the Gospel (Demonstratio Evangelica).* Ed. and trans. W. J. Ferrar. Grand Rapids: Baker Book House, 1981.

Faris, Donald L. *Trojan Horse: The Homosexual Ideology and the Christian Church.* Burlington, Ont.: Welch, 1990.

Fee, Gordon. *The First Epistle to the Corinthians.* Grand Rapids: Eerdmans, 1987.

Field, J. Fraser. "Social Consequences of Gay Rights Laws Can't Be Ignored." *Vancouver Sun,* 28 August 1997, Section A, p. 15.

Flynn, Eileen. *AIDS: A Catholic Call for Compassion.* Kansas City: Sheed & Ward, 1985.

Forstein, Marshall. "Homophobia." *Psychiatric Annals* 18/1 (January 1988): 33–36.

Fortune, Marie Marshall. *Sexual Violence: The Unmentionable Sin.* New York: Pilgrim Press, 1983.

Foucault, Michel. *The History of Sexuality. Vol. 2: The Use of Pleasure.* New York: Pantheon Books, 1985.

Fox, Robert Lane. *Pagans and Christians.* New York: Alfred A. Knopf, 1987.

Freud, Sigmund. "The Disposition to Obsessional Neurosis." In vol. 12 of *The Standard Edition of the Complete Psychological Works of Sigmund Freud,* ed. James Strachey, 311–26. London: Hogarth Press, 1958.

————. "Letter 277" (so-called "Letter to an American Mother"), 9 April 1935. In *Letters of Sigmund Freud.* ed. Ernst L. Freud, trans. Tania and James Stern, 423–24. New York: Basic Books, 1960.

————. "Three Essays on the Theory of Sexuality." In vol. 7 of *The Standard Edition of the Complete Psychological Works of Sigmund Freud,* ed. James Strachey, 125–243. London: Hogarth Press, 1953.

Furnish, Victor Paul. *The Moral Teaching of Paul: Selected Issues.* 2d ed. Nashville: Abingdon Press, 1985.

————. "The Bible and Homosexuality: Reading the Texts in Context." In *Homosexuality in the Church: Both Sides of the Debate,* ed. Jeffrey S. Siker, 18–35. Louisville, Ky.: Westminster John Knox Press, 1994.

———. "What Does the Bible Say about Homosexuality?" In *Caught in the Crossfire: Helping Christians Debate Homosexuality*, ed. Sally B. Geis and Donald E. Messer, 57–66. Nashville: Abingdon Press, 1994.

Galbraith, John Kenneth. *Anatomy of Power*. Boston: Houghton Mifflin, 1983.

Gallagher, John, and Chris Bull. *Perfect Enemies: The Religious Right, the Gay Movement, and the Politics of the 1990s*. New York: Crown Publishers, 1996.

Gallagher, Maggie. *Enemies of Eros: How the Sexual Revolution Is Killing Family, Marriage, and Sex and What We Can Do about It*. Chicago: Bonus, 1989.

Gay, Peter. *The Enlightenment: An Interpretation*. New York: Alfred A. Knopf, 1969.

Geis, Sally B., and Donald E. Messer, eds. *Caught in the Crossfire: Helping Christians Debate Homosexuality*. Nashville: Abingdon Press, 1994.

Gillespie, Thomas W. "Pastoral Dilemma." In *Homosexuality and Christian Community*, ed. Choon-Leong Seow, 113–22. Louisville, Ky.: Westminster John Knox Press, 1996.

Glaser, Chris. *Uncommon Calling: A Gay Christian's Struggle to Serve the Church*. Louisville, Ky.: Westminster John Knox Press, 1996.
———. "Are Gay Unions Christian Covenants?" In *Caught in the Crossfire: Helping Christians Debate Homosexuality*, ed. Sally B. Geis and Donald E. Messer, 141–48. Nashville: Abingdon Press, 1994.

Goergen, Donald. *The Sexual Celibate*. New York: Seabury Press, 1974.

Gonsiorek, John C., and James D. Weinrich, eds. *Homosexuality: Research Implications for Public Policy*. Newbury Park, Calif.: Sage Publications, 1991.

Gottlieb, Fred. "The Council on National Affairs." *American Journal of Psychiatry* 150/2 (February 1993): 376–77.

Grant, George, and Horne, Mark A. *Legislating Immorality: The Homosexual Movement Comes Out of the Closet*. Chicago: Moody Press, 1993.

Gray, John. *The Legacy of Canaan: The Ras Shamra Texts and Their Relevance to the Old Testament*. 2d ed. Leiden: E. J. Brill, 1965.

Green, Richard. *The "Sissy Boy Syndrome" and the Development of Homosexuality*. New Haven, Conn.: Yale University Press, 1987.

Greenberg, David F. *The Construction of Homosexuality*. Chicago: University of Chicago Press, 1988.

Gregory of Nyssa. "Canonical Epistle to Letoius, Bishop of Melitene." In *The Seven Ecumenical Councils of the Undivided Church*, ed. Henry R. Percival. Vol. 14 of *The Nicene and Post-Nicene Fathers*, ed. Philip Schaff and Henry Wace, 611. Grand Rapids: Eerdmans, 1974.

Grenz, Stanley J. *The Moral Quest: Foundations of Christian Ethics.* Downers Grove, Ill.: InterVarsity Press, 1997.

———. *Sexual Ethics: An Evangelical Perspective.* Rev. ed. Louisville, Ky.: Westminster John Knox Press, 1997.

———. *Theology for the Community of God.* Nashville: Broadman & Holman, 1995.

Grenz, Stanley J., and Roy D. Bell. *Betrayal of Trust: Sexual Misconduct in the Pastorate.* Downers Grove, Ill.: InterVarsity Press, 1995.

Gudorf, Christine E. *Body, Sex, and Pleasure: Reconstructing Christian Sexual Ethics.* Cleveland: Pilgrim Press, 1994.

Haldeman, Douglas C. "Sexual Orientation Conversion Therapy for Gay Men and Lesbians: A Scientific Examination." In *Homosexuality: Research Implications for Public Policy,* ed. John C. Gonsiorek and James D. Weinrich, 149–60. Newbury Park, Calif.: Sage Publications, 1991.

Halperin, David M. *One Hundred Years of Homosexuality and Other Essays on Greek Love.* New York: Routledge, 1990.

Hamer, Dean H.; Stella Hu; Victoria L. Magnuson; Nan Hu; and Angela M. L. Pattatucci. "Linkage between DNA Markers on the X Chromosome and Male Sexual Orientation." *Science* 261 (1993): 321–27.

Hanigan, James P. *Homosexuality: The Test Case for Christian Sexual Ethics.* Mahwah, N.J.: Paulist Press, 1988.

Harvey, John F. Review of Boswell, *Christianity, Social Tolerance, and Homosexuality.* In *Linacre Quarterly* 48/3 (August 1981): 265–75.

Hatterer, Lawrence J. *Changing Homosexuality in the Male: Treatment for Men Troubled by Homosexuality.* New York: McGraw-Hill, 1970.

Hays, Richard B. *The Moral Vision of the New Testament.* San Francisco: Harper, 1996.

———. "Awaiting the Redemption of Our Bodies: Drawing on Scripture and Tradition in the Church Debate on Homosexuality." *Latimer* 110 (June 1992): 20–30.

———. "Relations Natural and Unnatural: A Response to John Boswell's Exegesis of Romans 1." *Journal of Religious Ethics* 14/1 (Spring 1986): 184–215.

Herzer, Manfred. "Kertbeny and the Nameless Love." *Journal of Homosexuality* 12/1 (Fall 1986): 1–26.

Hettlinger, Richard F. *Living with Sex: The Student's Dilemma.* New York: Seabury Press, 1966.

Hoffman, Martin. "Homosexuality." In *Human Sexuality in Four Per-*

spectives, ed. Frank A. Beach, 164–89. Baltimore: Johns Hopkins University Press, 1977.

Horner, Tom. *Jonathan Loved David: Homosexuality in Biblical Times.* Philadelphia: Westminster Press, 1978.

Hunt, Mary E. "Lovingly Lesbian: Toward a Feminist Theology of Friendship." In *Sexuality and the Sacred: Sources for Theological Reflection,* ed. James B. Nelson and Sandra P. Longfellow, 169–82. Louisville, Ky.: Westminster John Knox Press, 1994.

Isay, Richard. *Being Homosexual.* New York: Farrar, Straus & Giroux, 1989.

———. "Psychoanalytic Theory and the Therapy of Gay Men." In *Homosexuality/Heterosexuality: Concepts of Sexual Orientation,* ed. David P. McWhirter, Stephanie A. Sanders, and June Machover Reinisch, 283–303. New York: Oxford University Press, 1990.

Jenson, Joseph. "Human Sexuality in the Scriptures." In *Human Sexuality and Personhood.* Chicago: Franciscan Herald Press, 1981.

Johansson, Warren, and William A. Percy. "Homosexuality." In *Handbook of Medieval Sexuality,* ed. Vern L. Bullough and James A. Brundage, 155–89. New York: Garland Publishing, 1996.

Jones, H. Kimball. *Toward a Christian Understanding of the Homosexual.* New York: Association Press, 1966.

Jones, Stanton L. "Addendum." In *Homosexuality in the Church: Both Sides of the Debate,* ed. Jeffrey S. Siker, 107–12. Louisville, Ky.: Westminster John Knox Press, 1994.

———. "Homosexuality according to Science." In *The Crisis of Homosexuality,* ed. J. Isamu Yamamoto, 103–14. Wheaton, Ill.: Victor Books, 1990.

Jones, Stanton L., and Don E. Workman. "Homosexuality: The Behavioral Sciences and the Church." *Journal of Psychology and Theology* 17/3 (Fall 1989): 213–25.

Jurgens, W. A., ed. and trans. *The Faith of the Early Fathers.* Collegeville, Minn.: Liturgical Press, 1970.

Kagan, Jerome. "Psychology of Sex Differences." In *Human Sexuality in Four Perspectives,* ed. Frank A. Beach, 87–114. Baltimore: Johns Hopkins University Press, 1977.

Kanoti, George A., and Anthony R. Kosnik. "Homosexuality: Ethical Aspects." *Encyclopedia of Bioethics,* ed. Warren T. Reich, 2:671–77. New York: Free Press, 1978.

Karlen, Arno. *Homosexuality: A New View.* New York: W. W. Norton, 1971.

Keeling, Michael. "A Christian Basis for Gay Relationships." In *Towards a Theology of Gay Liberation,* ed. Malcolm Macourt, 100–7. London: SCM Press, 1977.

Kennedy, John W. "Episcopalians Tone Down Sexuality Statement." *Christianity Today* (3 October 1994): 70.

King, Michael, and Elizabeth McDonald. "Homosexuals Who Are Twins: A Study of Forty-Six Probands," *British Journal of Psychiatry* 160 (March 1992): 407–9.

Kinsey, Alfred C.; Wardell B. Pomeroy; and Clyde E. Martin. *Sexual Behavior in the Human Male.* Philadelphia: W. B. Saunders, 1948.

Kirk, Jerry R. *The Homosexual Crisis in the Mainline Church.* Nashville: Thomas Nelson, 1978.

Kon, Igor S. *The Sexual Revolution in Russia from the Age of the Czars to Today.* Trans. James Riordan. New York: Free Press, 1995.

Kotva, Joseph J., Jr. "Scripture, Ethics, and the Local Church: Homosexuality as a Case Study." *Conrad Grebel Review* 7/1 (Winter 1989): 41–61.

Kroeger, Catherine Clark. "Are Gay Unions Christian Covenants?" In *Caught in the Crossfire: Helping Christians Debate Homosexuality,* ed. Sally B. Geis and Donald E. Messer, 132–40. Nashville: Abingdon Press, 1994.

Kronemeyer, Robert. *Overcoming Homosexuality.* New York: Macmillan, 1980.

Lance, H. Darrell. "The Bible and Homosexuality." *American Baptist Quarterly* 8/2 (June 1989): 140–51.

Levan, Christopher. "Homosexuality and Sin." In *Theological Reflections on Ministry and Sexual Orientation,* ed. Pamela Dickey Young, 56–83. Burlington, Ont.: Trinity Press, 1990.

LeVay, S. "A Difference in Hypothalamic Structure between Heterosexual and Homosexual Men." *Science* 253 (1991): 1034–37.

Lewin, Tamar. "Sex in America: Faithfulness in Marriage Thrives after All." *New York Times,* 7 October 1994, Section A, p. 1.

Livingood, John M., ed. *National Institute of Mental Health Task Force on Homosexuality: Final Report and Background Papers.* Rockville, Md.: National Institute of Mental Health, 1972.

Lucian. "Dialogues of Courtesans." In vol. 7 of *Lucian in Eight Volumes,* trans. M. D. MacLeod, 355–467. Loeb Classical Library. Cambridge, Mass.: Harvard University Press, 1961.

Luther, Martin. *Lectures on Genesis: Chapters 15—20.* Vol. 3 of *Luther's Works,* ed. Jaroslav Pelikan, trans. George V. Schick. St. Louis: Concordia, 1961.

Macourt, Malcolm, ed. *Towards a Theology of Gay Liberation.* London: SCM, 1977.

Magnuson, Roger J. *Are Gay Rights Right? Making Sense of the Controversy.* Rev. ed. Portland, Oreg.: Multnomah, 1990.

Malick, David E. "The Condemnation of Homosexuality in Romans 1:26–27." *Bibliotheca Sacra* 150 (July–September 1993): 327–40.

Marcus, Eric. *Is It a Choice? Answers to Three Hundred of the Most Frequently Asked Questions about Gays and Lesbians.* San Francisco: HarperSanFrancisco, 1993.

Martin, Dale B. "Heterosexism and the Interpretation of Romans 1:18–32." *Biblical Interpretation* 3/3 (October 1995): 332–55.

Maslow, Abraham. "Self-Esteem (Dominance-Feeling) and Sexuality in Women." In *Sexual Behavior and Personality Characteristics,* ed. Manfred F. DeMartino, 71–112. New York: Citadel Press, 1963.

Masters, William H., and Virginia E. Johnson. *Homosexuality in Perspective.* New York: Bantam Books, 1982.

McCormick, Cheryl M., and Sandra F. Witelson. "Functional Cerebral Asymmetry and Sexual Orientation in Men and Women." *Behavioral Neuroscience* 108/3 (June 1994): 525–31.

McManus, Michael. "Homosexuals Anonymous Gives Gay Christians a Way Out." *Sioux Falls (S.D.) Argus Leader,* 7 March 1987, Section A, p. 9.

McNeill, John J. *The Church and the Homosexual.* 3d ed. Boston: Beacon Press, 1988. Originally published by Sheed, Andrews, & McMeel, Kansas City, 1976.

———. *Taking a Chance on God: Liberating Theology for Gays, Lesbians, and Their Lovers, Families, and Friends.* Boston: Beacon Press, 1988.

———. "Homosexuality: Challenging the Church to Grow." *Christian Century* 104/8 (11 March 1987): 242–46.

McNeill, John T., and Helena M. Gamer, eds. and trans. *Medieval Handbooks of Penance.* New York: Octagon Books, 1965.

McWhirter, David P.; Stephanie A. Sanders; and June Machover Reinisch, eds. *Homosexuality/Heterosexuality: Concepts of Sexual Orientation.* New York: Oxford University Press, 1990.

Meeks, Wayne A. "The Image of the Androgyne: Some Uses of a Symbol in Earliest Christianity." History of Religions 13 (1974): 165–208.

Meier, Paul D. "Counseling Homosexuals." *Fundamentalist Journal* 4/3 (March 1985): 20–21.

Michael, Robert T.; John H. Gagnon; Edward O. Laumann; and Gina Kolata. *Sex in America: A Definitive Survey.* Boston: Little, Brown & Co., 1994.

Moberly, Elizabeth R. *Homosexuality: A New Christian Ethic.* Cambridge, Eng.: James Clarke & Co., 1983.

Morrow, William. "Sexual Ethics and Biblical Principles: A Response to *Dirt, Greed and Sex.* " In *Theological Reflections on Ministry and Sexual Orientation,* ed. Pamela Dickey Young, 26–55. Burlington, Ont.: Trinity Press, 1990.

Murray, Jacqueline. "Twice Marginal and Twice Invisible: Lesbians in the Middle Ages." In *Handbook of Medieval Sexuality,* ed. Vern L. Bullough and James A. Brundage, 191–222. New York: Garland Publishing, 1996.

Nelson, James B. *Embodiment.* Minneapolis: Augsburg, 1978.

———. "Are Christianity and Homosexuality Incompatible?" In *Caught in the Crossfire: Helping Christians Debate Homosexuality,* ed. Sally B. Geis and Donald E. Messer, 99–109. Nashville: Abingdon Press, 1994.

Nelson, James B., and Sandra P. Longfellow, eds. *Sexuality and the Sacred: Sources for Theological Reflection.* Louisville, Ky.: Westminster John Knox Press, 1994.

Nicolosi, Joseph. *Reparative Therapy of Male Homosexuality: A New Clinical Approach.* Northvale, N.J.: Jason Aronson, 1991.

———. "What Does Science Teach about Human Sexuality?" In *Caught in the Crossfire: Helping Christians Debate Homosexuality,* ed. Sally B. Geis and Donald E. Messer, 67–77. Nashville: Abingdon Press, 1994.

Origen. *Commentarii in epistulam ad Romanos.* In Origenes, *Römerbriefkommentar,* trans. Theresia Heither. Vol. 2 of *Fontes Christiani.* Freiburg im Breisgau: Herder, 1992.

Ovid. *Metamorphoses.* Trans. Frank Justus Miller. Loeb Classical Library. Cambridge, Mass.: Harvard University Press, 1916.

Packard, Vance. *The Sexual Wilderness.* New York: David McKay Co. 1968.

Paglia, Camille. *Sexual Personae: Art and Decadence.* New Haven, Conn.: Yale University Press, 1990.

Petersen, William L. "On the Study of "Homosexuality" in Patristic Sources." In *Studia Patristica 20,* ed. Elizabeth A. Livingstone, 283–88. Leuven: Peeters, 1989.

Phaedrus. *The Fables of Phaedrus.* Trans. P. F. Widdows. Austin, Tex.: University of Texas Press, 1992.

Pharr, Clyde, trans. *The Theodosian Code and Novels and the Sirmondian Constitutions.* Princeton, N.J.: Princeton University Press, 1952.

Pharr, Suzanne. *Homophobia: A Weapon of Sexism.* Inverness, Calif.: Chardon Press, 1988.

Photius. *Bibliotheca.* Trans. N. G. Wilson. London: Duckworth, 1994.

Pillard, Richard C., and James D. Weinrich. "Evidence of Familial Nature of Male Homosexuality." *Archives of General Psychiatry* 43/8 (August 1986): 808–12.

Pittenger, Norman. "What It Means to Be Human." In *Towards a Theology of Gay Liberation,* ed. Malcolm Macourt, 83–90. London: SCM Press, 1977.

Plato. *Laws. Vol. 2.* Trans. R. G. Bury. Loeb Classical Library, ed. G. P. Wood. Cambridge, Mass.: Harvard University Press, 1926.

————. *Symposium.* Trans. W. R. M. Lamb. Loeb Classical Library. Cambridge, Mass.: Harvard University Press, 1925.

Pronk, Pim. *Against Nature? Types of Moral Argumentation regarding Homosexuality.* Trans. John Vriend. Grand Rapids: Eerdmans, 1993.

Ptolemy. *Tetrabiblos.* Trans. F. E. Robbins. Loeb Classical Library. Cambridge, Mass.: Harvard University Press, 1940.

Ragan, Bryant T. "The Enlightenment Confronts Homosexuality." In *Homosexuality in Modern France,* ed. Jeffrey Merrick and Bryant T. Ragan, 8–29. New York: Oxford University Press, 1996.

Reisman, Judith A., and Edward W. Eichel. *Kinsey, Sex and Fraud: The Indoctrination of a People.* Lafayette, La.: Lochinvar-Huntington House Publications, 1990.

Ricketts, Wendell. "Biological Research on Homosexuality: Ansell's Cow or Occam's Razor?" *Journal of Homosexuality* 9/4 (Summer 1984): 65–93.

Riordon, Michael. *The First Stone: Homosexuality and the United Church.* Toronto: McClelland & Stewart, 1990.

Saia, Michael R. *Counseling the Homosexual.* Minneapolis: Bethany House, 1988.

Sample, Tex. "Should Gays and Lesbians Be Ordained?" In *Caught in the Crossfire: Helping Christians Debate Homosexuality,* ed. Sally B. Geis and Donald E. Messer, 121–31. Nashville: Abingdon Press, 1994.

Satinover, Jeffrey. *Homosexuality and the Politics of Truth.* Grand Rapids: Baker Book House, 1996.

Scanzoni, Letha, and Virginia Ramey Mollenkott. *Is the Homosexual My Neighbor? A Positive Christian Response.* Rev. ed. San Francisco: HarperSanFrancisco, 1994. Originally published by Harper & Row, 1978.

Schmidt, Thomas E. *Straight and Narrow? Compassion and Clarity in the Homosexuality Debate.* Downers Grove, Ill.: InterVarsity Press, 1995.

Schrage, Wolfgang. *The Ethics of the New Testament,* trans. David E. Green. Philadelphia: Fortress Press, 1988.

Scroggs, Robin. *The New Testament and Homosexuality: Contextual Background for Contemporary Debate.* Philadelphia: Fortress Press, 1983.

Seow, Choon-Leong, ed. *Homosexuality and Christian Community.* Louisville, Ky.: Westminster John Knox Press, 1996.

Siker, Jeffrey S. "Homosexual Christians, the Bible, and Gentile Inclusion: Confessions of a Repenting Heterosexist." In *Homosexuality in the Church: Both Sides of the Debate,* ed. Jeffrey S. Siker, 178–94. Louisville, Ky.: Westminster John Knox Press, 1994.

Siker, Jeffrey S., ed. *Homosexuality in the Church: Both Sides of the Debate.* Louisville, Ky.: Westminster John Knox Press, 1994.

Smedes, Lewis B. *Sex for Christians: The Limits and Liberties of Sexual Living.* Rev. ed. Grand Rapids: Eerdmans, 1994.

Soards, Marion L. *Scripture and Homosexuality: Biblical Authority and the Church Today.* Louisville, Ky.: Westminster John Knox Press, 1995.

Socarides, Charles W., and Benjamin Kaufman. "Reparative Therapy" (letter to the editors with replies by Fred Gottlieb and Richard A. Isay). *American Journal of Psychiatry* 151/1 (January 1994): 157–59.

Spong, John Shelby. *Living in Sin? A Bishop Rethinks Human Sexuality.* San Francisco: Harper & Row, 1988.

Stackhouse, Max L. "The Heterosexual Norm." In *Homosexuality and Christian Community,* ed. Choon-Leong Seow, 133–43. Louisville, Ky.: Westminster John Knox Press, 1996.

Stafford, Tim. "Coming Out." *Christianity Today* 33/11 (18 August 1989): 16–21.

Sullivan, Andrew. "The Politics of Homosexuality." *The New Republic* 208/19 (10 May 1993): 23–37.

Sullivan, Andrew, ed. *Same-Sex Marriage: Pro and Con, a Reader.* New York: Vintage Books, 1997.

Swaab, D. F., and M. A. Hofman. "An Enlarged Suprachiasmatic Nucleus in Homosexual Men." *Brain Research* 537 (1990): 141–48.

Tam, Ekman P. C. "Counseling with Gay Men and Lesbians: An Integrative Approach." *Pastoral Sciences* 16 (1997): 163–79.

Tannahill, Reay. *Sex in History.* London: Hamish Hamilton, 1980.

Tanner, Norman P., ed. *Decrees of the Ecumenical Councils.* London: Sheed & Ward, 1990.

Tatian. *Oratio ad Graecos and Fragments,* trans. Molly Whittaker. Oxford: Clarendon Press, 1982.

Tertullian. "The Chaplet." In *Tertullian: Disciplinary, Moral, and Ascetical Works,* trans. Edwin A. Quain. Vol. 40 of *The Fathers of the Church,* 223–67. Washington, D.C.: Catholic University of America Press, 1959.

———. "The Five Books against Marcion." Trans. Peter Holmes. In vol. 3 of *The Ante-Nicene Fathers of the Christian Church,* ed. Alexander Roberts and James Donaldson, rev. A. Cleveland Coxe, 269–475. Grand Rapids: Eerdmans, 1976.

———. "On the Pallium." Trans. S. Thelwall. In vol. 4 of *The Ante-Nicene Fathers of the Christian Church,* ed. Alexander Roberts and James Donaldson, rev. A. Cleveland Coxe, 5–13. Grand Rapids: Eerdmans, 1976.

Thielicke, Helmut. *Ethics of Sex.* Trans. John W. Doberstein. New York: Harper & Row, 1964.

Tillich, Paul. *Morality and Beyond.* New York: Harper & Row, 1963.

Trible, Phyllis. *God and the Rhetoric of Sexuality.* Philadelphia: Fortress Press, 1978.

Tripp, C. A. *The Homosexual Matrix.* New York: McGraw-Hill, 1975. Second ed.: New American Library, 1987.

Ukleja, P. Michael. "Homosexuality and the Old Testament." *Bibliotheca Sacra* 140/559 (July–September 1983): 259–66.

Vara, Richard. "Uneasy Peace Reigns over Episcopal Convention." *Houston Chronicle,* 3 September 1994, Religion section, p. 1.

Weinberg, George. *Society and the Healthy Homosexual.* New York: St. Martin's Press, 1972.

Wenham, G. J. "The Old Testament Attitude to Homosexuality." *Expository Times* 102/12 (September 1991): 359–63.

White, Mel. *Stranger at the Gate: To Be Gay and Christian in America.* New York: Simon & Schuster, 1994.

Williams, Bruce A. "Homosexuality and Christianity: A Review Discussion." *The Thomist* 46/4 (October 1982): 609–25.

Williams, Don. *The Bond That Breaks: Will Homosexuality Split the Church?* Los Angeles: BIM, 1978.

Wink, Walter. "Biblical Perspectives on Homosexuality." *Christian Century* 96/36 (7 Nov. 1979): 1082–86.

Witham, Larry. "Episcopal Bishops Divided on Sexuality." *Washington Times,* 10 September 1994, final edition, Section A, p. 13.

Wolf, James G., ed. *Gay Priests.* San Francisco: Harper & Row, 1989.

Woods, Richard. *Another Kind of Love: Homosexuality and Spirituality.* Chicago: Thomas Moore Press, 1977.

Worthen, Anita, and Bob Davies. *Someone I Love Is Gay.* Downers Grove, Ill.: InterVarsity Press, 1996.

Wortman, Julie A. "Sex—Getting It Straight?" *Witness* 77/10 (October 1994): 21.

Wright, David F. "Homosexuals or Prostitutes? The Meaning of *Arsenokoitai* (1 Cor. 6:9, 1 Tim. 1:10)." *Vigiliae Christianae* 38/2 (June 1984): 125–53.

Zaas, Peter. "1 Cor. 6:9ff.: Was Homosexuality Condoned in the Corinthian Church?" In *Society of Biblical Literature 1979 Seminar Papers,* ed. Paul J. Achtemeier, 2:205–12. Missoula, Mont.: Scholars Press, 1979.

INDEX OF SCRIPTURE

INDEX OF AUTHORS

INDEX OF SUBJECTS